Francis Frith's

Weston-super-Mare

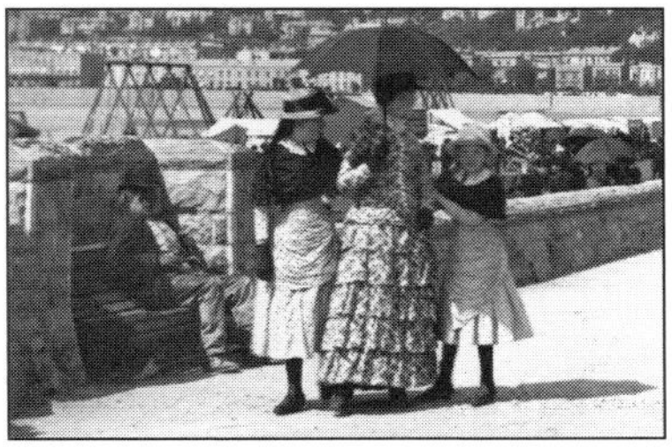

Photographic Memories

Francis Frith's
Weston-super-Mare

Sharon Poole

THE FRANCIS FRITH COLLECTION®

First published in the United Kingdom in 2001 by
Frith Book Company Ltd

Hardback Edition 2001
ISBN 1-85937-409-3

Paperback Edition 2001
ISBN 1-85937-306-2

Reprinted in Paperback 2004

British Library Cataloguing in Publication Data

Francis Frith's Weston-super-Mare
Sharon Poole

Frith Book Company Ltd
Frith's Barn, Teffont,
Salisbury, Wiltshire SP3 5QP
Tel: +44 (0) 1722 716 376
Email: info@francisfrith.co.uk
www.francisfrith.co.uk

Printed and bound in Great Britain

Front Cover: **Weston-super-Mare, The Sands 1913** 65160

The colour-tinting is for illustrative purposes only, and is not intended to be historically accurate

AS WITH ANY HISTORICAL DATABASE THE FRITH ARCHIVE IS CONSTANTLY BEING CORRECTED AND IMPROVED AND THE PUBLISHERS WOULD WELCOME INFORMATION ON OMISSIONS OR INACCURACIES

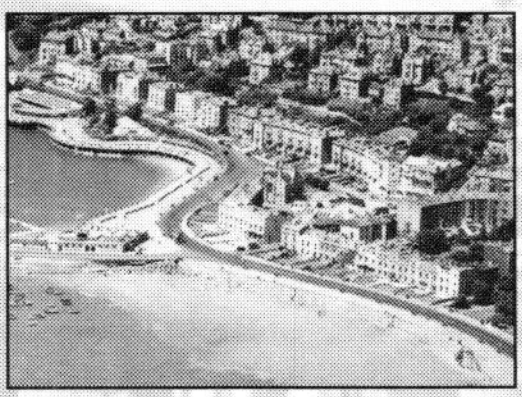

Contents

Francis Frith: Victorian Pioneer 7

Frith's Archive - A Unique Legacy 10

Weston-super-Mare - An Introduction 12

The Town 17

The Sea Front 29

Glentworth Bay & Marine Lake 46

Anchor Head 58

Birnbeck Pier, Woods & Toll Road 62

Around Weston-super-Mare 68

Index 87

Free Mounted Print Voucher 91

Francis Frith: *Victorian Pioneer*

FRANCIS FRITH, Victorian founder of the world-famous photographic archive, was a complex and multi-talented man. A devout Quaker and a highly successful Victorian businessman, he was both philosophical by nature and pioneering in outlook.

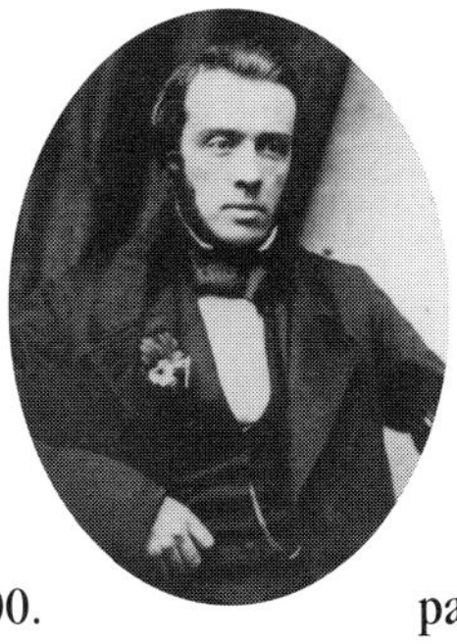

By 1855 Francis Frith had already established a wholesale grocery business in Liverpool, and sold it for the astonishing sum of £200,000, which is the equivalent today of over £15,000,000. Now a multi-millionaire, he was able to indulge his passion for travel. As a child he had pored over travel books written by early explorers, and his fancy and imagination had been stirred by family holidays to the sublime mountain regions of Wales and Scotland. 'What a land of spirit-stirring and enriching scenes and places!' he had written. He was to return to these scenes of grandeur in later years to 'recapture the thousands of vivid and tender memories', but with a different purpose. Now in his thirties, and captivated by the new science of photography, Frith set out on a series of pioneering journeys to the Nile regions that occupied him from 1856 until 1860.

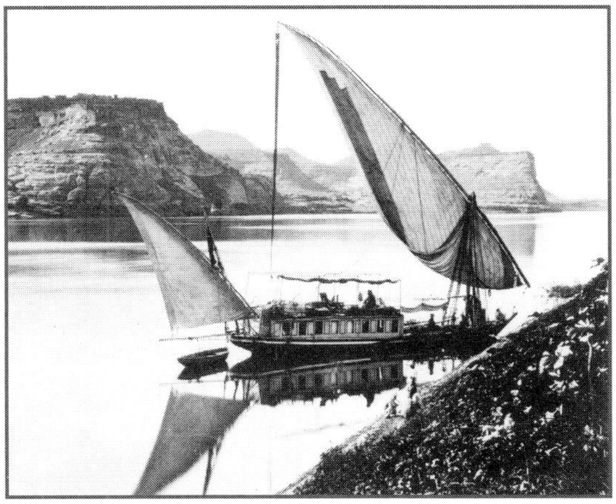

Intrigue and Adventure

He took with him on his travels a specially-designed wicker carriage that acted as both dark-room and sleeping chamber. These far-flung journeys were packed with intrigue and adventure. In his life story, written when he was sixty-three, Frith tells of being held captive by bandits, and of fighting 'an awful midnight battle to the very point of surrender with a deadly pack of hungry, wild dogs'. Sporting flowing Arab costume, Frith arrived at Akaba by camel sixty years before Lawrence, where he encountered 'desert princes and rival sheikhs, blazing with jewel-hilted swords'.

During these extraordinary adventures he was assiduously exploring the desert regions bordering the Nile and patiently recording the antiquities and peoples with his camera. He was the first photographer to venture beyond the sixth cataract. Africa was still the mysterious 'Dark Continent', and Stanley and Livingstone's historic meeting was a decade into the future. The conditions for picture taking confound belief. He laboured for hours in his wicker dark-room in the sweltering heat of the desert, while the volatile chemicals fizzed dangerously in their trays. Often he was forced to work in remote tombs and caves where conditions were cooler. Back in London he exhibited his photographs and was 'rapturously cheered' by members of the Royal Society. His reputation as a photographer was made overnight. An eminent modern historian has likened their impact on the population of the time to that on our own generation of the first photographs taken on the surface of the moon.

Venture of a Life-Time

Characteristically, Frith quickly spotted the opportunity to create a new business as a specialist publisher of photographs. He lived in an era of immense and sometimes violent change. For the poor in the early part of Victoria's reign work was a drudge and the hours long, and people had precious little free time to enjoy themselves. Most had no transport other than a cart or gig at their disposal, and had not travelled far beyond the boundaries of their own town or village. However, by the 1870s, the railways had threaded their way across the country, and Bank Holidays and half-day Saturdays had been made obligatory by Act of Parliament. All of a sudden the ordinary working man and his family were able to enjoy days out and see a little more of the world.

With characteristic business acumen, Francis Frith foresaw that these new tourists would enjoy having souvenirs to commemorate their days out. In 1860 he married Mary Ann Rosling and set out with the intention of photographing every city, town and village in Britain. For the next thirty years he travelled the country by train and by pony and trap, producing fine photographs of seaside resorts and beauty spots that were keenly bought by millions of Victorians. These prints were painstakingly pasted into family albums and pored over during the dark nights of winter, rekindling precious memories of summer excursions.

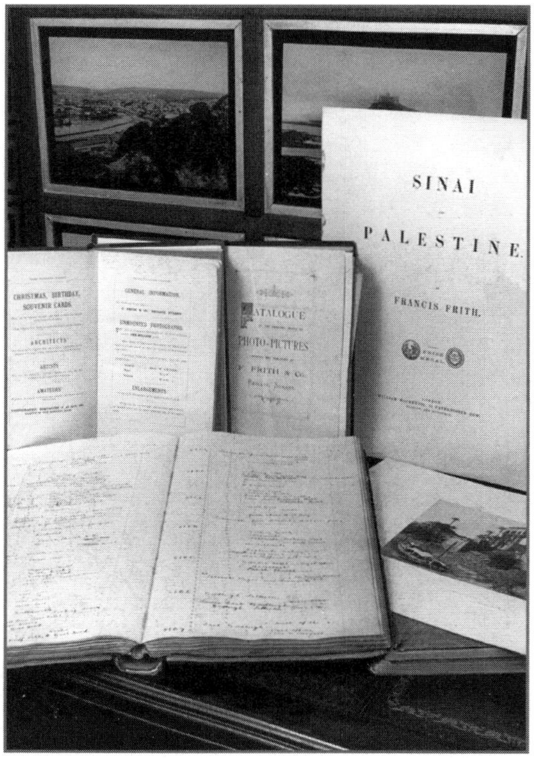

The Rise of Frith & Co

Frith's studio was soon supplying retail shops all over the country. To meet the demand he gathered about him a small team of photographers, and published the work of independent artist-photographers of the calibre of Roger Fenton and Francis Bedford. In order to gain some understanding of the scale of Frith's business one only has to look at the catalogue issued by Frith & Co in 1886: it runs to some 670 pages, listing not only many thousands of views of the British Isles but also many photographs of most European countries, and China, Japan, the USA and Canada – note the sample page shown on page 9 from the hand-written *Frith & Co* ledgers detailing pictures taken. By 1890 Frith had created the greatest specialist photographic publishing company in the

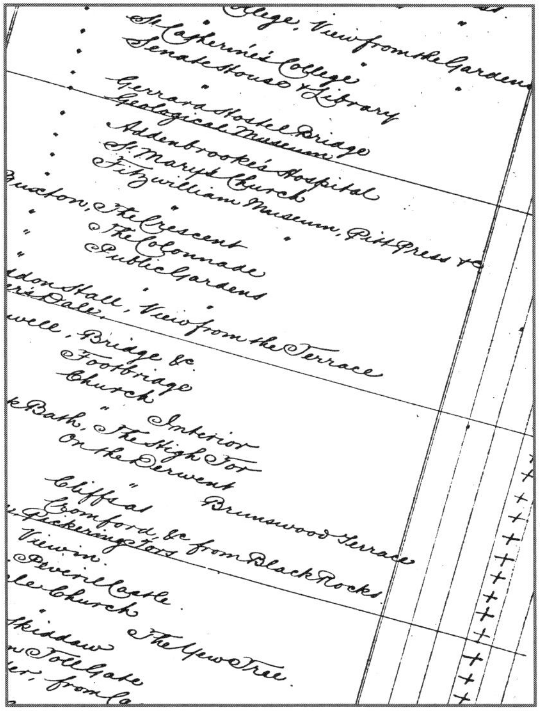

St Catherine's College
Senate House & Library
Gerrard Hostel Bridge
Geological Museum
Addenbrooke's Hospital
St Mary's Church
Fitzwilliam Museum, Pitt Press &c
The Crescent
The Colonnade
Public Gardens
View from the Terrace
Bridge &c.
Footbridge
Church
Interior
The High Tor
On the Derwent
Cliffs at
Brunswood Terrace
Cromford, &c from Black Rocks
Pickering Tors
Peveril Castle
Church
The Yew Tree
Skiddaw
Toll Gate

world, with over 2,000 outlets – more than the combined number that Boots and WH Smith have today! The picture on the right shows the *Frith & Co* display board at Ingleton in the Yorkshire Dales (left of window). Beautifully constructed with a mahogany frame and gilt inserts, it could display up to a dozen local scenes.

Postcard Bonanza

The ever-popular holiday postcard we know today took many years to develop. In 1870 the Post Office issued the first plain cards, with a pre-printed stamp on one face. In 1894 they allowed other publishers' cards to be sent through the mail with an attached adhesive halfpenny stamp. Demand grew rapidly, and in 1895 a new size of postcard was permitted called the court card, but there was little room for illustration. In 1899, a year after Frith's death, a new card measuring 5.5 x 3.5 inches became the standard format, but it was not until 1902 that the divided back came into being, with address and message on one face and a full-size illustration on the other. *Frith & Co* were in the vanguard of postcard development, and Frith's sons Eustace and Cyril continued their father's monumental task, expanding the number of views offered to the public and recording more and more places in Britain, as the coasts and countryside were opened up to mass travel.

Francis Frith died in 1898 at his villa in Cannes, his great project still growing. The archive he created continued in business for another seventy years. By 1970 it contained over a third of a million pictures of 7,000 cities, towns and villages. The massive photographic record Frith has left to us stands as a living monument to a special and very remarkable man.

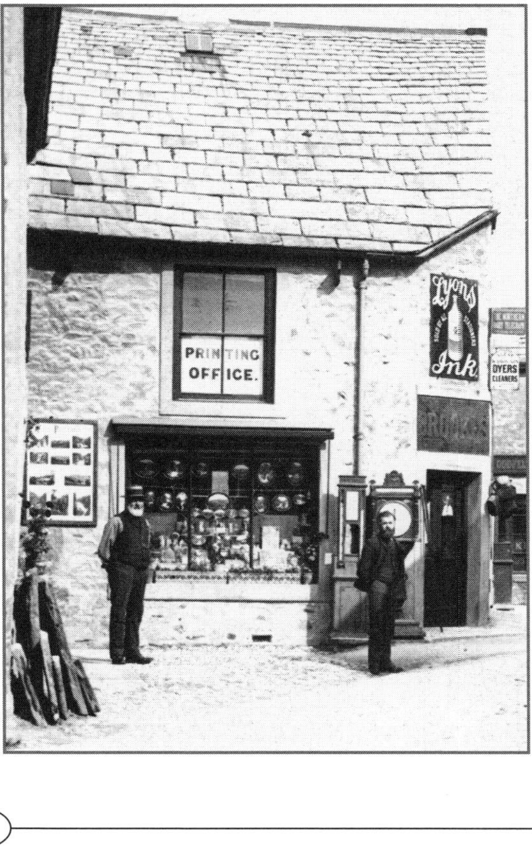

Frith's Archive: *A Unique Legacy*

Francis Frith's legacy to us today is of immense significance and value, for the magnificent archive of evocative photographs he created provides a unique record of change in 7,000 cities, towns and villages throughout Britain over a century and more. Frith and his fellow studio photographers revisited locations many times down the years to update their views, compiling for us an enthralling and colourful pageant of British life and character.

We tend to think of Frith's sepia views of Britain as nostalgic, for most of us use them to conjure up memories of places in our own lives with which we have family associations. It often makes us forget that to Francis Frith they were records of daily life as it was actually being lived in the cities, towns and villages of his day. The Victorian age was one of great and often bewildering change for ordinary people, and though the pictures evoke an impression of slower times, life was as busy and hectic as it is today.

We are fortunate that Frith was a photographer of the people, dedicated to recording the minutiae of everyday life. For it is this sheer wealth of visual data, the painstaking chronicle of changes in dress, transport, street layouts, buildings, housing, engineering and landscape that captivates us so much today. His remarkable images offer us a powerful link with the past and with the lives of our ancestors.

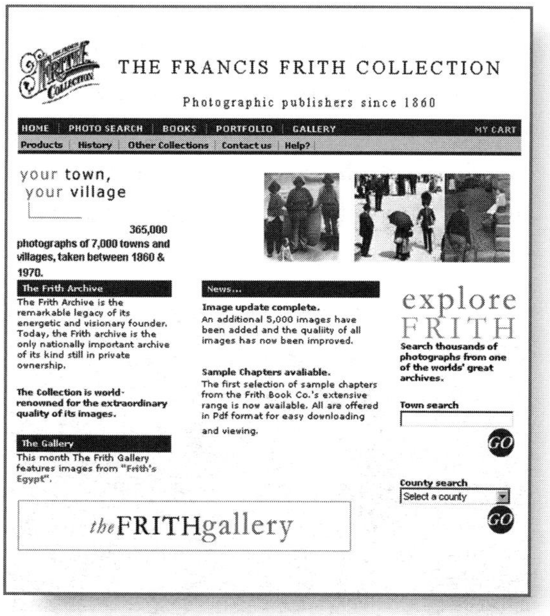

See Frith at www.francisfrith.co.uk

Today's Technology

Computers have now made it possible for Frith's many thousands of images to be accessed almost instantly. In the Frith archive today, each photograph is carefully 'digitised' then stored on a CD Rom. Frith archivists can locate a single photograph amongst thousands within seconds. Views can be catalogued and sorted under a variety of categories of place and content to the immediate benefit of researchers.

Inexpensive reference prints can be created for them at the touch of a mouse button, and a wide range of books and other printed materials assembled and published for a wider, more general readership - in the next twelve months over a hundred Frith local history titles will be published! The day-to-day workings of the archive are very different from how they were in Francis Frith's time: imagine the herculean task of sorting through eleven tons of glass negatives as Frith had to do to locate a particular sequence of pictures! Yet the archive still prides itself on maintaining the same high standards of excellence laid down by Francis Frith, including the painstaking cataloguing and indexing of every view.

It is curious to reflect on how the internet now allows researchers in America and elsewhere greater instant access to the archive than Frith himself ever enjoyed. Many thousands of individual views can be called up on screen within seconds on one of the Frith internet sites, enabling people living continents away to revisit the streets of their ancestral home town, or view places in Britain where they have enjoyed holidays. Many overseas researchers welcome the chance to view special theme selections, such as transport, sports, costume and ancient monuments.

We are certain that Francis Frith would have heartily approved of these modern developments in imaging techniques, for he himself was always working at the very limits of Victorian photographic technology.

The Value of the Archive Today

Because of the benefits brought by the computer, Frith's images are increasingly studied by social historians, by researchers into genealogy and ancestory, by architects, town planners, and by teachers and schoolchildren involved in local history projects.

In addition, the archive offers every one of us an opportunity to examine the places where we and our families have lived and worked down the years. Highly successful in Frith's own era, the archive is now, a century and more on, entering a new phase of popularity.

The Past in Tune with the Future

Historians consider the Francis Frith Collection to be of prime national importance. It is the only archive of its kind remaining in private ownership and has been valued at a million pounds. However, this figure is now rapidly increasing as digital technology enables more and more people around the world to enjoy its benefits.

Francis Frith's archive is now housed in an historic timber barn in the beautiful village of Teffont in Wiltshire. Its founder would not recognize the archive office as it is today. In place of the many thousands of dusty boxes containing glass plate negatives and an all-pervading odour of photographic chemicals, there are now ranks of computer screens. He would be amazed to watch his images travelling round the world at unimaginable speeds through network and internet lines.

The archive's future is both bright and exciting. Francis Frith, with his unshakeable belief in making photographs available to the greatest number of people, would undoubtedly approve of what is being done today with his lifetime's work. His photographs, depicting our shared past, are now bringing pleasure and enlightenment to millions around the world a century and more after his death.

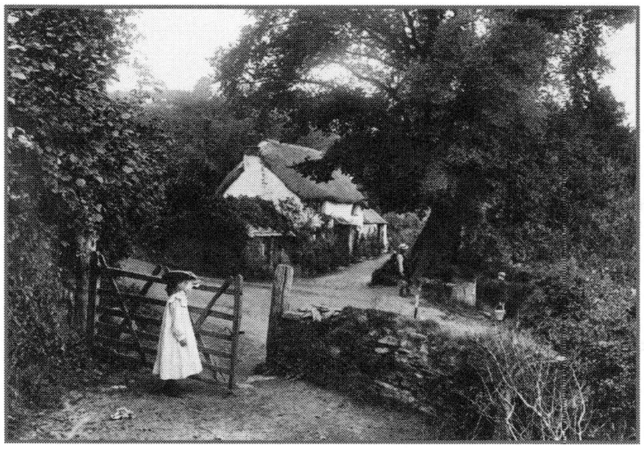

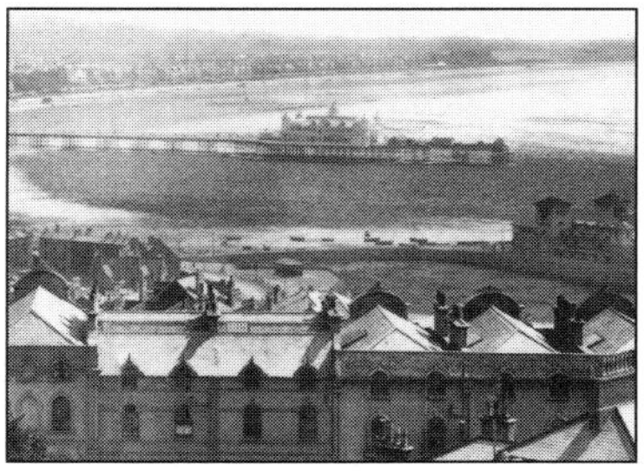

Weston-super-Mare - *An Introduction*

WESTON is usually thought of as a Victorian town. It is true that one of two major phases of growth and building occurred during this time; the other being during the inter-war period. However, it is easy to forget Weston's ancient past and discount altogether the 18th century, when visitors first began to arrive at this small seaside village.

The most visible monument to past residents is the Iron Age hillfort of Worlebury, which overlooks the present town from the hill. Here, people lived a simple life, growing crops, keeping farm animals on the top of the hill, and fishing from the rich waters of the Bristol Channel. Their way of life ended when the hillfort was overrun and the inhabitants massacred in about AD45. We do not know who killed them; it could have been Roman soldiers, or perhaps another Iron Age tribe. It might even have been in-fighting amongst themselves.

Evidence of earlier occupation in the area was uncovered as the Victorians gradually began to develop the town. Stone Age flints and axes have been found on the hill, and Bronze Age burial urns uncovered around Ashcombe.

Romano-British people lived on the lower slopes of Worle Hill. A Roman grave was found, overlaying earlier Iron Age pit burials north of Grove Park, and there is evidence of a small settlement in the area now covered by the Royal Crescent and Weston College. Other burial sites, both Roman and Dark Age, include Park Place, Greenfield Place and Ashcombe Park.

Over the next few hundred years, a village slowly established itself on the lower hill-slopes. The core of settlement was around the Norman Parish Church, dedicated to St John the Baptist. Around this, thatched cottages and farmsteads were built.

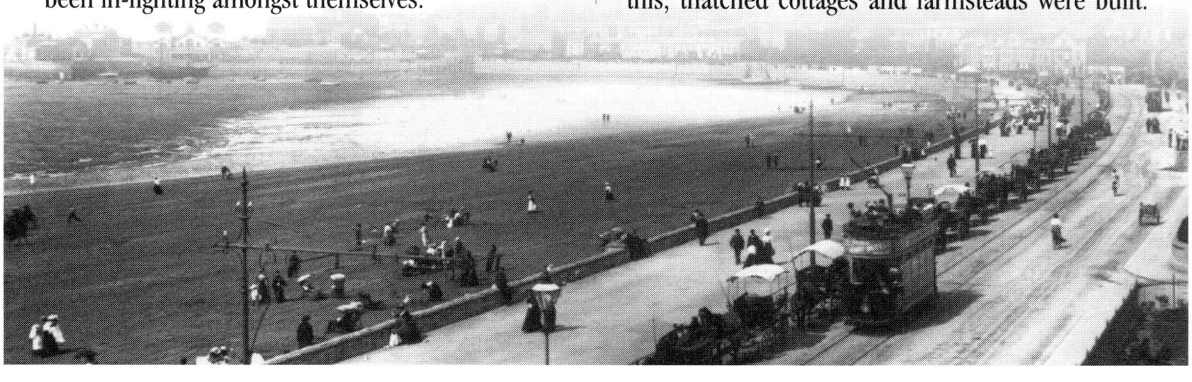

On the hilltop, animals would graze, while the slopes would be used for growing crops. Sprats, herring and eels were fished from the streams, rhynes and coastal waters, whilst on the lower marshlands, reeds and teasels would be harvested.

After the Norman invasion, property was distributed between supporters of William I. When the Domesday survey was recorded in 1086, Weston itself was not mentioned, being most likely part of the manor of Ashcombe, then held by Herluin from the Bishop of Countances. The first written reference to Weston occurs in the registers for the Dean and Chapter of Wells in 1226, with an entry referring to the Rector of Weston.

On the whole, national events passed this quiet corner of the West Country by. The Black Death left its mark around 1349, as is evidenced by the fact that the village had several rectors in short succession.

The first visitors to the immediate area, in any numbers, occurred in 1566. Prospecting miners had discovered deposits of calamine, a zinc ore used in the brass industry, on Worle Hill. This was very important in armament manufacture, so large quantities were mined and sent to Tintern for processing.

In 1696 the manors of Ashcombe and Weston were bought by John Pigott of Brockley. As well as farms and lands across North Somerset, the property included the small manor house at the Grove in Weston. The family never made it their main home but instead treated it as a summer retreat by the sea. The second son, Rev Wadham Pigott, made it his home after being appointed curate-in-charge at Weston Parish Church in January 1790. He also acted as local squire since the elder brother, John, was frequently abroad. Later Wadham became Squire in his own right and took an active part in the development of the village.

Before the 17th century, no one had imagined that bathing in seawater might be good for you. Inland spas had been the holiday resorts of Britain throughout the 17th and early 18th centuries, with the rich visiting places such as Harrogate and Bath to drink - and sometimes bathe in - the natural mineral springs. Elegant Assembly Rooms, pump-rooms, circulating libraries and theatres had been built; these were soon copied by other spa towns.

At the end of the 17th century some doctors, mainly those practising at spas without hot-springs, began to 'discover' the curative powers of cold-water bathing. Slowly resorts developed, usually at places close to a large inland town, for travel was difficult. The first visitors began to arrive in the late 18th century, coming to Weston from Bath and Bristol.

When in 1789 George III took a course of sea bathing at Weymouth, everyone in society wished to do the same. Some of Weston's early holiday-makers included philanthropist Hannah More and the classical scholar Dr Langhorne. It is even believed the artist J W Turner came to paint here. In

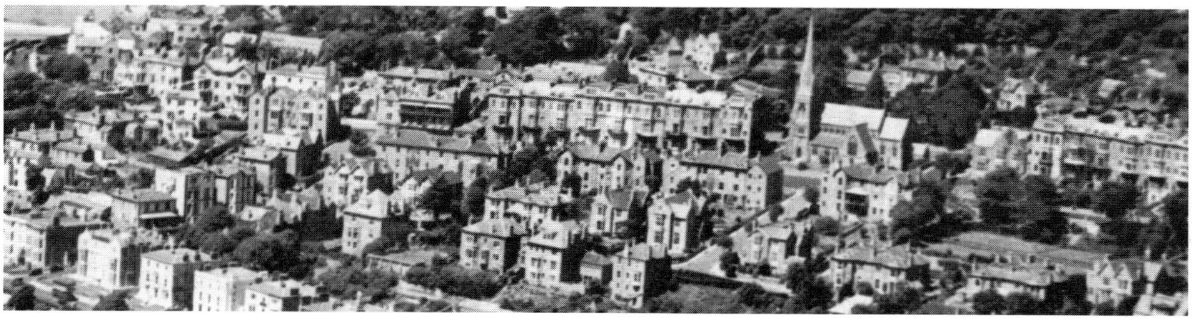

fact, those early visitors left a valuable legacy. Most ladies, and many gentlemen, were taught to paint and the watercolours they have left us are our only record of what places looked like at this time, before the invention of photography.

The Rev Leeves of Wrington built a summer holiday home on the beach in 1791. This survives today as the Thatched Cottage Restaurant. Weston's first hotel, The Royal, was built in 1810, and still welcomes guests today. As more visitors arrived, local people began to supplement their income by renting out rooms, apartments and even whole houses; only wealthy people had either time or means to travel and often brought servants with them, requiring a lot of accommodation.

It was still a requirement of resorts, whether inland or coastal, to have a baths complex, and in Weston, the rocky island of Knightstone was chosen as the site. The first baths opened there in July 1820 and offered hot and cold salt water bathing. A lodging house was built on the island, together with a refreshment room and reading room. Although accessible at low tide, people had to be rowed over at high tide by local boatmen. Later a causeway was built and in September 1830 Dr Edward Long Fox of Bristol purchased Knightstone. Dr Fox was assisted in his work by his son, Dr Francis Ker Fox, and the pair spent money and time developing the facilities on offer. An exercise courtyard was created and a new elegant baths building erected 'for the purpose of introducing fresh and salt water, hot and cold vapour and shower, sulphur and every description of medicated baths'. This fine building has recently been restored.

The beach offered an alternative to the formal routines of the bath house. As Victorian modesty prevailed over 18th-century freedom, people stopped bathing naked and the bathing machine was invented. This was a hut on wheels, drawn down to the water while the occupant changed inside. The bather could then descend straight into the water unseen from the beach. Men's and ladies machines were kept well separated. In Weston, the men's were opposite the Grand Atlantic Hotel and the ladies' in Glentworth Bay. The bathing machines disappeared from Weston in 1903, hastened in their destruction by a big storm.

Railways made the seaside holiday possible for everyone. Weston was one of the first resorts to get a rail link, when the Bristol & Exeter Railway arrived in 1841. Initially, the attraction of railway travel had been pitched at the wealthy and exclusive market. Later it became the means for mass travel. The first Bank Holiday in 1871 heralded a new tradition of annual mass migration to the sea. Four years later, the first excursions from Birmingham were run.

From this time the seaside holiday began to take the familiar form it has today, and Weston developed to meet those needs. New housing was built, both on the hillside for wealthier new

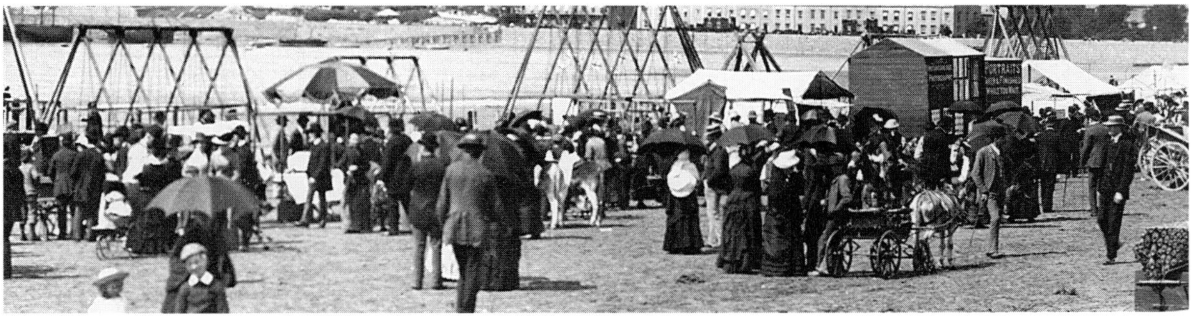

residents, and on the levels, where terraces of cheaper homes housed tradesmen, shopkeepers and those servicing the tourist trade. New churches were built for the growing population, and shops and other facilities appeared. By the mid-19th century there was one feature that declared a resort had truly arrived - a Pier. The first to open was the Chain Pier at Brighton; subsequently, they sprang up all over the country as resorts competed to have the biggest and best. Several resorts had more than one and such was the case with Weston: Birnbeck Pier dates to 1867 and the Grand Pier to 1904. In recent times, the Weston Aquarium became Britain's newest pier upon opening in 1995.

The holiday itself tended to follow a pattern. Few people booked lodgings in advance. On arrival at the railway station, the drivers of wagonettes, who would know where lodgings were available, would transport disembarking passengers there. Once installed in accommodation, the new arrivals had a wealth of entertainment to choose from.

Around the country, donkeys had been used as beasts of burden on the beaches, carrying fishermen's catch into the town or carting seaweed to fields for fertiliser. In Weston, fishermen would go on donkeys and ponies to Birnbeck after every tide to collect the sprats and herring from the nets. Visitors would often hire a donkey to explore the outlying villages and with this trend the concept of seaside donkey rides was born. On the sands, attractions included swing-boats and other fairground style amusements. Stalls were set up selling all description of things - buckets, spades and seaside souvenirs. Food included such things as seafood, teas, ginger beers, mineral waters and ice cream.

The first seaside bands were provided by regiments of soldiers in the early 19th century, for they were stationed along the south coast in case of invasion by Napoleon. Soon, proper bandstands were built - Weston had several. Grove Park is the well-known one, but there was one each on Birnbeck and the Grand Piers, with another on Beach Lawns. Later, continental bands spent summer seasons in the resorts, German and Italian being the most popular. Concerts were free, although a chair would cost you 2d. A collection was held at the end. Other entertainment came from Pierrots, who first appeared in Britain in 1891, concert parties and novelty acts such as Professor Baur and his performing donkey, Domino.

During the 19th century, the population grew dramatically from around 100 to 20,000 residents. Edwardians looked for more fun and freedom than the previous generation. On Knightstone, a new swimming pool and a theatre were built. A purpose-built library and museum opened in the Boulevard and housing estates pushed the town boundaries ever outwards.

During the First World War, soldiers came to

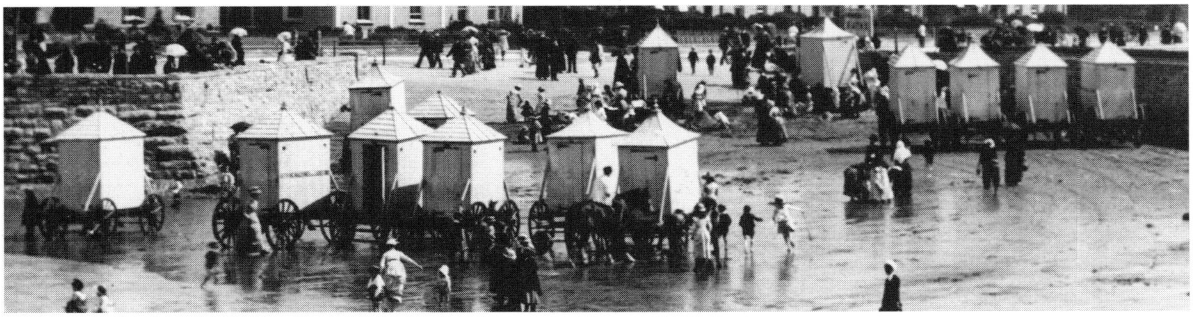

train on the beach, to drill and learn how to dig trenches. A Red Cross hospital for the wounded was set up at Ashcombe House and timber was felled in Weston Woods for pit props, shoring for trenches and the new aircraft industry.

In the inter-war years, Weston saw one of its most intense periods of growth. The Marine Lake, Winter Gardens Pavilion, open-air swimming pool, cinemas and airport were all built at this time. The airport was especially popular with Welsh workers, who could fly over to Weston at weekends.

During the Second World war, many beaches, especially those most at risk of invasion such as the south and east coasts, were off-limits to the public. Weston never suffered in this way and, although the piers were closed, there was still plenty to do.

After the War, most people still holidayed in Britain. More people had cars, but money was tight. However, a big threat lay just over the horizon. Easier and cheaper air travel began to make a foreign holiday possible for the first time for many people.

Another factor that had to be taken into account after the War was the change in tastes. American influences started to spread. Edwardian theatres were replaced with amusement arcades. Outdoors, putting greens and clock golf courses were laid out and features such as model railways and model villages were built.

By the 1970s, English resorts were in decline. Foreign holidays not only guaranteed sun but were cheap, as wages and consequently prices abroad were lower. People also wanted the new experiences and cultures that could only to be obtained by a foreign holiday. Seaside resorts have evolved along with this change, and new holiday patterns have developed as people take shorter breaks at home and longer holidays abroad.

Today, tourism is big business in terms of the income it generates and the number of people it employs. It cuts across all ages and across the social structure. People still like to spend their time at the seaside, and it still flourishes where other traditional industries have declined. After 250 years, our love affair with the sea remains a passionate one.

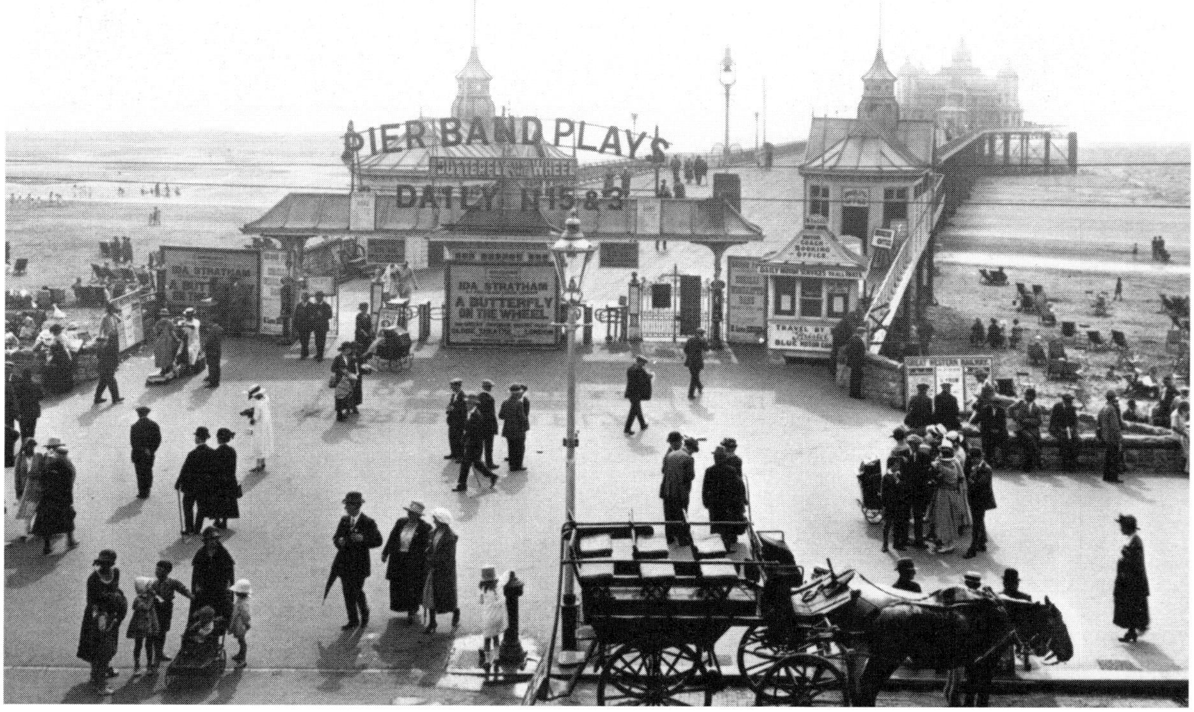

The Town

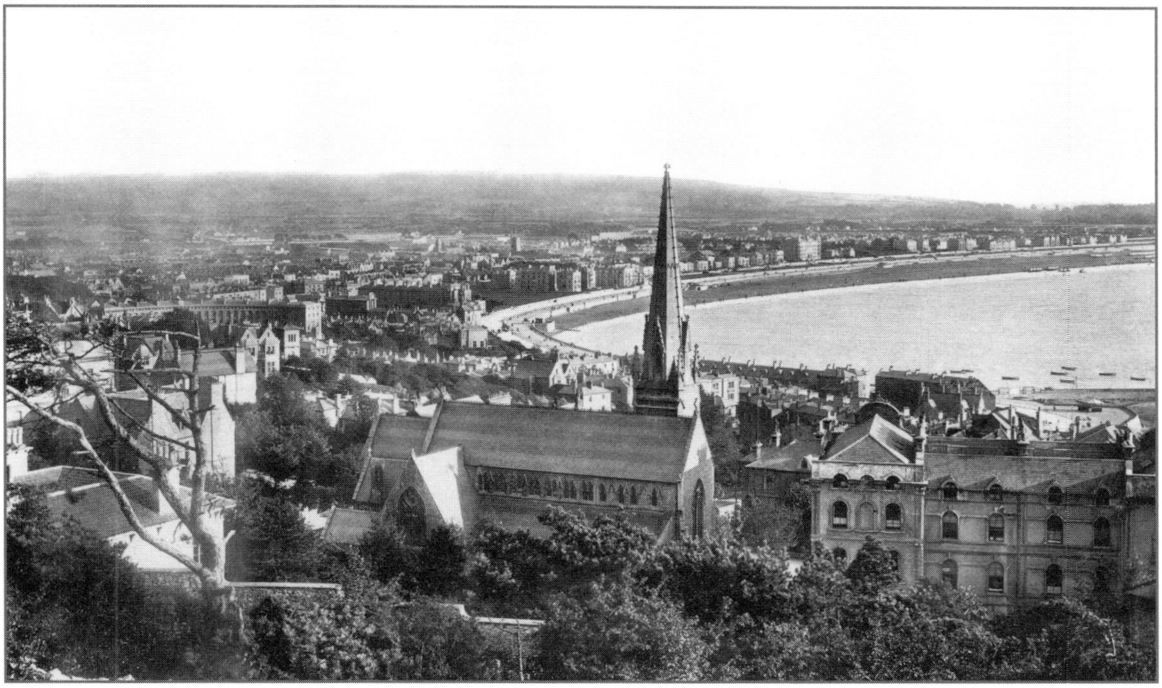

Weston-super-Mare, from the Encampment 1890 27875
This shows the natural sweep of the bay uninterrupted by the Grand Pier. The church in the foreground is Holy Trinity, built in the 1860s. You can see how defined the boundaries of the town were before the sprawl of development in the 20th century.

View from the Encampment 1904 53012
The Grand Pier now dominates the bay. It opened in June 1904, the same year that this picture was taken. At the landward end, an open space marks where the Winter Gardens would be built in 1927.

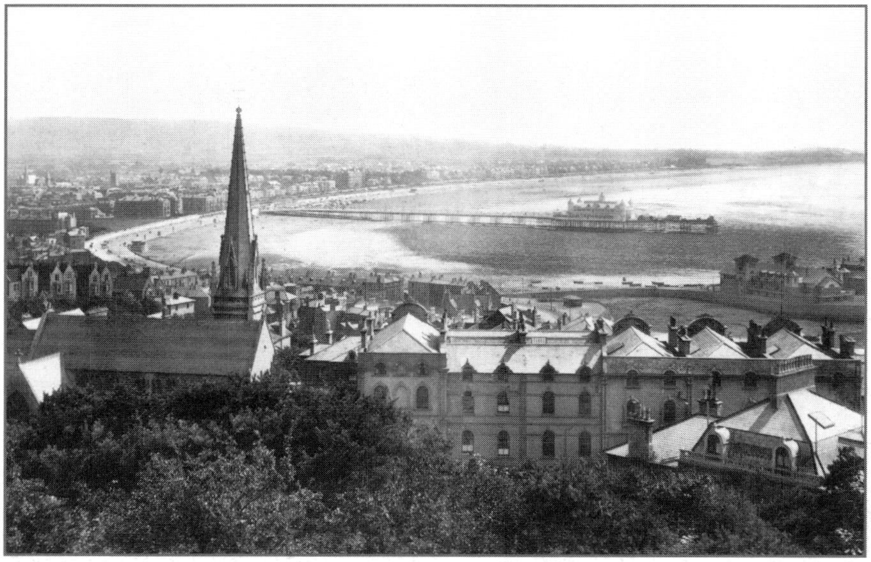

View from the Encampment 1913 65353
This view from Worlebury shows the remains of the stone ramparts of the Iron Age hillfort in the foreground. In the distance, the Grand Pier can be seen with the 450 metre extension built in 1907. This was so that paddle-steamers could dock there instead of having to travel round the bay to Birnbeck Pier.

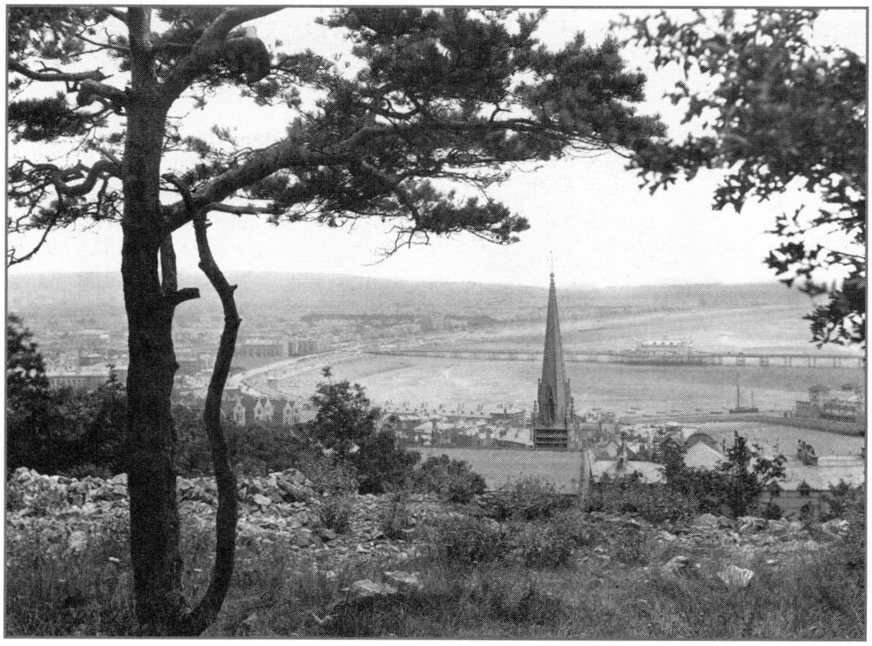

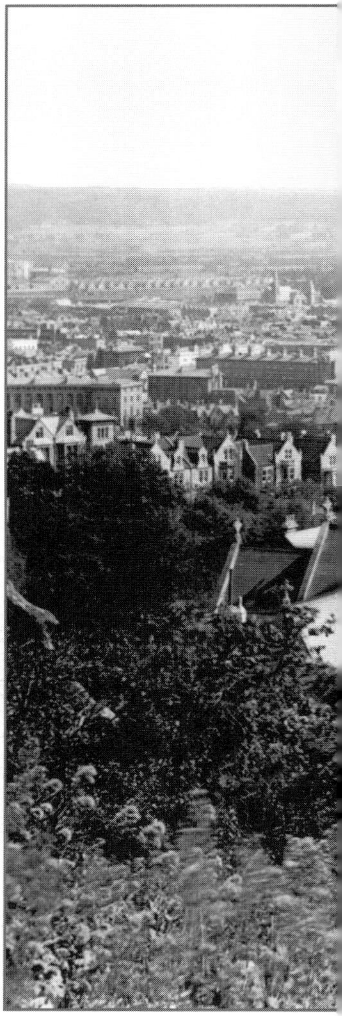

View from the Encampment 1923
74009
Another general view of Weston from the hill. The extension to the Grand Pier was removed in 1916 as the currents had proved too dangerous for steamers to safely berth there. The town is pictured just before the big developments of the 1920s and 1930s which saw the building of the Marine Lake, Open Air Pool, Winter Gardens and airport.

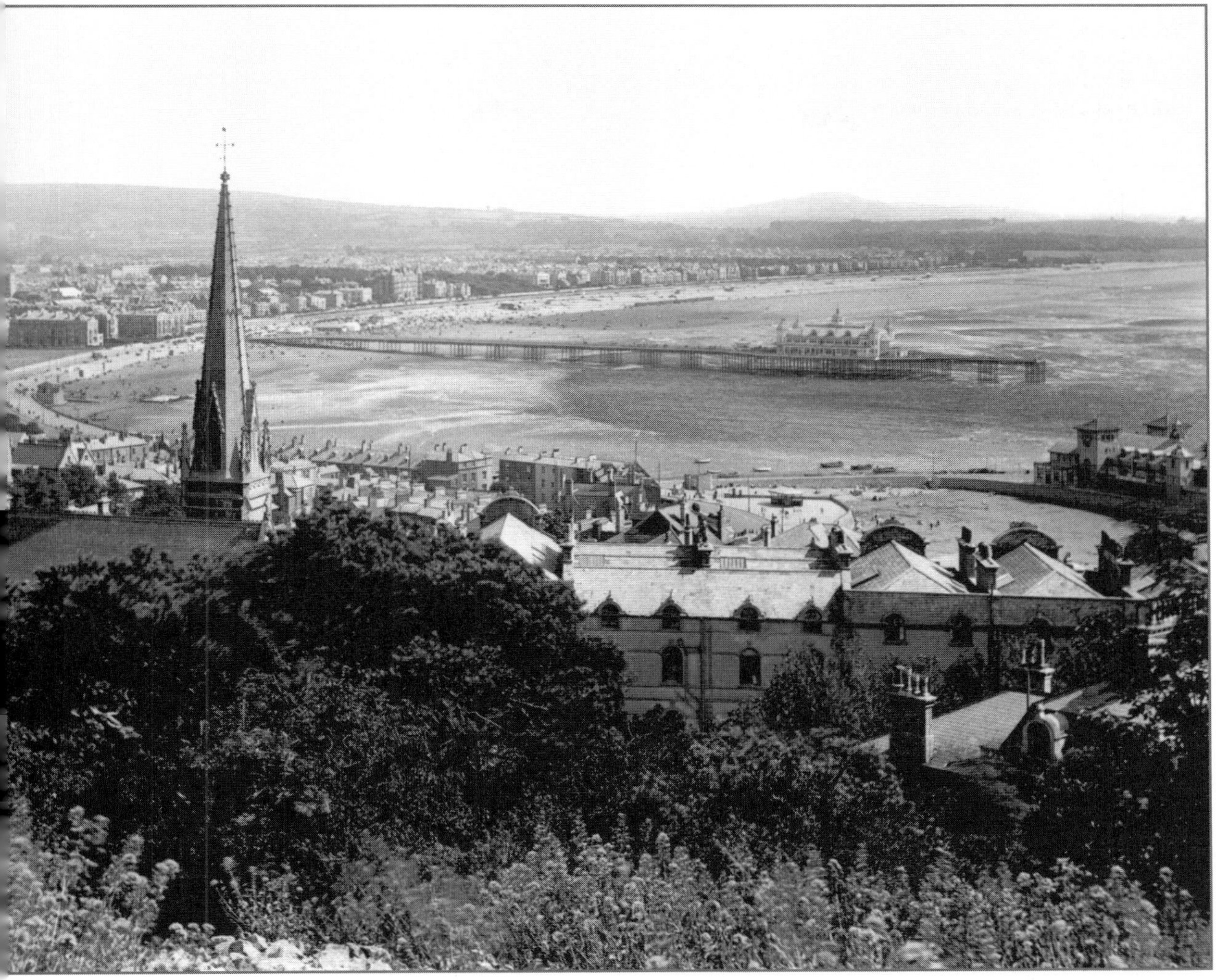

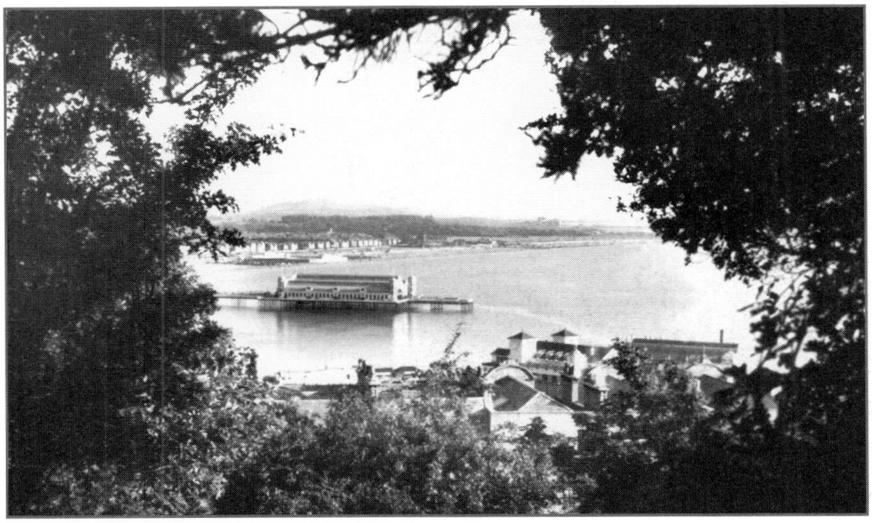

A Peep Through the Trees c1955 W69034

A picturesque scene, showing the Grand Pier and Knightstone framed by trees in Weston Woods. The pavilion on the Grand Pier was opened in 1933, and replaced the one shown in the previous pictures, which was destroyed by fire in 1930. Instead of a theatre, this pavilion housed amusement machines and a fun fair.

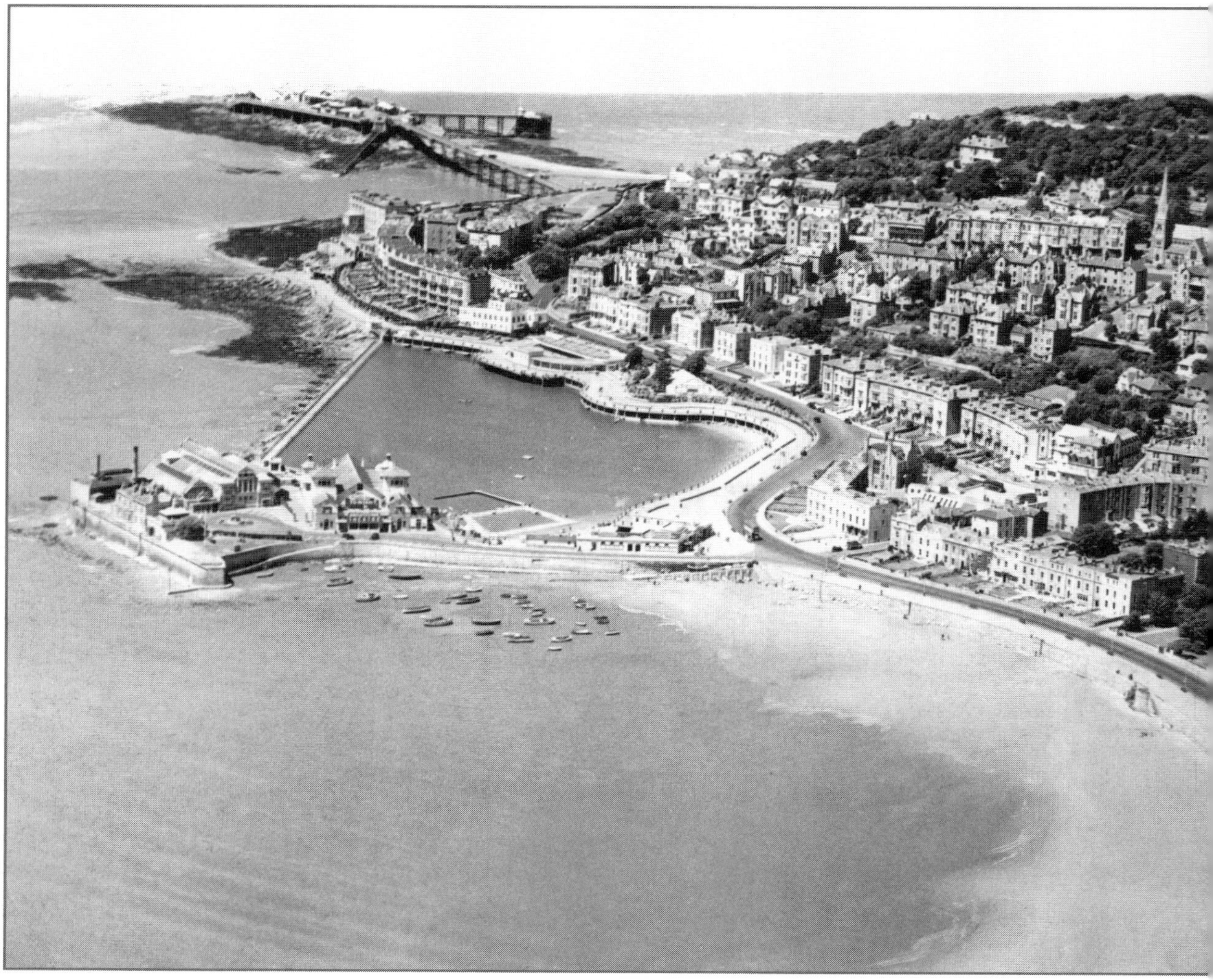

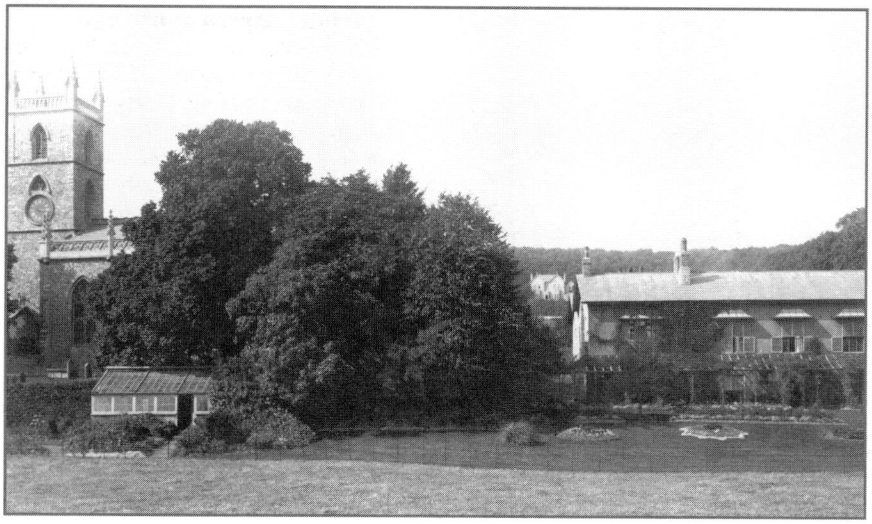

St John's Church and Rectory 1887 20340
The rectory, now known as Glebe House, is Weston's oldest surviving building, with parts dating back to the 17th century. During the English Civil War the rector, Christopher Sadbury, imprisoned rebel villagers here. In May 1889, the building was sold when a new rectory was built just to the north west of the church.

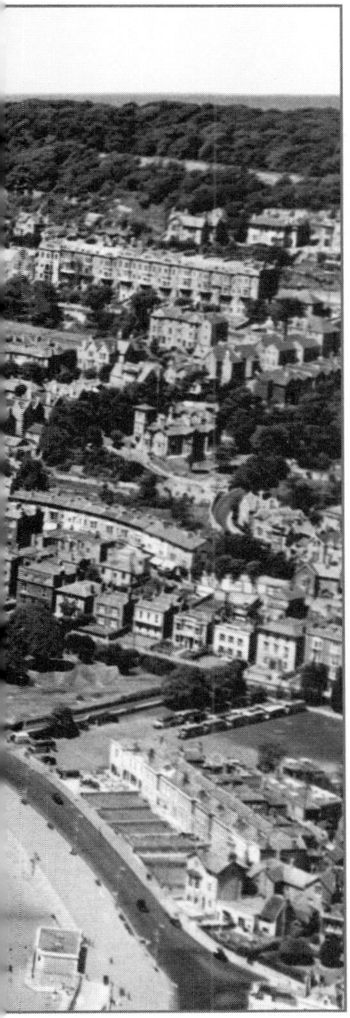

Overhead View c1959 W69083 This aerial shot shows the whole of the northern part of the town. In the distance is Birnbeck Pier with the steamer jetty to the north, and the lifeboat slipway on the south. In the distance a paddle steamer can be seen leaving the pier on its way to Wales. In the centre, the Marine Lake links Claremont with Knightstone, while to the right, the elegance of the mid 19th-century terraces and crescents is still apparent.

St John's Church 1887 20339
Weston's Parish Church was built in 1824. It replaced a Norman church that had become run down and semi-derelict. Rather than repair it, the decision was taken to rebuild. On the left is Oriel Terrace, built in 1847, while the grounds of Glebe House are on the right. The cast iron garden railings were all lost during World War Two, when they were removed for salvage.

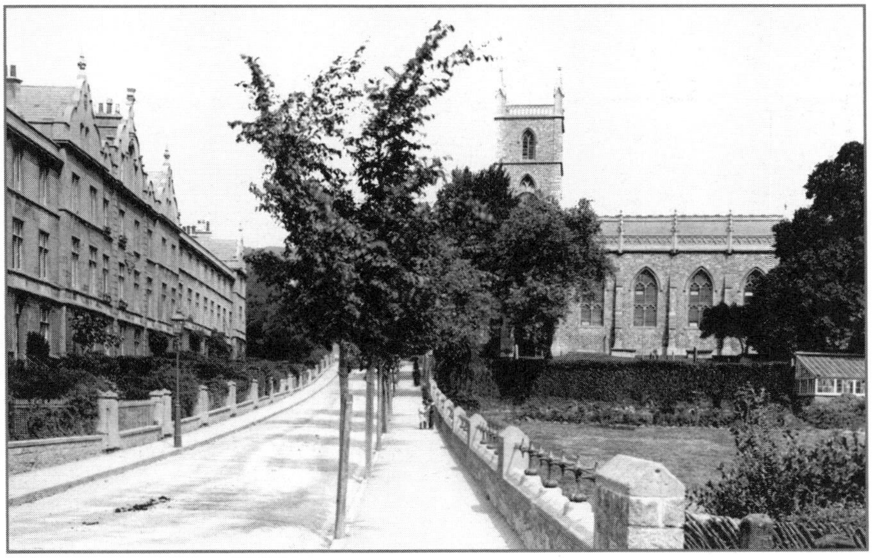

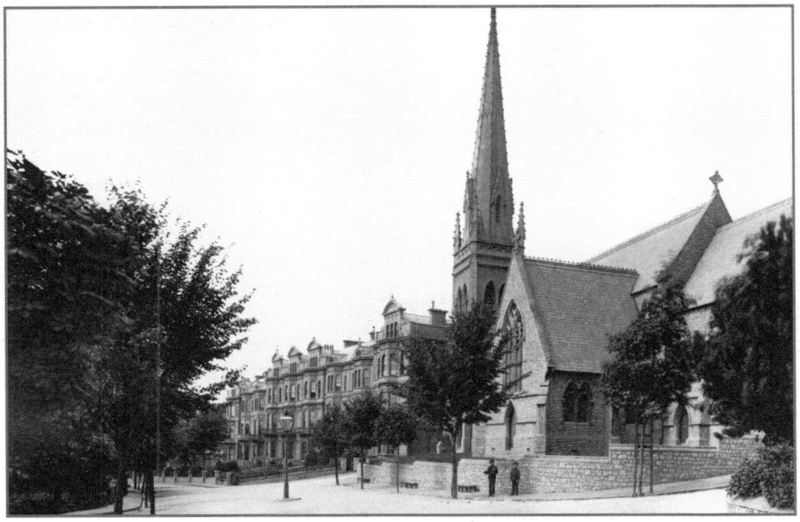

Trinity Church 1887 20341
This is Weston's third new Victorian church, opening in 1862. It was the centrepiece of the "Cliftonville" area around Shrubbery and Atlantic Roads. The church was derogatively known as the "Bonnet Shop" due to the high fashion worn by its wealthy congregation.

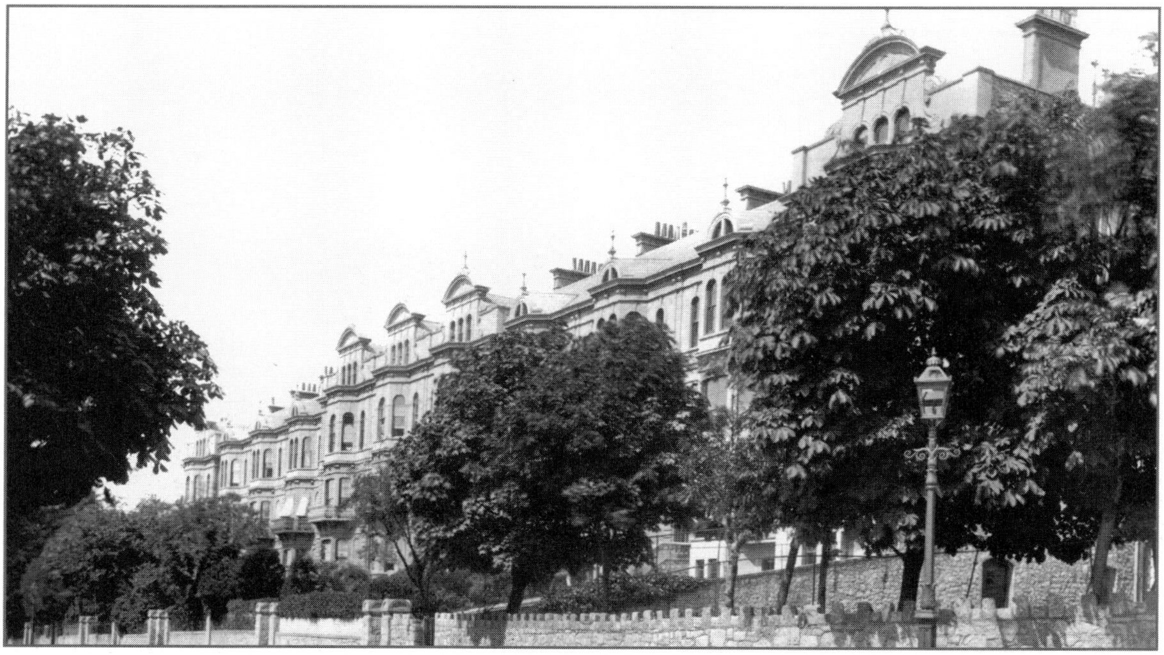

Atlantic Terrace 1887 20342
Part of the 'Cliftonville' area, these smart terraces housed the wealthy colonels, surgeons and Indian Army officers who retired to the seaside here. They enjoyed outstanding views across Weston Bay. Notice the particularly fine, cast-iron gas lamp on the corner just outside the grounds of St Faith's private school.

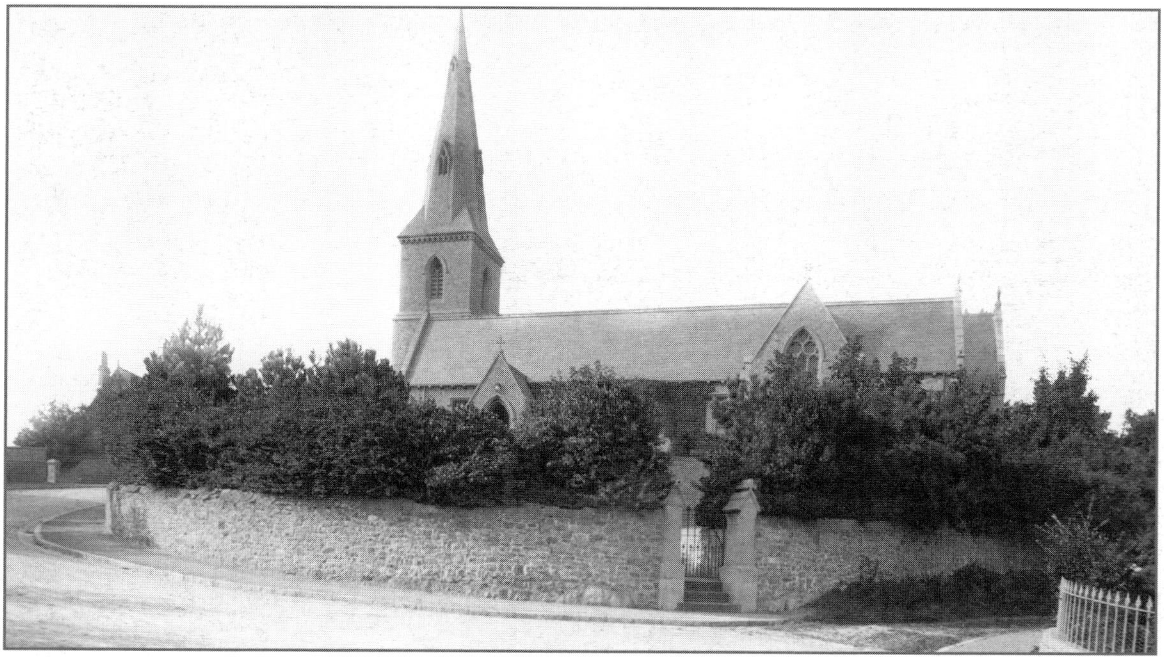

Christ Church 1887 20338
Christ Church was Weston's second new church, opening in 1855 to serve the new estates around Montpelier. Unusually, the church was built before the houses. The Parish of Christ Church stretches down to Baker Street and Alfred Street, where the school and church hall were built.

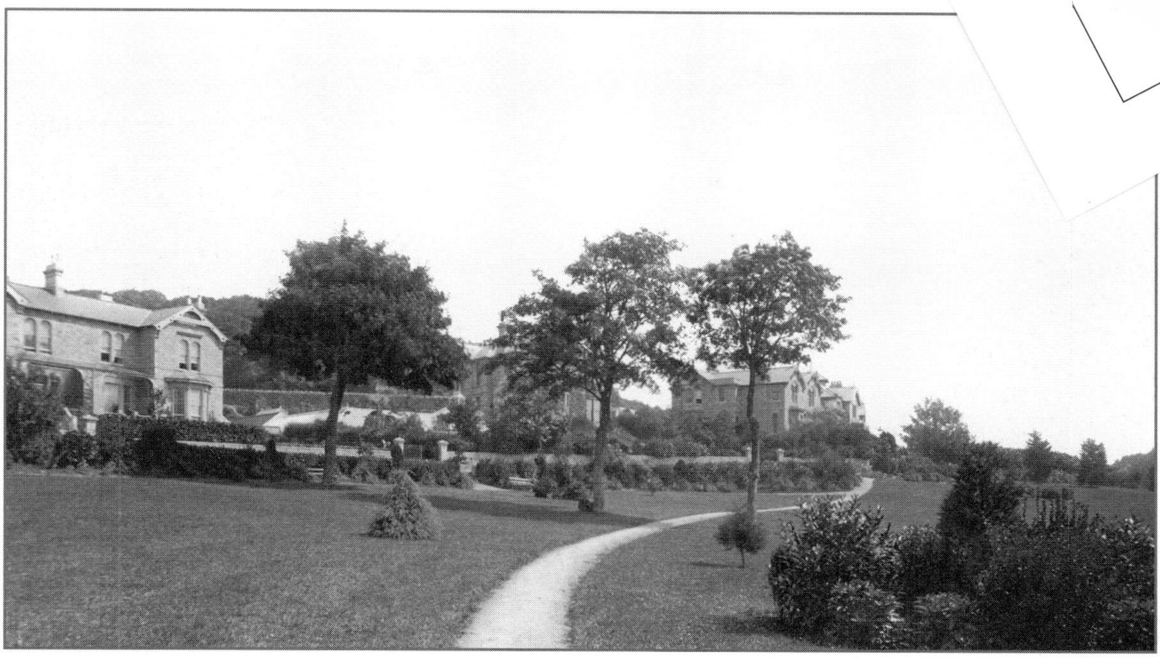

Eastfield Park 1887 20343

This small exclusive estate was built in the 1870s. Besides the large private gardens attached to each house, there was this attractive communal private park, carefully landscaped with the shrubs and trees beloved of Victorian gardeners. The houses themselves were designed for large families, with extensive servants quarters.

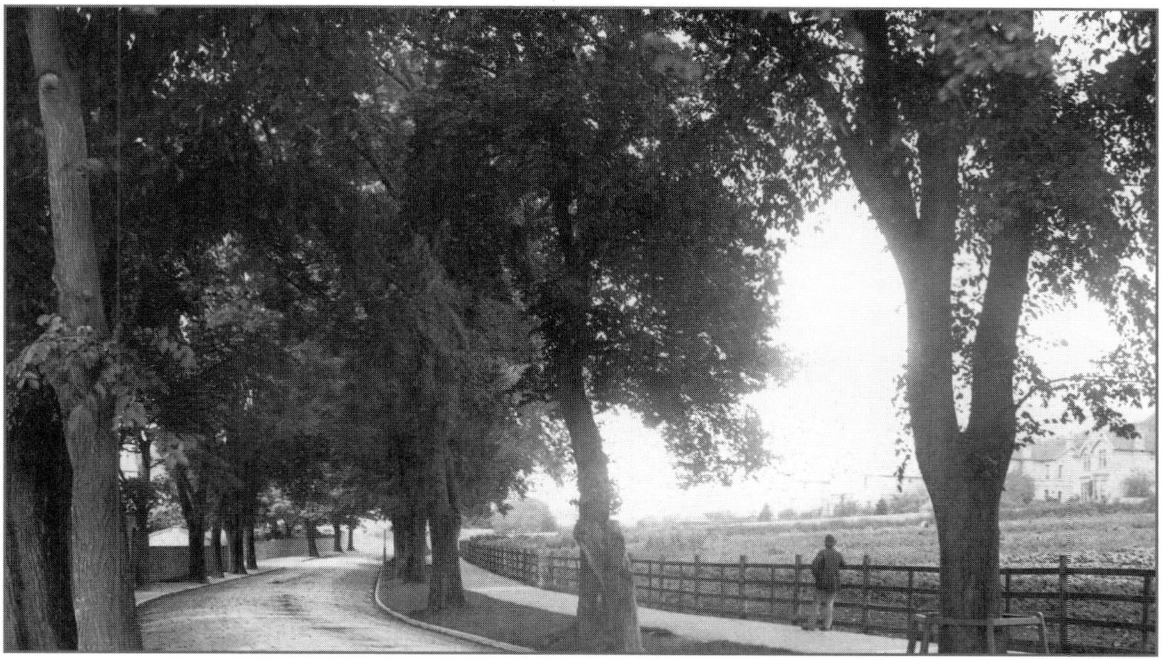

On the Bristol Road 1887 20347

This rural scene shows the houses of Eastfield Park in the distance on the right. To the left can just be glimpsed the entrance to Weston Cemetery. On the left, between the cemetery and Milton, would have been farmland, now all built on; whilst to the right, there were no other buildings between these and The Lodge, home of the Earl of Cavan.

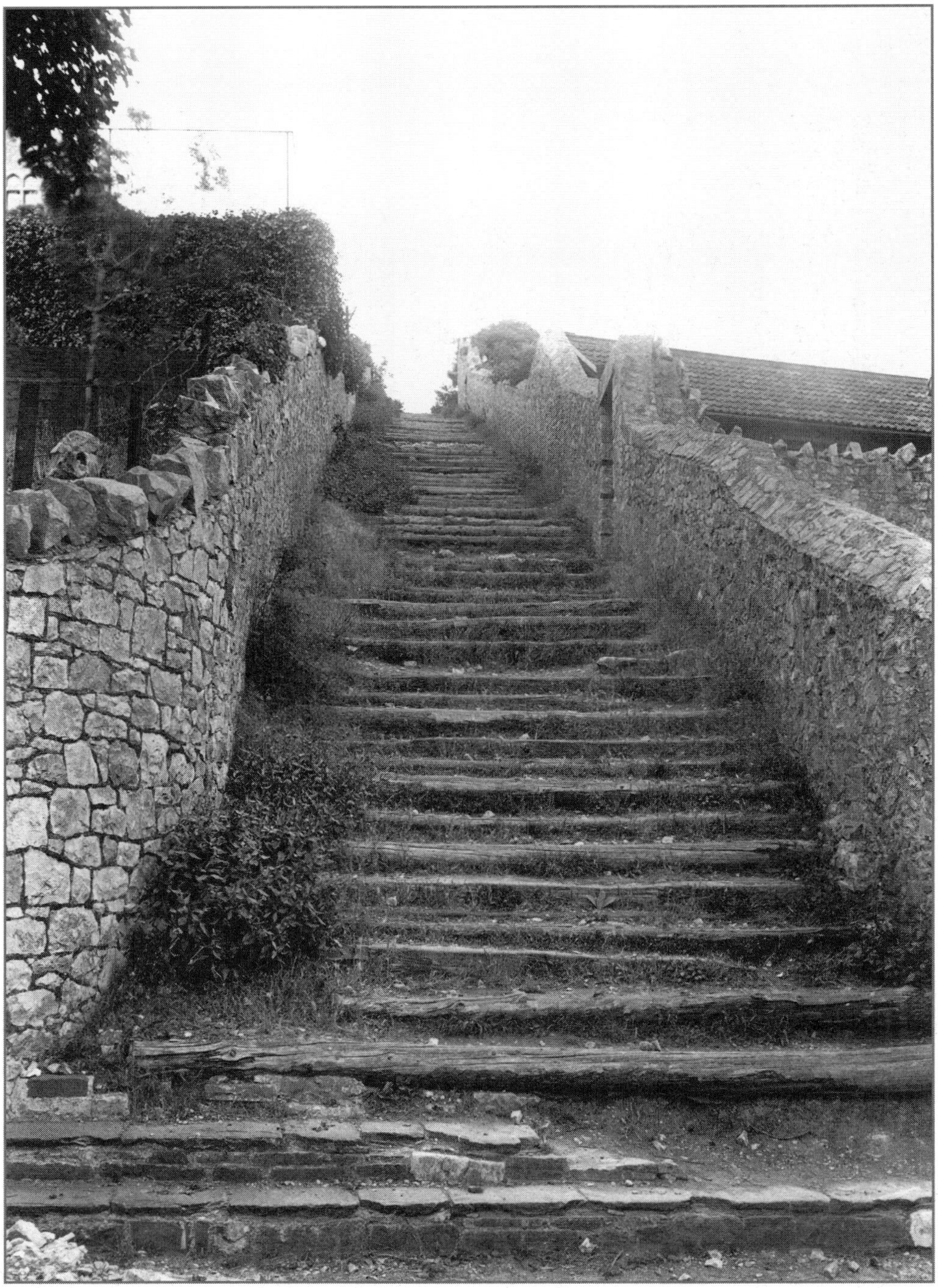

Steps to the Encampment 1913 65360
These rough timber steps led up from Camp Road to one of the prehistoric entrances of the Iron Age hillfort of Worlebury. They have since been replaced by concrete ones.

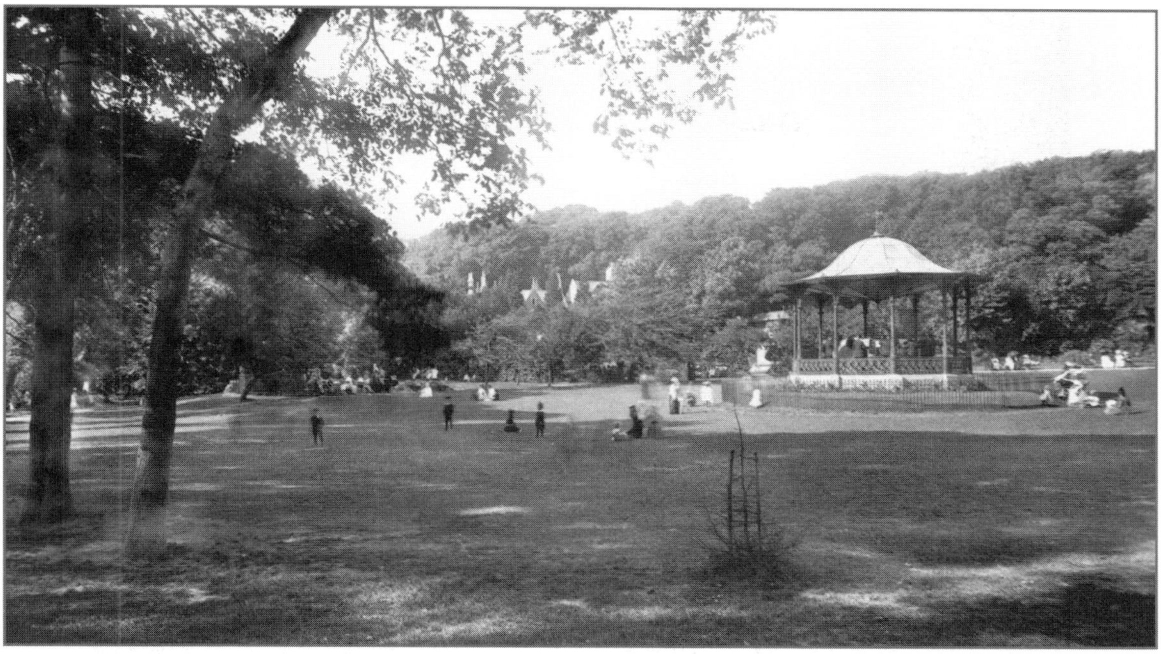

Grove Park 1892 31248
This was once The Grove, the private grounds surrounding Grove House, home of the Lord of the Manor. The Town acquired the house and parkland in 1889, and the attractive cast iron bandstand was built a year later from parts cast at Hills Brothers Sun Foundry at Alloa. It was a focal point for the celebration of national and local events.

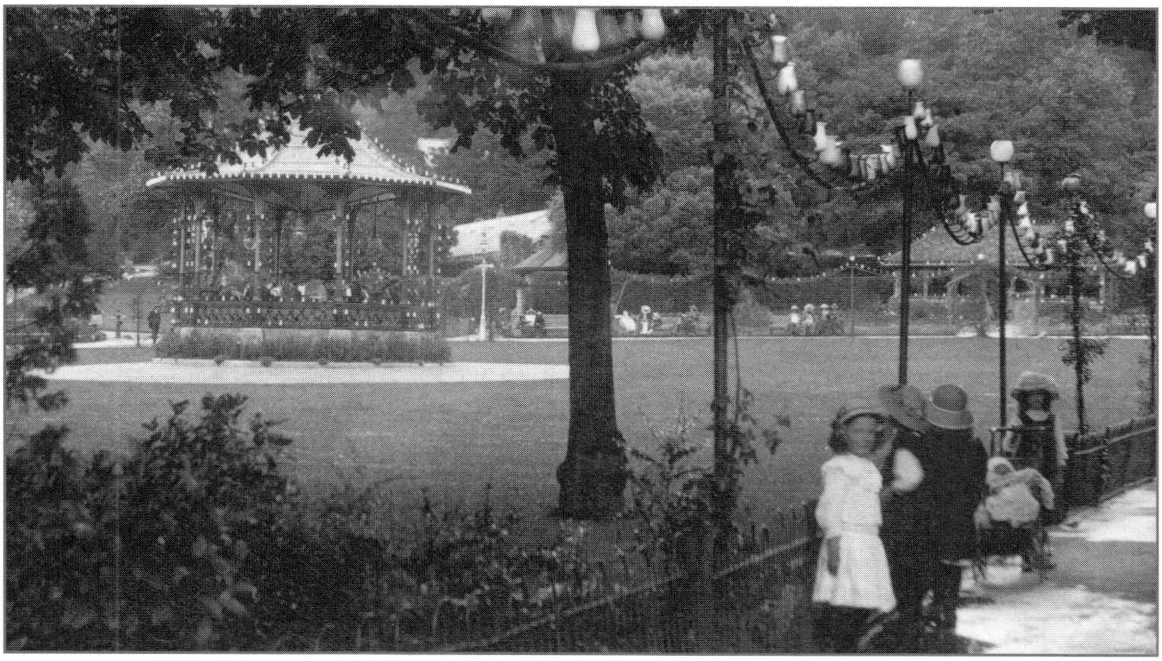

Grove Park 1913 65162
Here you can clearly see the coloured glass fairy lights, lit by electricity at night to create a fairyland feel. The group of children includes a girl with her doll in a pushchair. Dolls of this period usually had bisque (or unglazed) china heads with a composition body, and were easily broken.

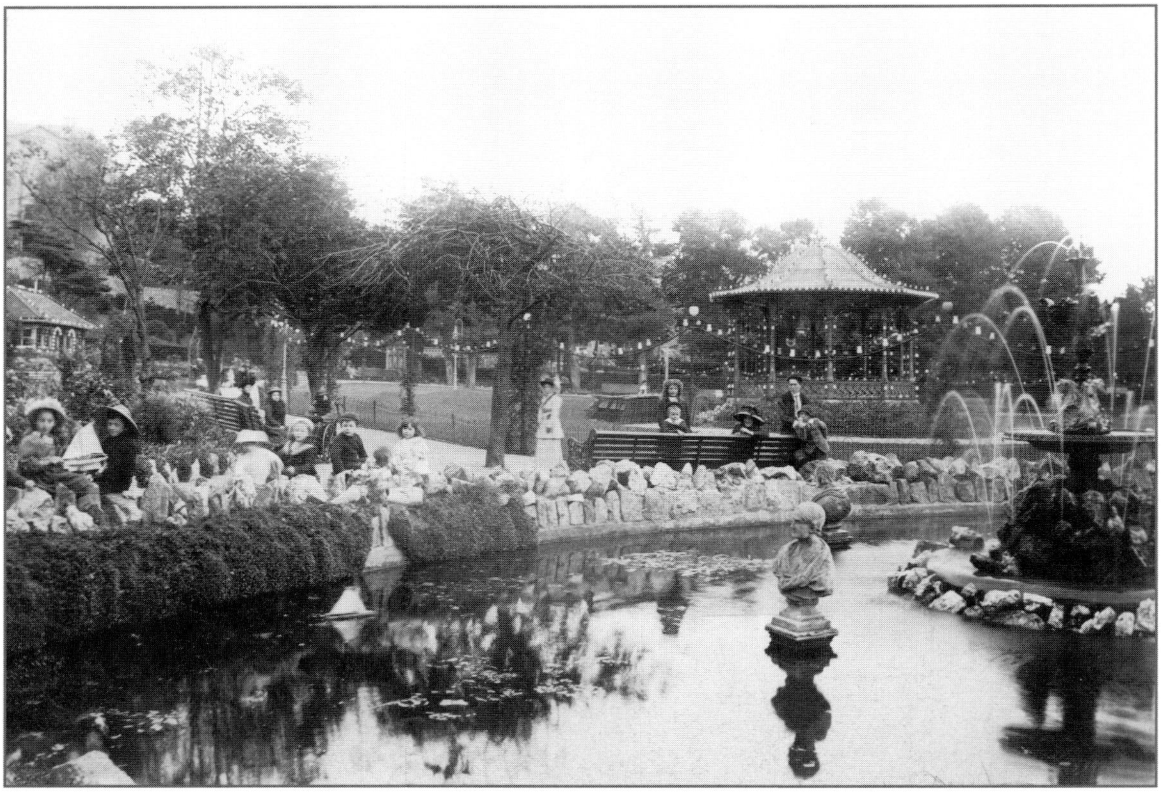

Grove Park 1913 65163
Stone busts of Shakespeare, Bacon, Locke, Voltaire, Newton and others stand in the pond. Today only one remains in a nearby flower-bed. In the 1700s these busts belonged to Sir Hugh Walpole in Twickenham. They were taken to Brockley Hall by John Hugh Smyth Pigott, who bought them in 1842, and were then placed in Prince Consort Gardens in 1864. They were finally moved to the grounds of Grove House in 1882 after one was vandalised.

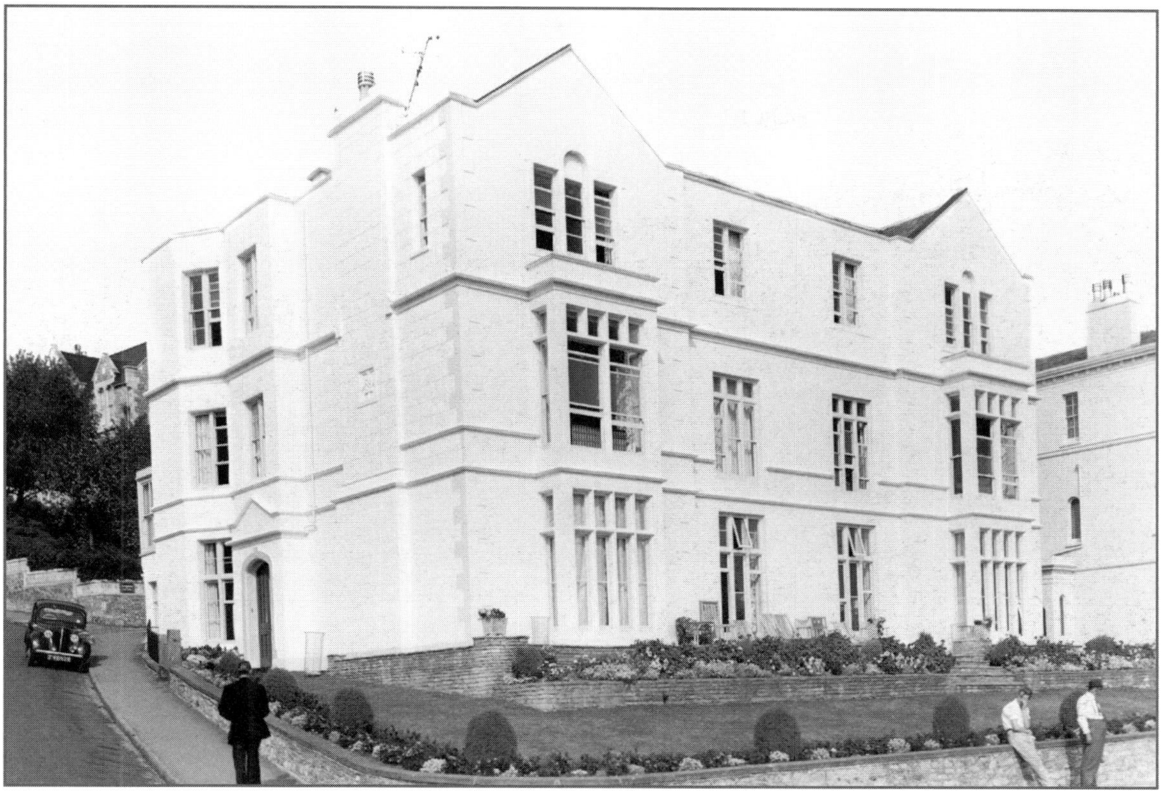

Stanley House
Bristol Aeroplane Co Welfare Dept c1955 W69503
Originally Elizabethan Villas and then the Madeira Hotel, this building, built in the 1840s, is on the corner of Birnbeck and Paragon Roads. The Bristol Aeroplane Company set up in the town during the Second World War. In the 1950s they were the largest single employer in the West Country, making aluminium prefabricated buildings as well as aircraft.

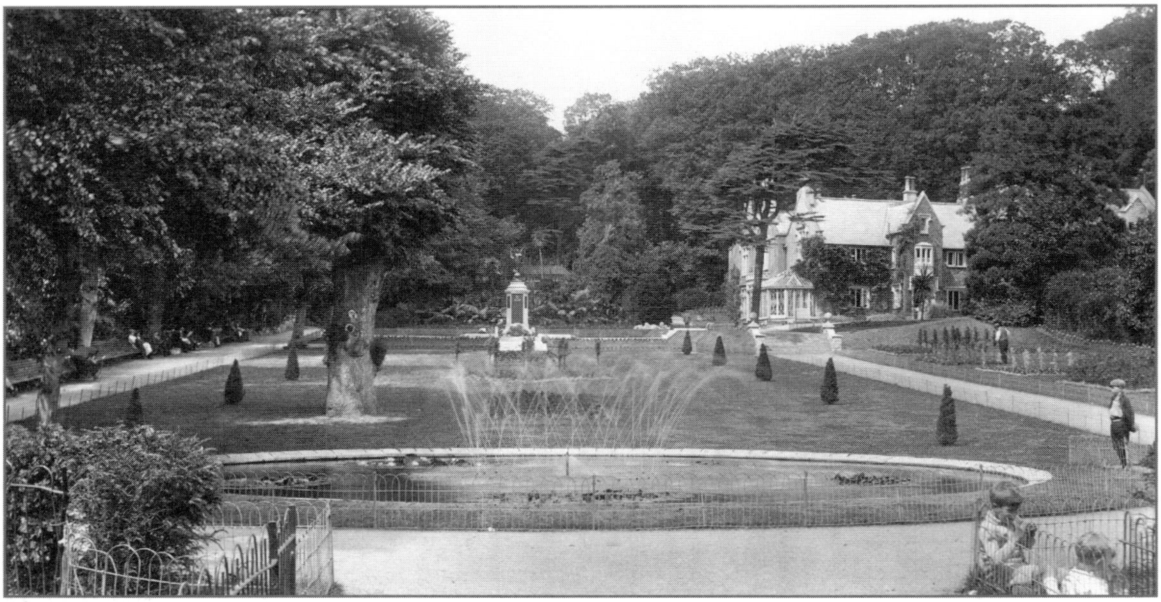

Grove Park 1923 74031
This manor house was bought by the Pigotts of Brockley in 1696. When the Town bought the house and land in 1889, it was decided to house the library here until the new one in the Boulevard opened in 1900. Later it became a cafe and a private house. The house was badly damaged by incendiary bombs during World War Two, and in the 1950s all but the coach house was demolished.

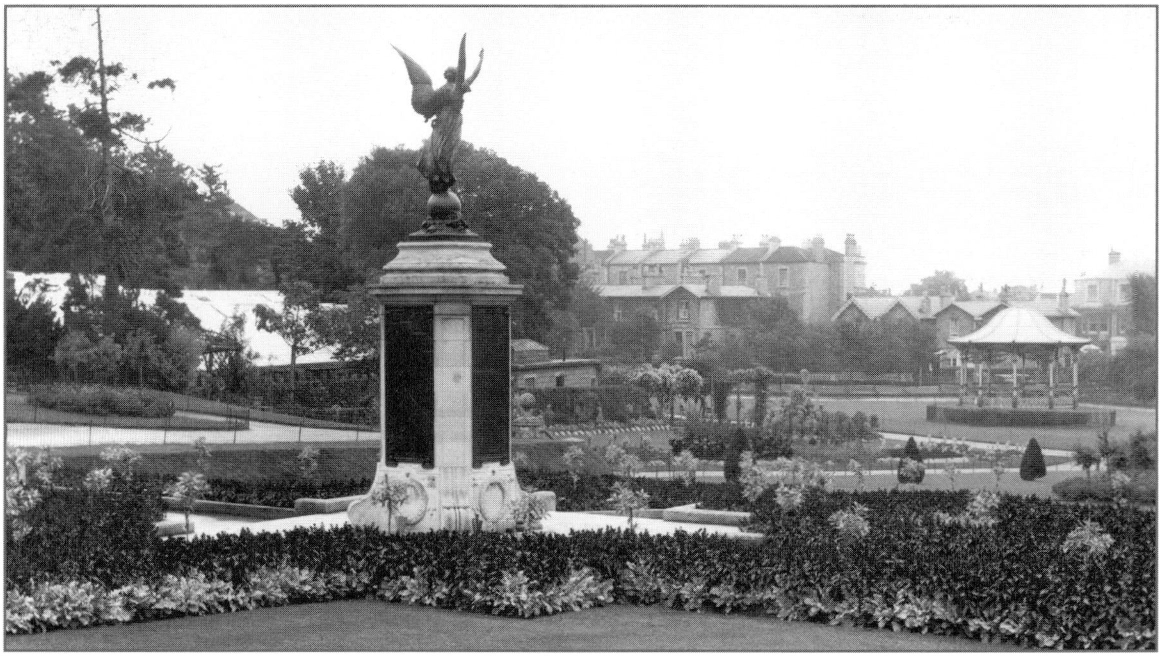

The War Memorial, Grove Park c1950 W69008
This First World War memorial, with its Portland stone terraces, was designed by the eminent sculptor Alfred Drury and installed in 1922. On top of the column is a bronze casting of winged Victory standing on a globe with one hand bearing the victor's palm, now sadly broken off.

The Sea Front

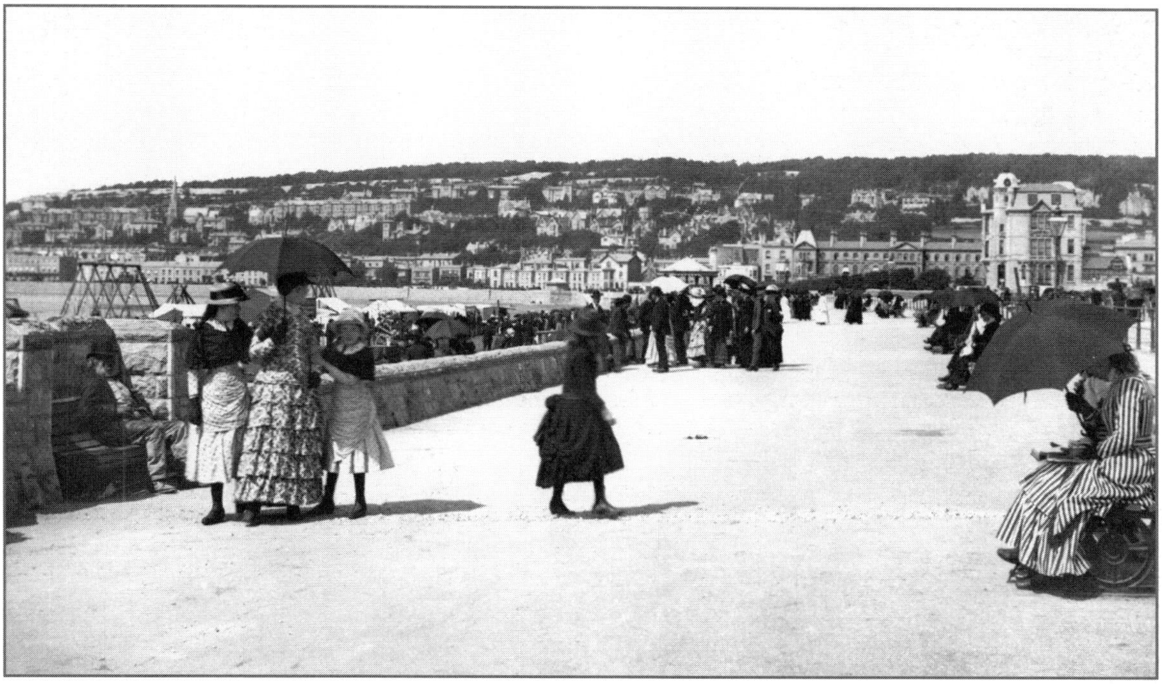

Marine Parade 1887 20329

This promenade with its wide walkway and low wall was built in 1883. Two miles long, it stretches from the Royal Hospital right around the bay to Birnbeck Pier, and was a major feat of engineering in its day. Note the two women in their 'seaside' dresses. These were usually made from cottons rather than the usual silks, which would have been damaged by the salty seaside air.

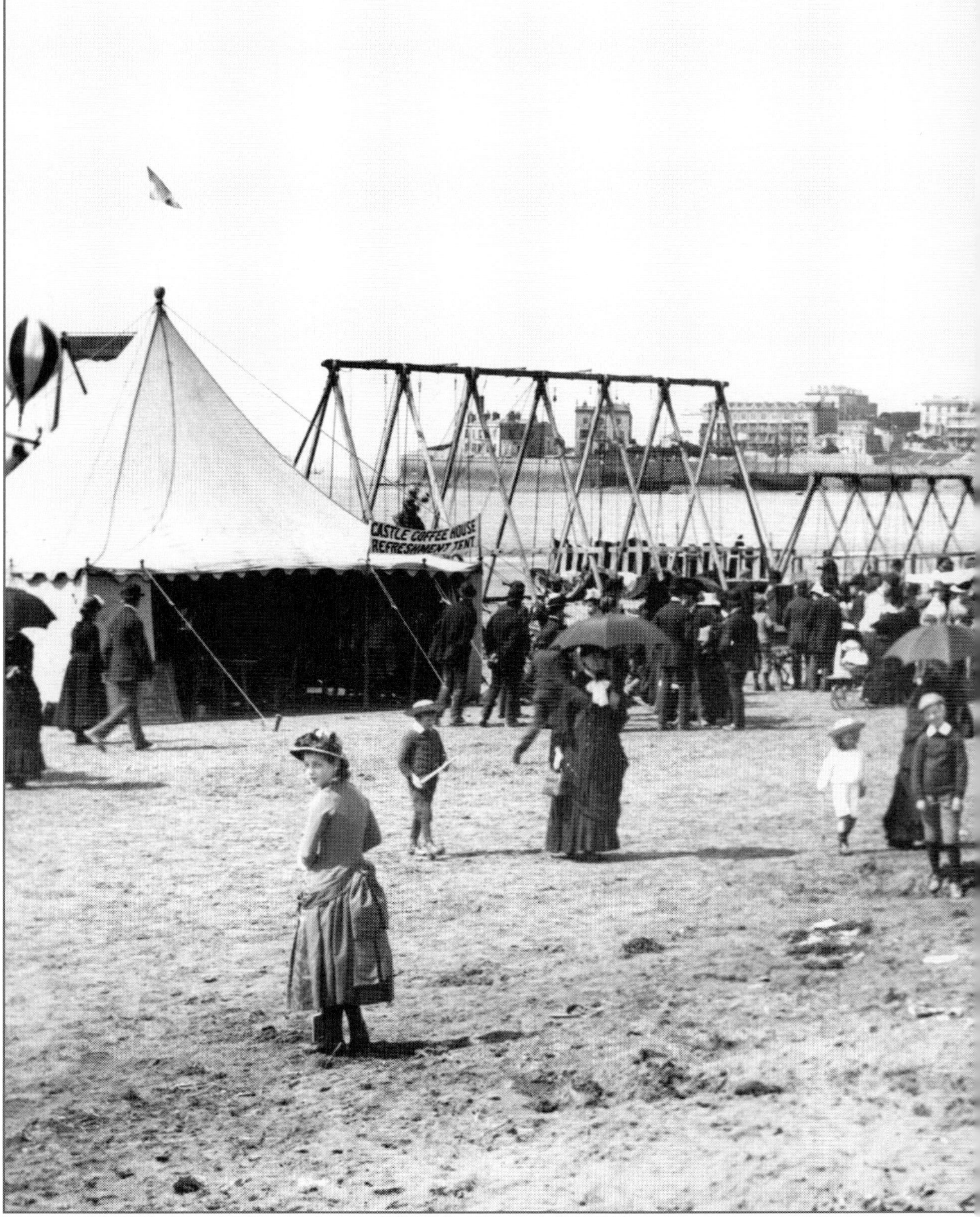
CASTLE COFFEE HOUSE
REFRESHMENT TENT

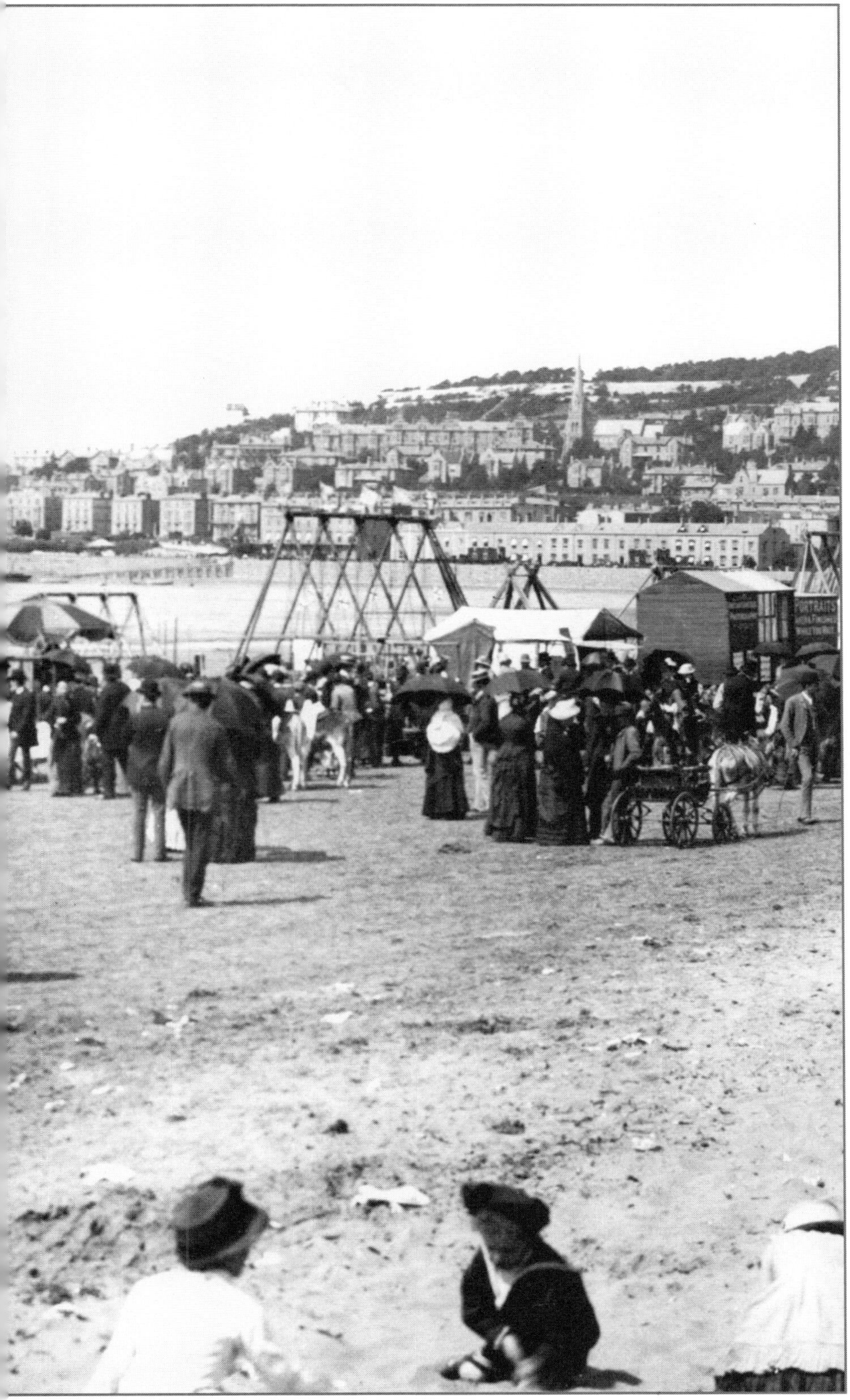

The Sands 1887 20318
Here you can see the wide range of entertainment on offer on the beach. On the left, the tea tent was run by the Castle Coffee House, based in Castle Street. To the right is a small shed advertising portraits 'painted and finished while you wait'. In these days before the Box Brownie camera was developed, there was often a beach photographer offering photographic portraits as well.

The Parade 1901 47874
Another view that clearly shows the 1883 promenade and sea wall. Before this was built, the beach stretched much further inland and sand dunes often formed as far as Regent Street. On the sands, donkeys wait for riders, as they have done since the earliest days of the resort.

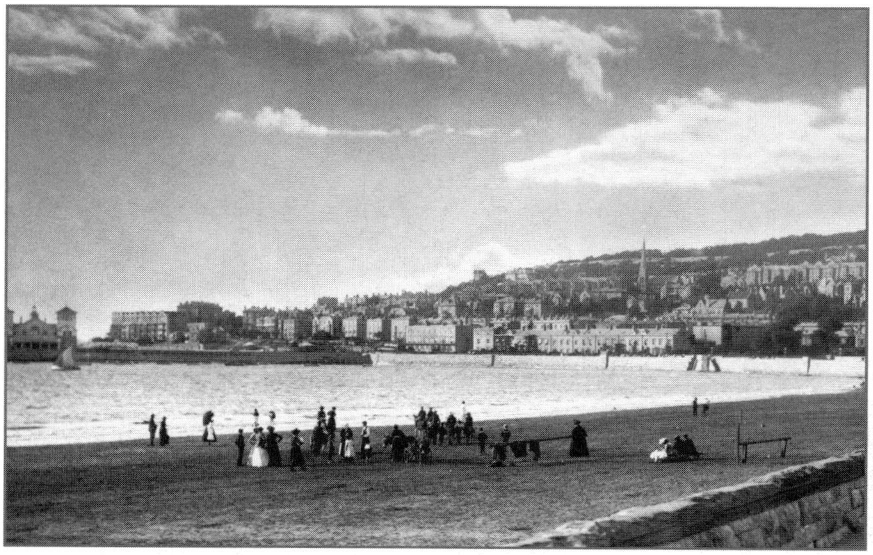

The Marine Parade 1902 48771
Taken from the southern corner of Victoria Square, this view shows the promenade just before the Grand Pier was built. In the foreground one of the new electric trams is passing a row of horse wagonettes. Competition between the two was fierce, with cabbies often driving slowly in front of a tram to delay it. On Knightstone you can see the new swimming baths and theatre.

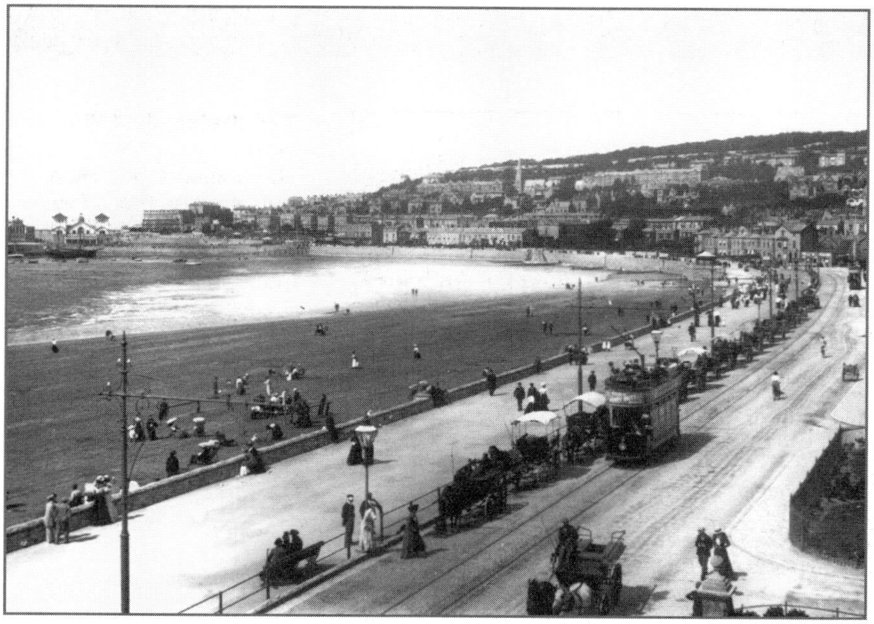

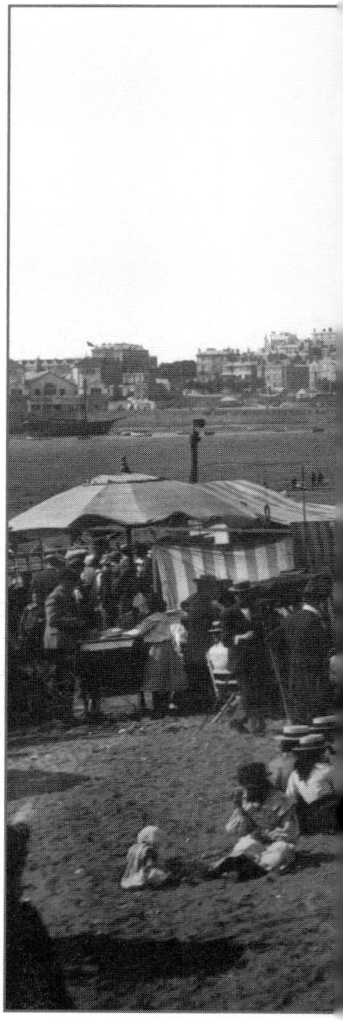

The Sands 1902 48773
This shows a packed beach with striped umbrellas marking the variety of stalls. These sold everything from teas and soft drinks to shellfish and souvenirs. There were also temporary stages set up with concert parties, pierrots and other entertainers. The crowds here appear to be centred around one of these.

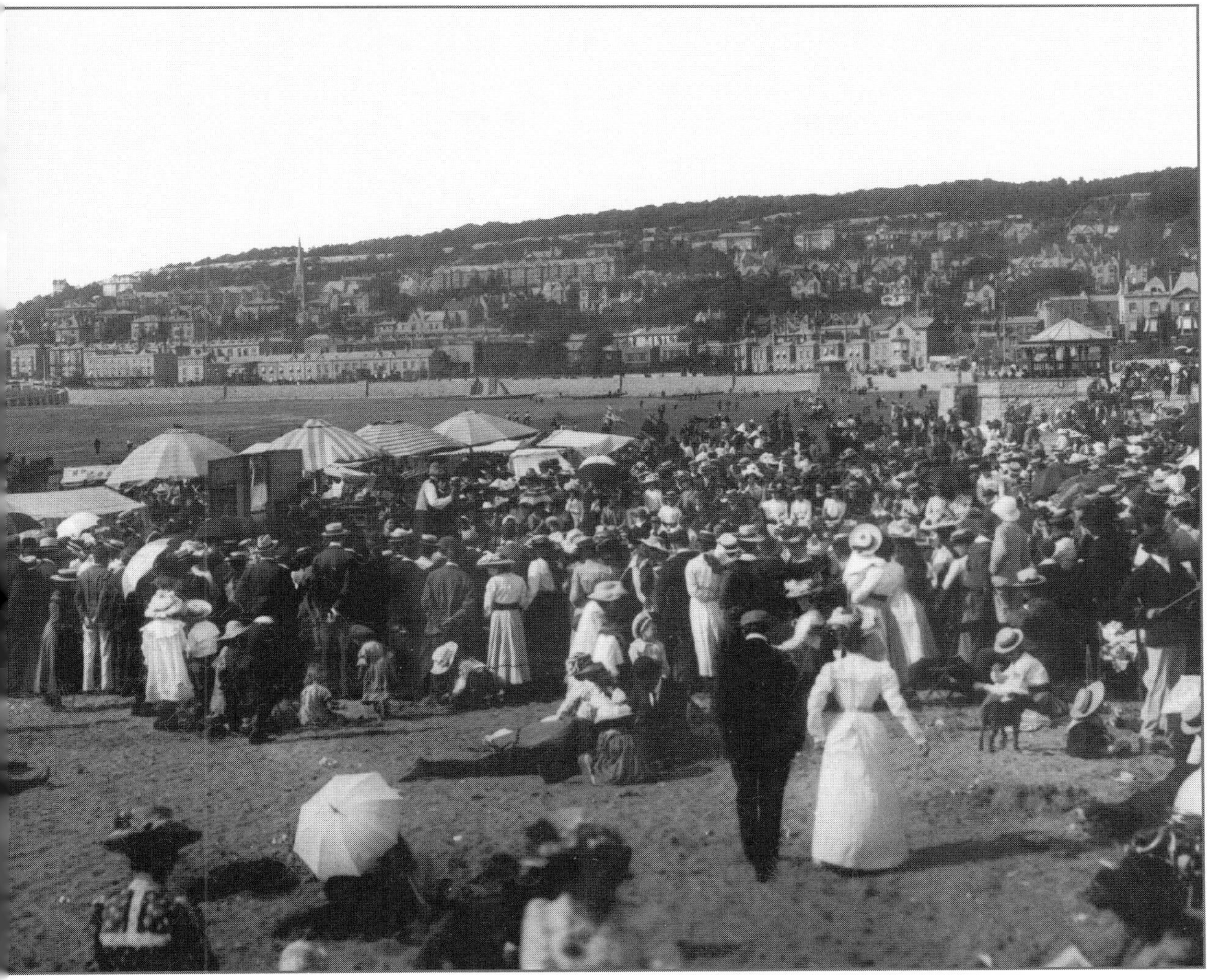

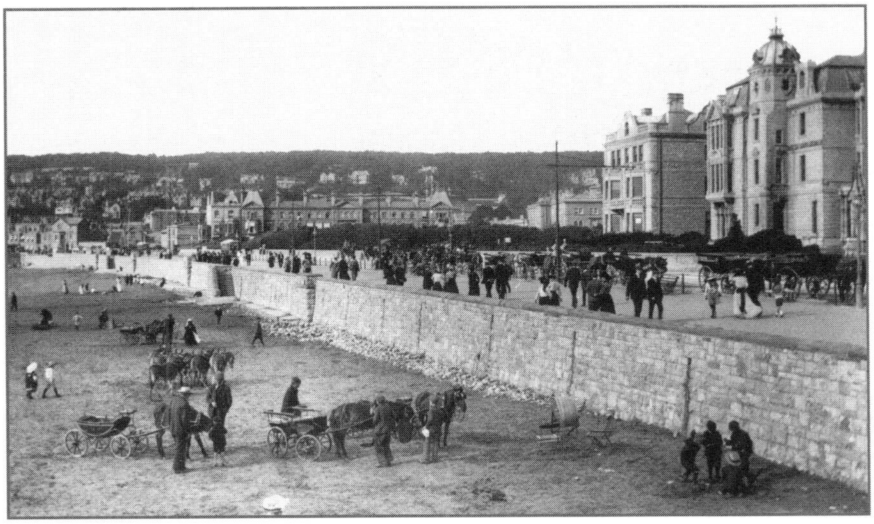

The Esplanade 1904

53006

This photograph is taken from the new Grand Pier. The previous year a great storm wrecked much of the sea front including the promenade shown here. Note the tiny donkey carts, used to give rides to children. A line of shrubs marks out Roger's Field. The Winter Gardens Pavilion would be built here in the 1920s.

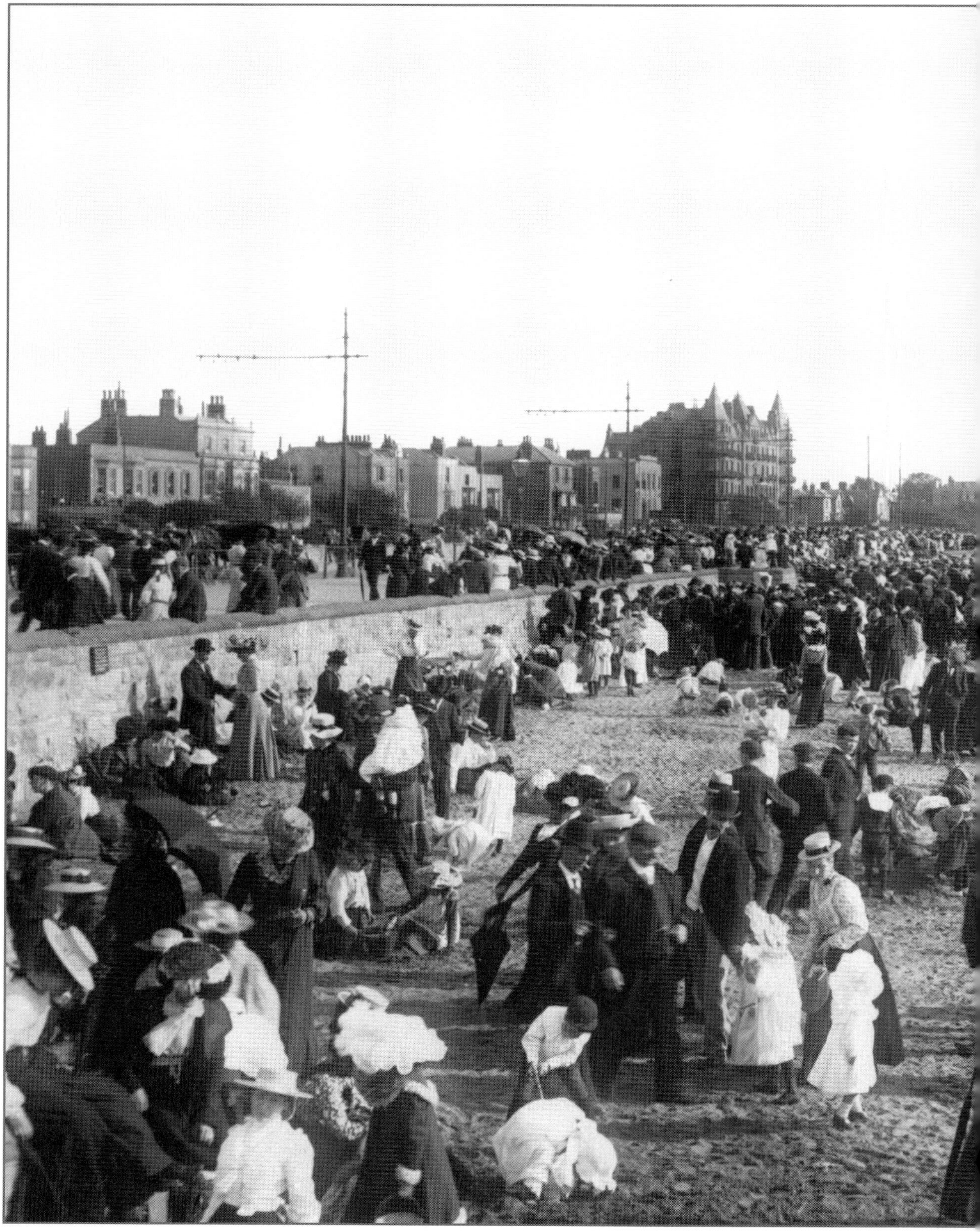

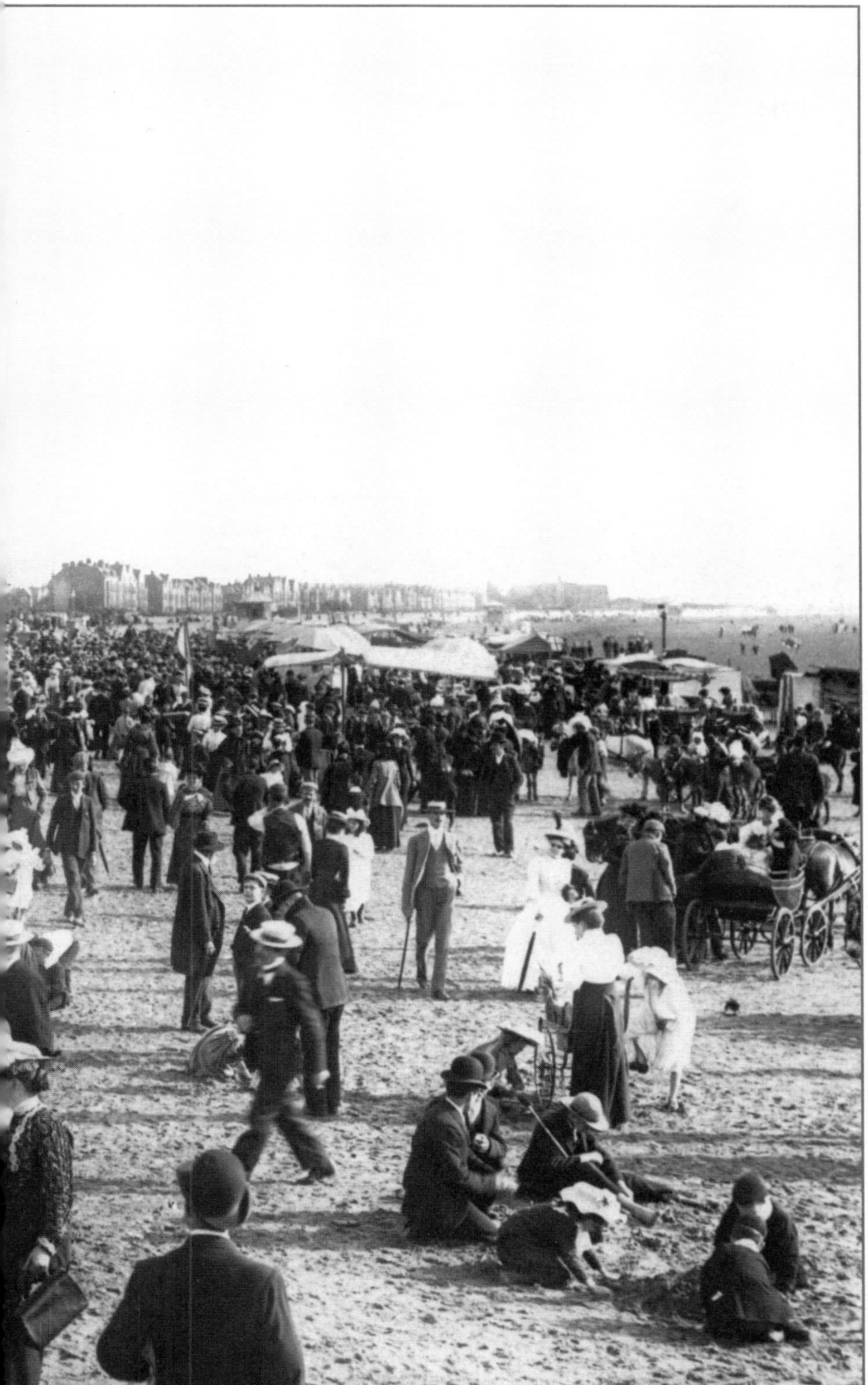

The Sands 1902 48777
Another view of happy holidaymakers. The costume here is interesting. Not a single person can be seen without a hat: the gentlemen wear bowlers, boaters or caps, while the ladies and children favour a variety of designs. For women, a sun tan was highly undesirable, as it marked you as an outdoor worker and therefore of lower class.

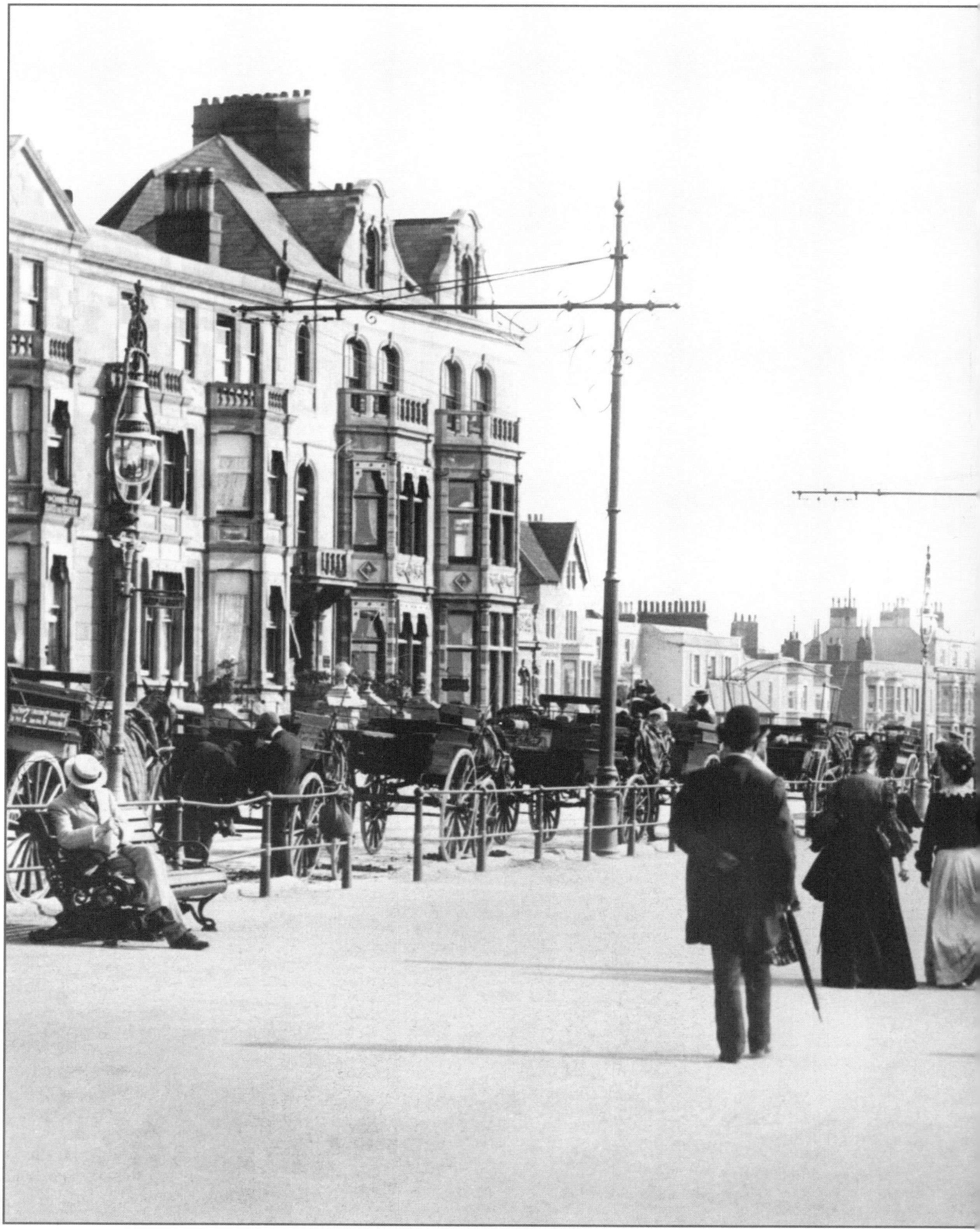

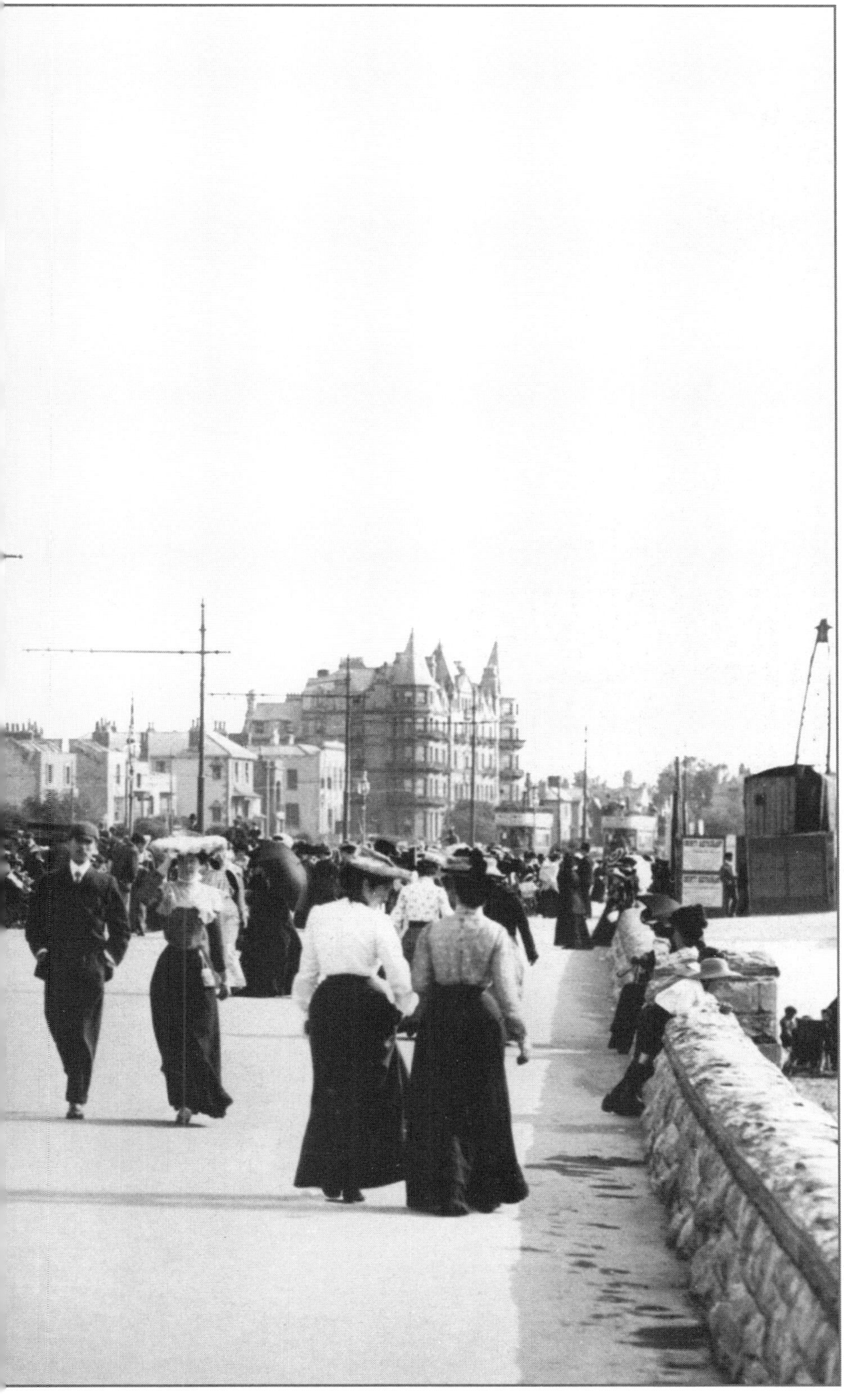

The Esplanade 1904
53015
Horse-drawn wagonettes are lined up for business under the iron gantries carrying the electric tram cables. On the right a sign reads 'Grand Pier Works', an indication that the new pier was in the process of being built. Because Birnbeck Pier was so out of the way for visitors arriving by rail, this pier was built at the end of Regent Street.

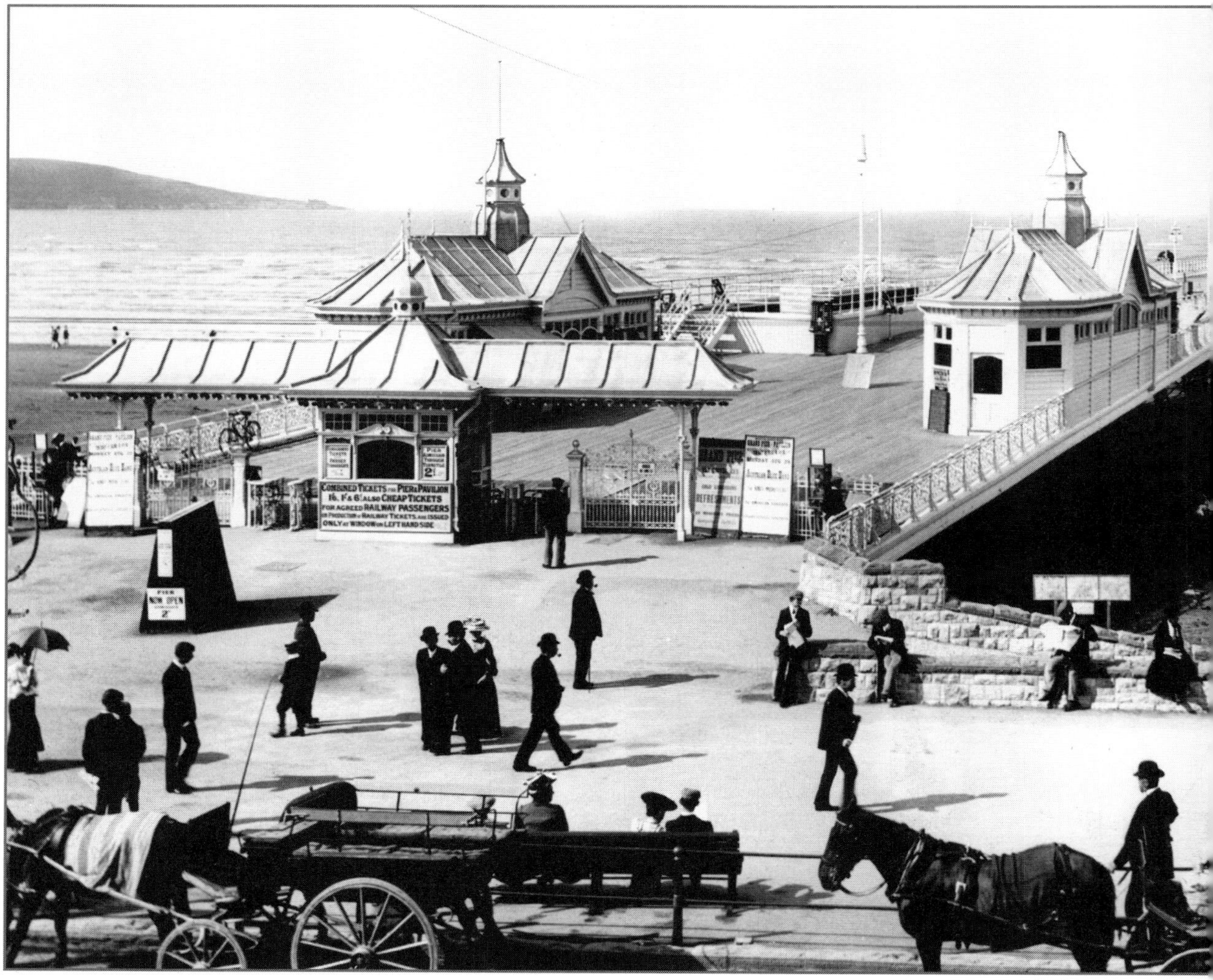

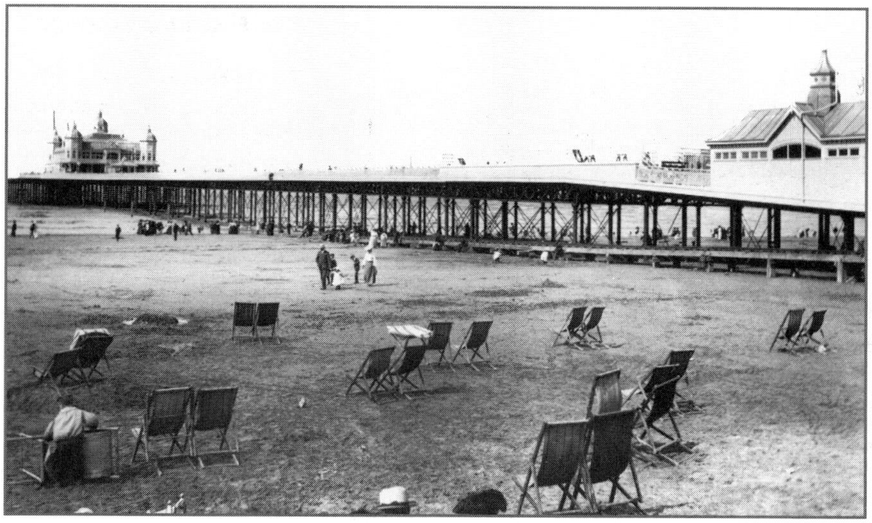

The Grand Pier 1904

53014

This picture of the new pier was taken shortly after it opened. The trackway used in its construction can still be seen on the beach. The pavilion at the end of the pier housed a 2,000-seat theatre where all the top music hall stars of the day appeared.

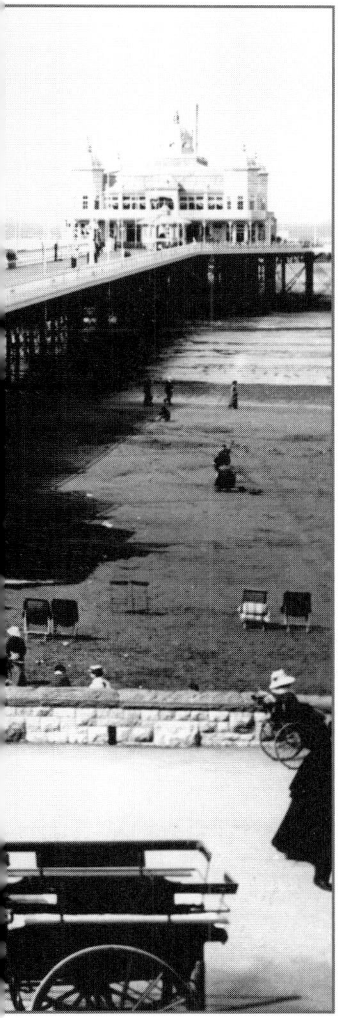

The Grand Pier 1904 53003
The newly opened Grand Pier here looks very pristine. Admission was 2d, or between 6d and 1s 6d (2½p-7½p) for a combined ticket to the pier and pavilion. The small pavilion to the right of the entrance was a booking office for Bristol Tramways & Carriage Co motor taxis and charabancs, which offered excursions into the countryside.

From the Pier 1904
53007
This view shows the fine sweep of Weston Bay. From the left, we can see Knightstone Harbour, then Birnbeck and Knightstone Roads as far as Park Place. The steeple of Holy Trinity Church, built in the 1860s, rises in the centre. In the lower right is an interesting cane pushchair.

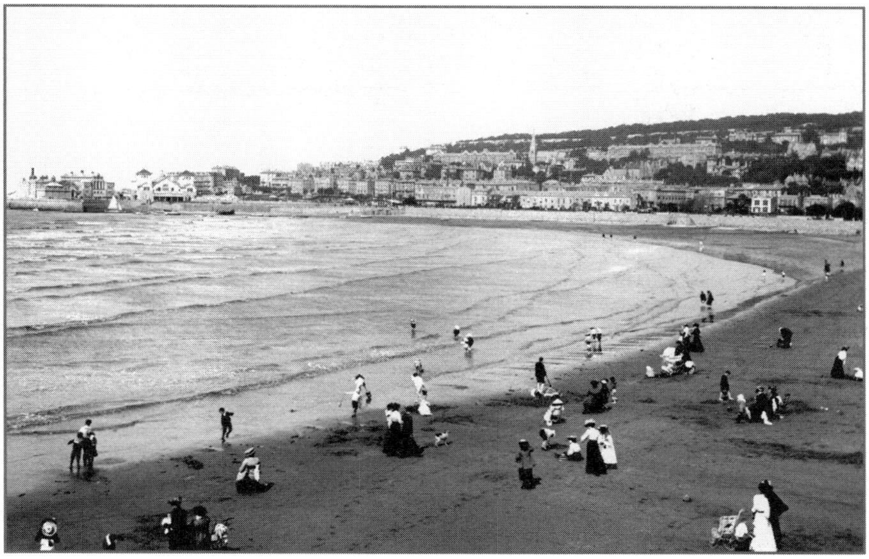

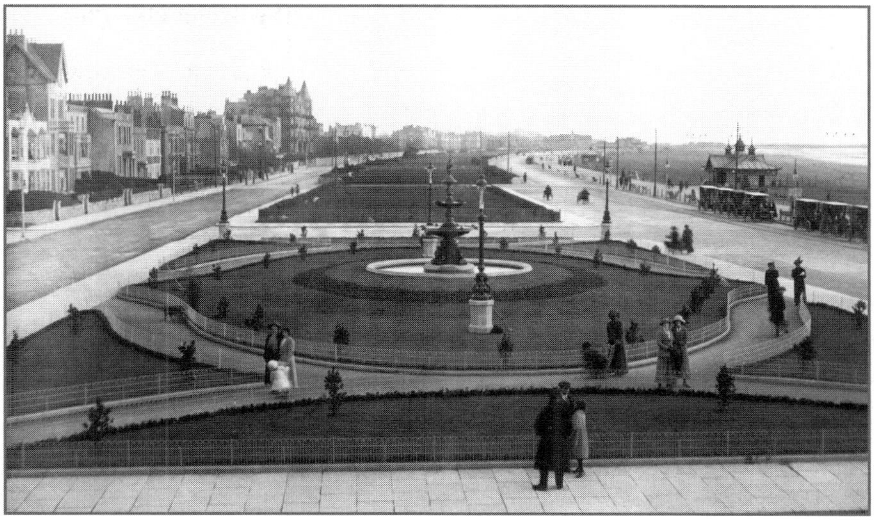

The Beach Lawns c1920
48770A
This open space was originally a private communal garden for the houses of Beach Road. The fine cast iron fountain in the centre was donated to the town by Mr Macfarlane when the gardens opened to the public in 1910. It was made at the Coalbrookdale factory in Telford, Shropshire.

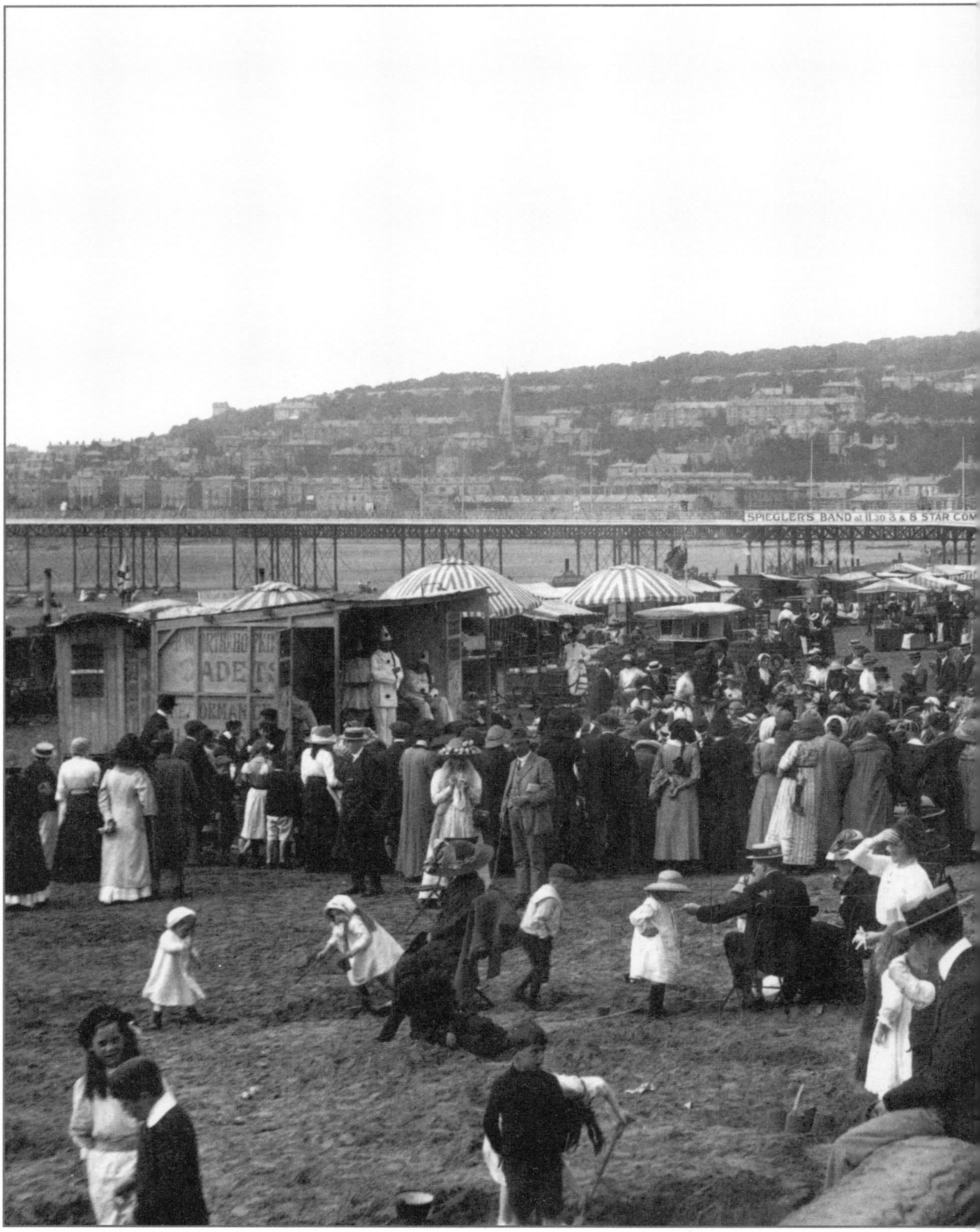
SPIEGLER'S BAND at 11.30 3 & 8 STAR COM

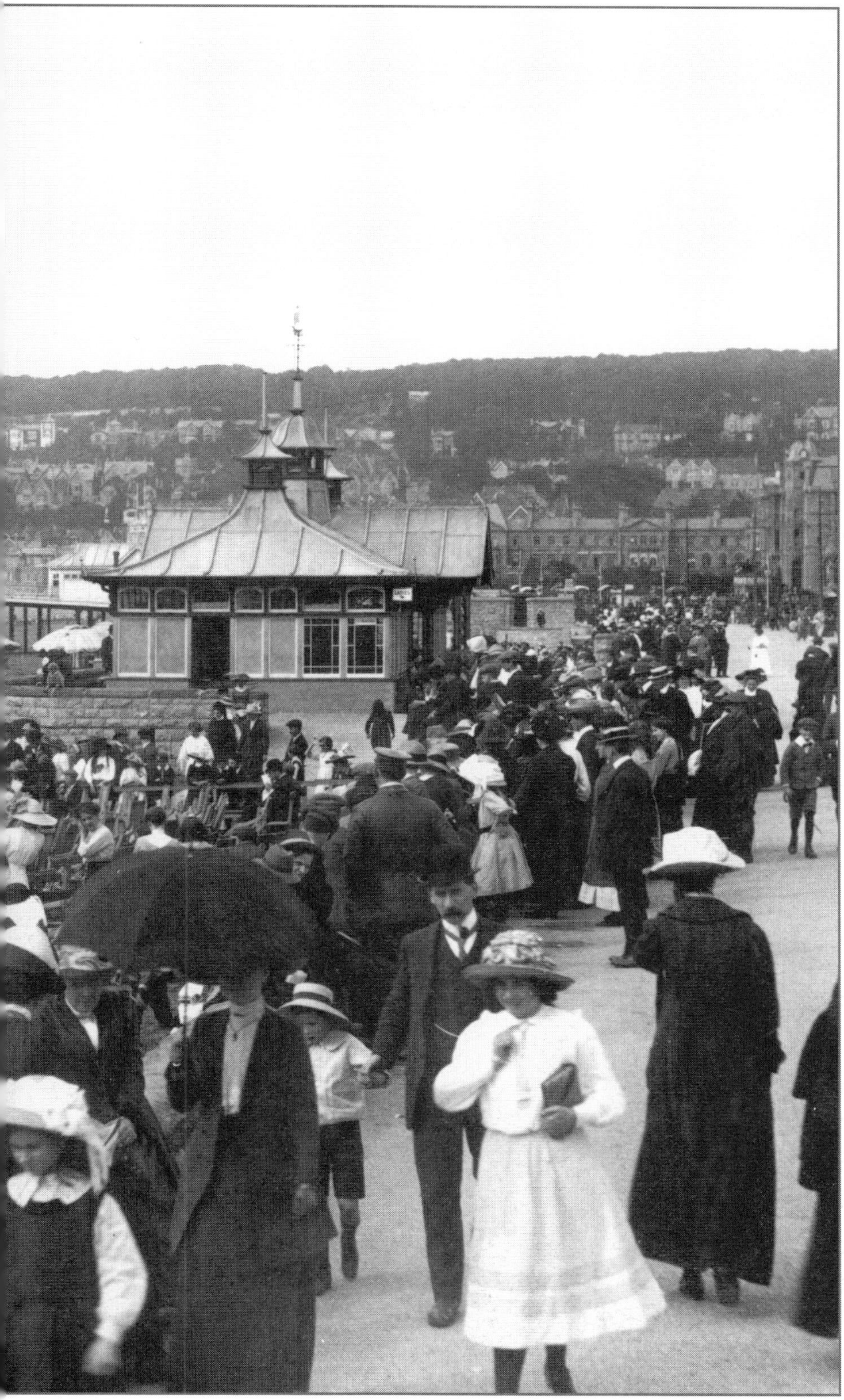

The Sands 1913 65160
Another crowded day on Weston Beach. In the background a banner on the side of the Grand Pier advertises Spiegler's Band. Continental bands, particularly German, Italian and Austrian ones, were very popular. A pierrot show is playing to an audience from an open-air stage on the left, while children busy themselves in the age-old tradition of building sandcastles.

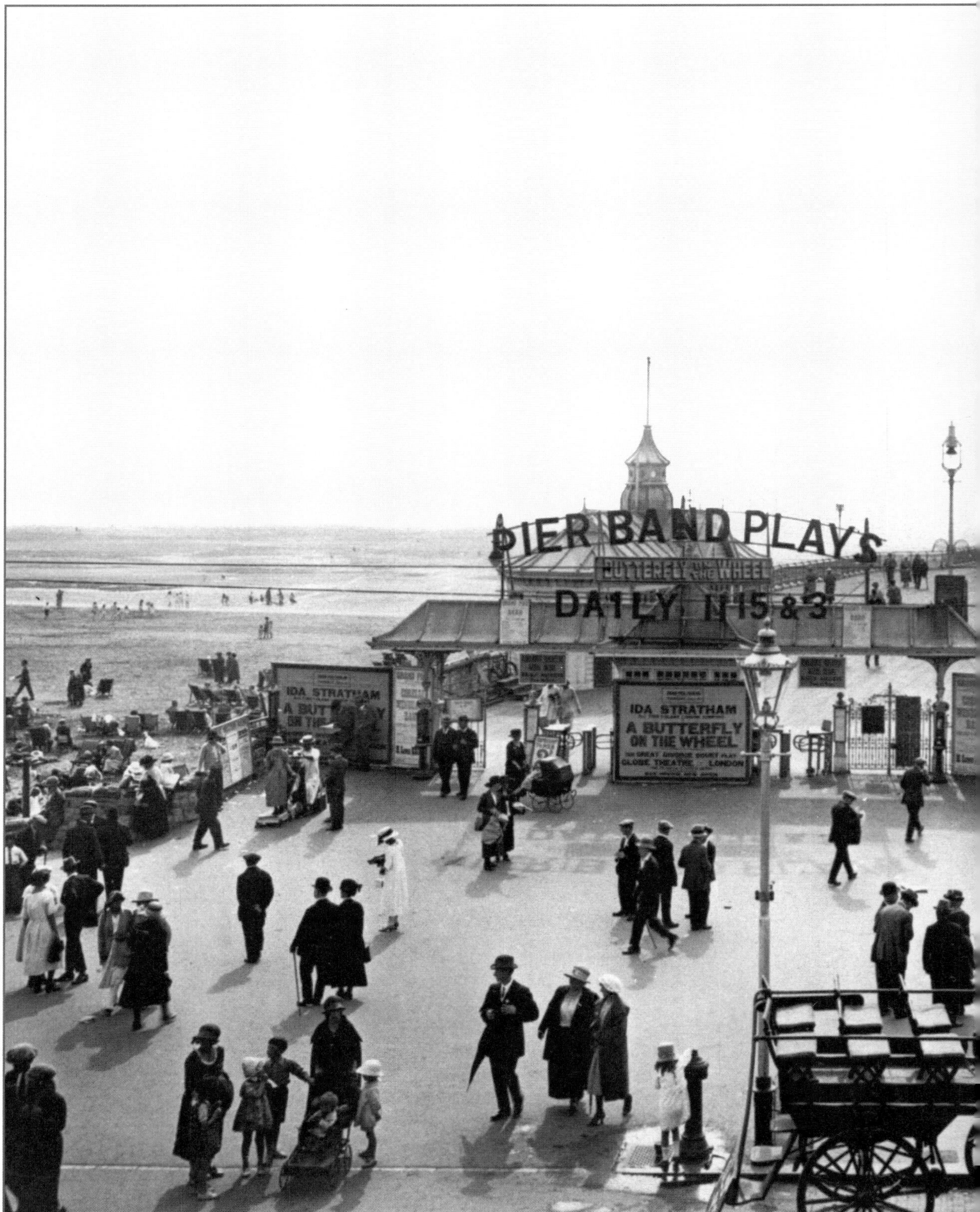
PIER BAND PLAYS
DAILY 11 15 & 3
IDA STRATHAM
A BUTTERFLY ON THE WHEEL
GLOBE THEATRE LONDON

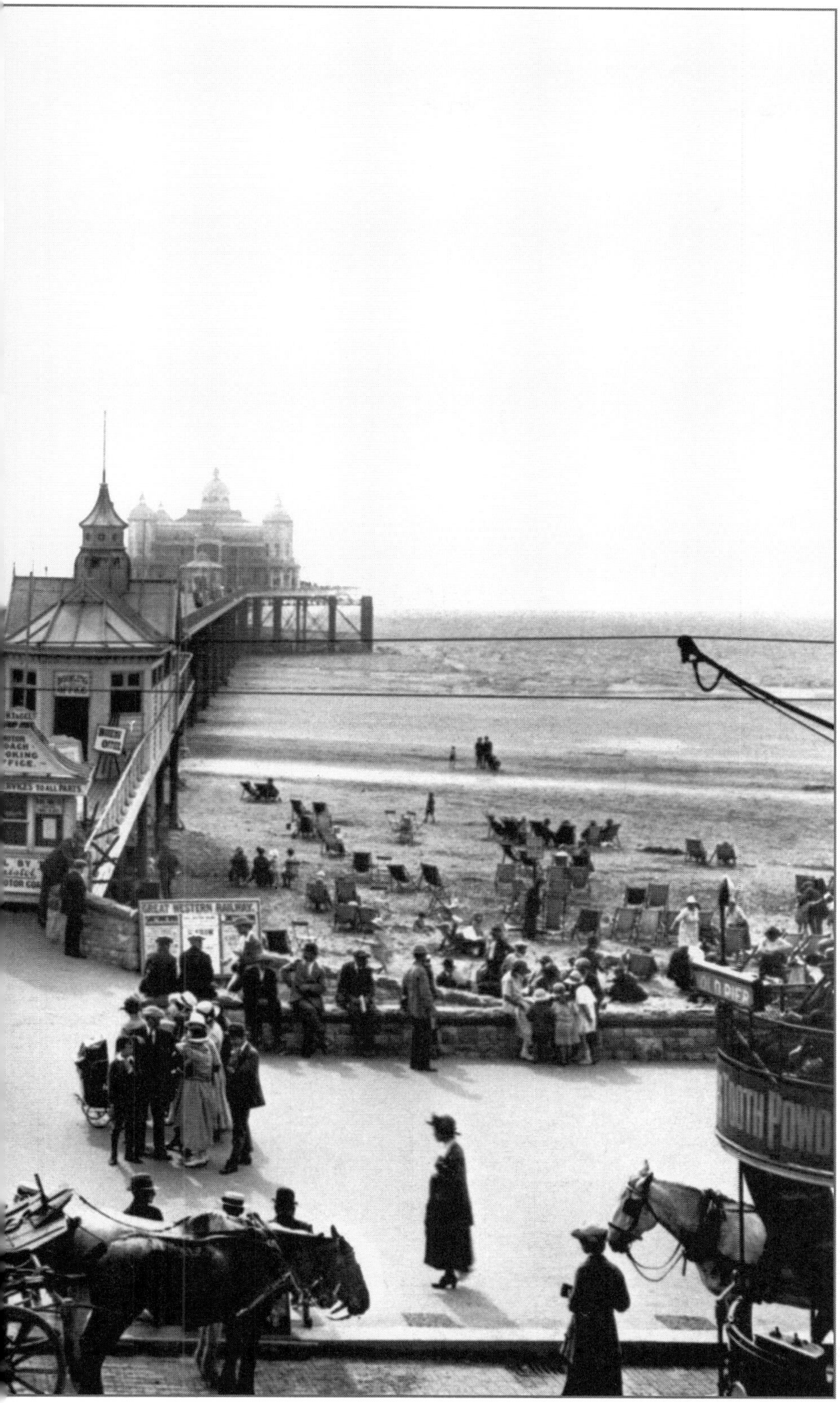

The Grand Pier 1923
74018
This picture is a delight to transport enthusiasts. In the foreground one of the last horse-drawn wagonettes waits for customers. These took tourists out to Cheddar and Burrington. Disappearing on the right is a tram on its way to the Old Pier, while just on the right of the pier entrance is the booking office for Bristol Blue Motor Coaches and posters for the Great Western Railway.

The Grand Pier 1935 87148
The new Grand Pier Pavilion is seen here, two years after its opening. The old pavilion burnt down in a spectacular fire in 1930. After years of arguments over whether and where to rebuild, this structure was decided upon. It is the largest pavilion on any pier and is still open today. Note the old-style telephone kiosk facing the Beach Hotel's Soda Fountain.

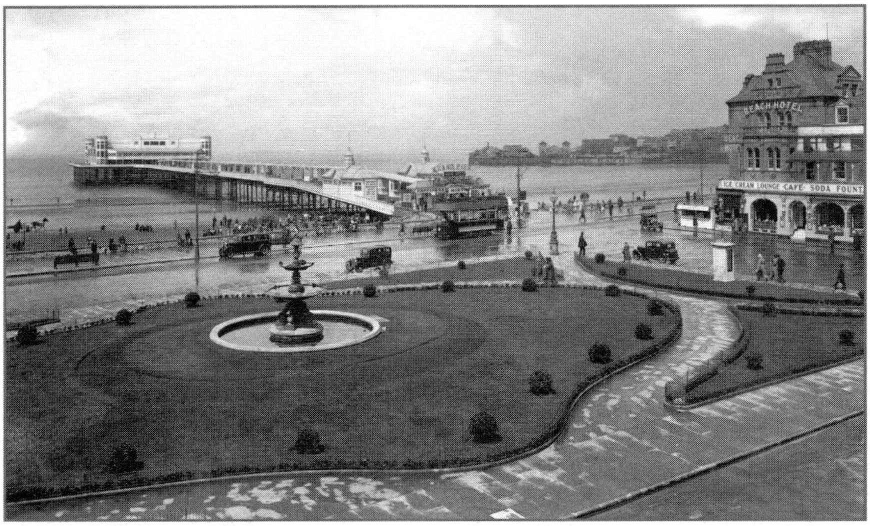

The Promenade c1955 W69017
In the 1950s, English seaside resorts still enjoyed as much popularity as in their heyday at the turn of the 20th century. These were the final years before cheap and easy air travel lured people abroad for their holidays. Note the extra storeys that have been added to the terraces in Knightstone Road.

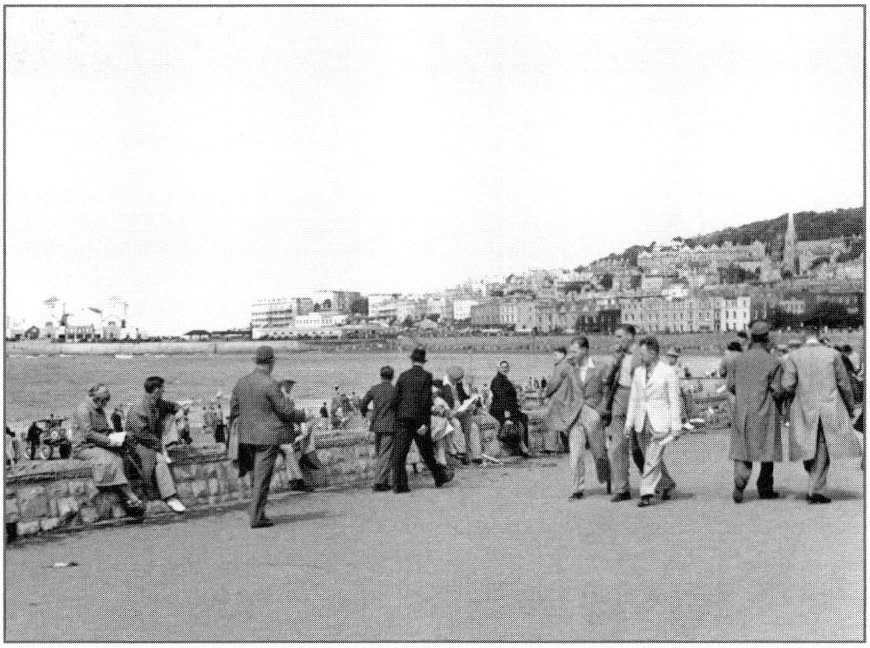

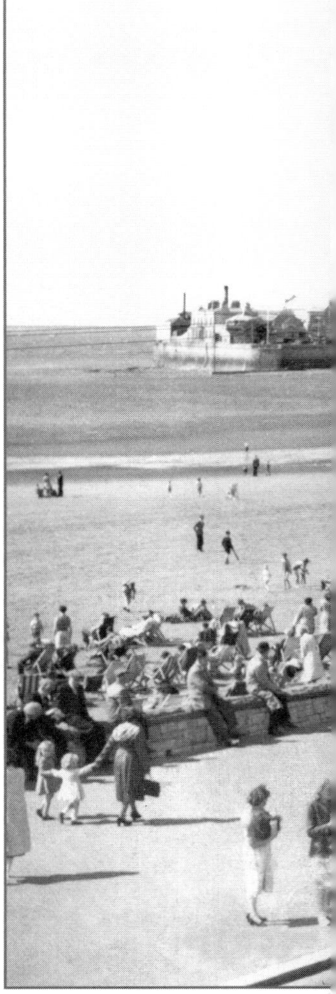

The Promenade c1955
W69068
In this scene, buses have replaced the trams that once plied their trade up and down the seafront. They last ran in 1937. There are also more private cars and 'No parking' signs have been installed along the promenade. Note the interesting style of lamps with their five-sided shades.

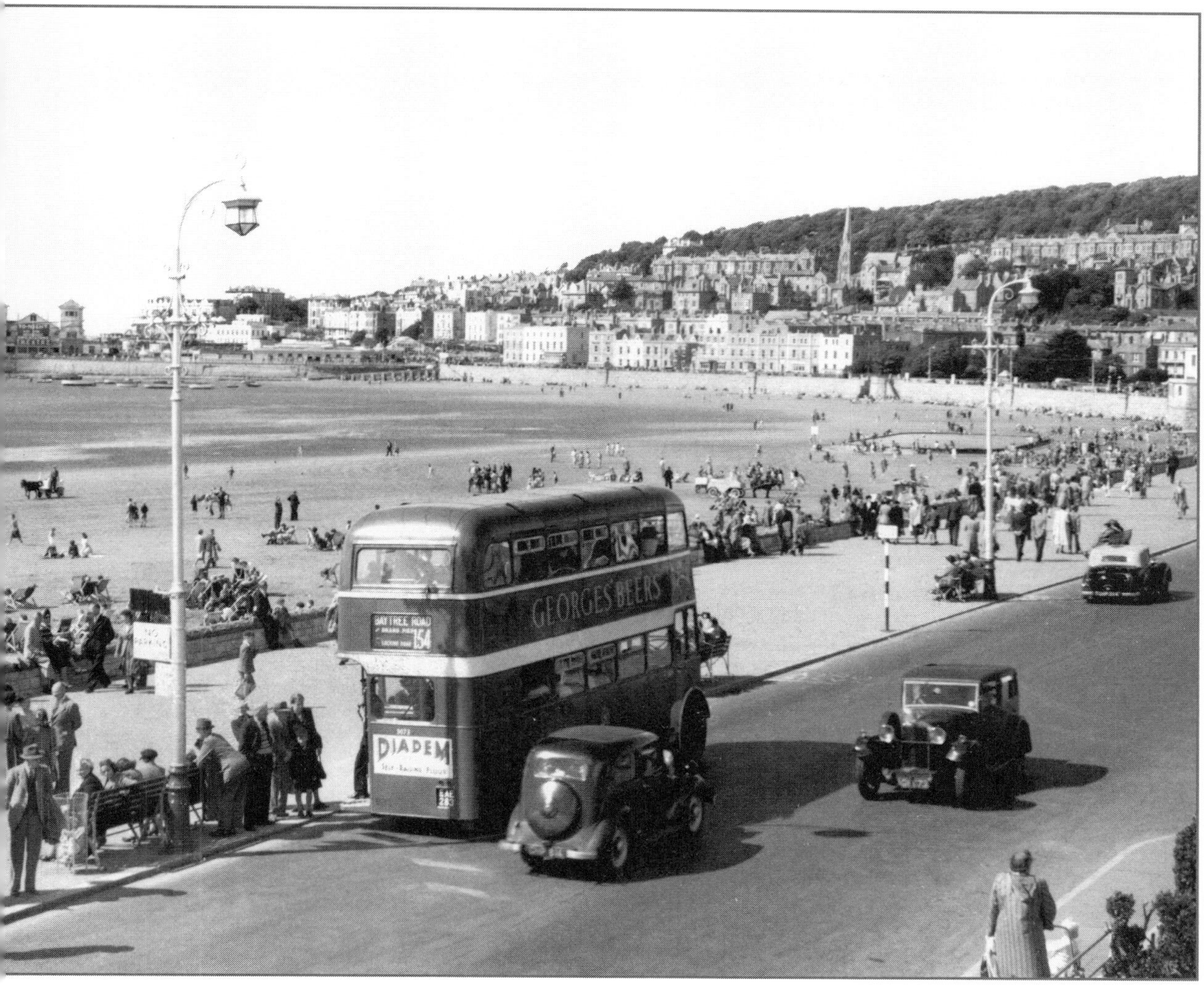

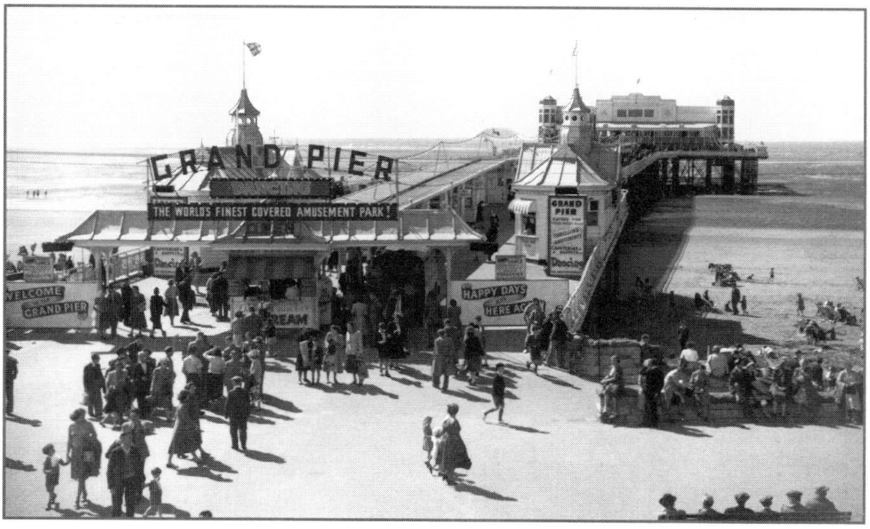

The Grand Pier c1955
W69079
A few alterations have taken place to the Edwardian entrance to the Grand Pier in this photograph. The turnstiles have been removed and you can just see the central windbreak and shelter that was built down the length of the pier in the early 1950s.

Glentworth Bay & Marine Lake

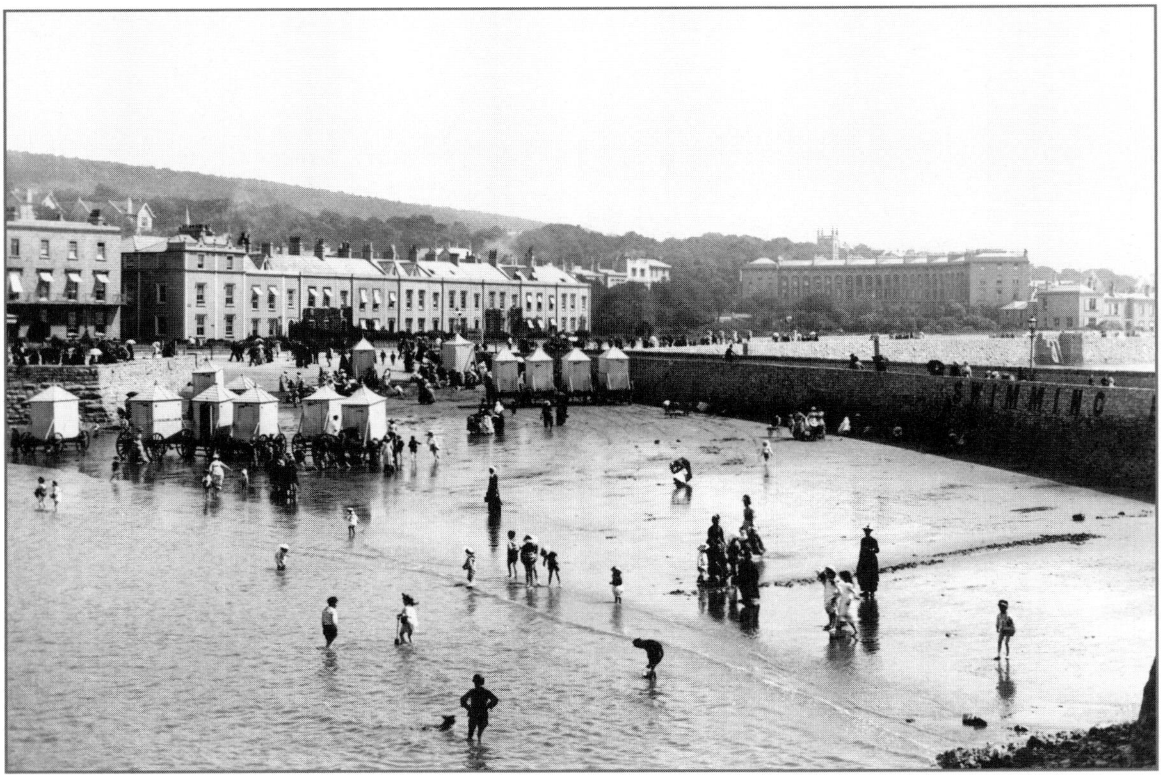

Glentworth Bay 1887 20324
These bathing machines were for the exclusive use of women. Those for men were a mile or so further south. These huts were wheeled down to the water while you changed into your bathing costume. You could then descend at the other end, unseen from the beach. They were already considered old-fashioned when they were wrecked in a gale in 1903, and so were never replaced.

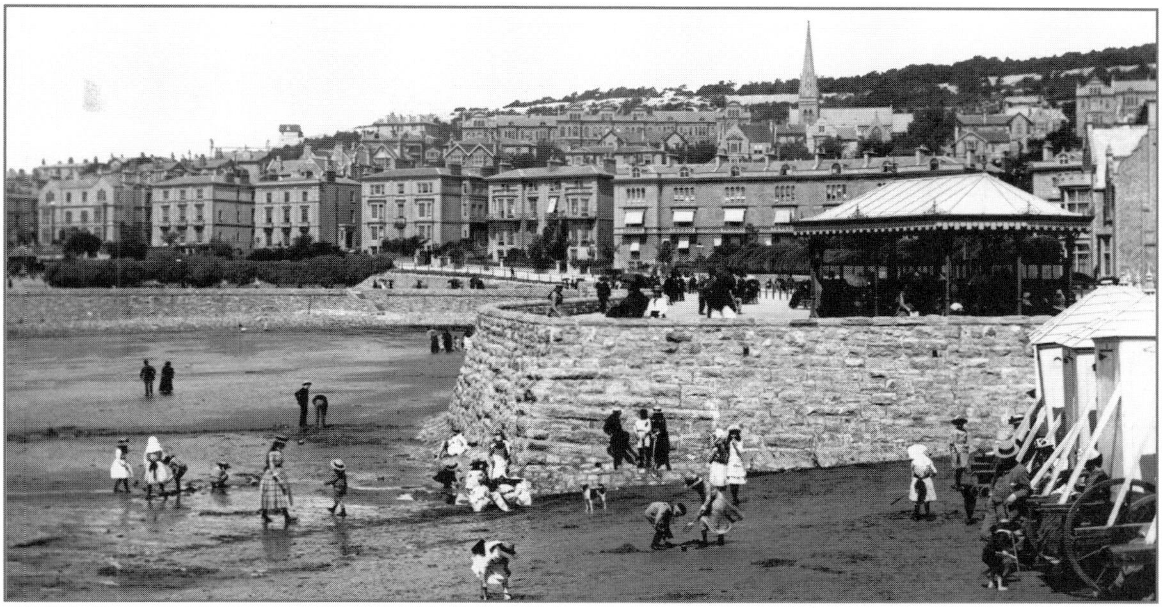

Glentworth Bay 1887 20323
This part of the beach, north of Knightstone, was more sheltered and secluded than the main sands and was therefore popular with women and children. On the promenade is one of the series of prefabricated cast iron shelters that were installed in the 1880s. When this one was removed it found a new home as the pavilion for Ashcombe Bowling Club.

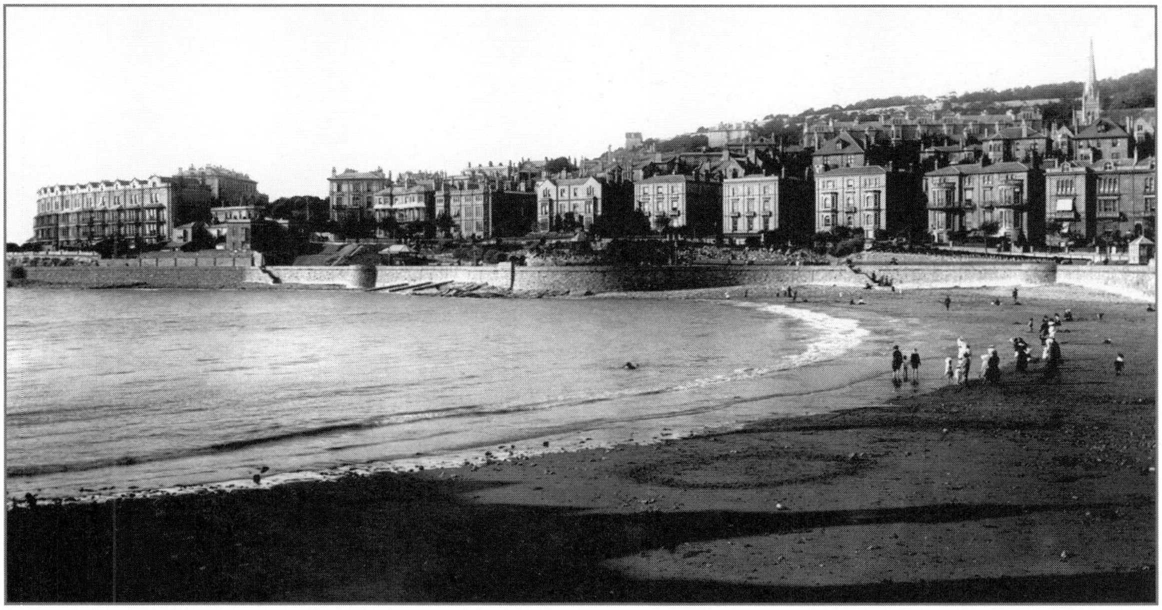

Glentworth Bay 1901 47875
This clearly shows the fine sweep of elegant buildings that lined Glentworth Bay and the hillside. All these buildings were constructed between 1840 and 1870 and display a harmony somewhat lost today. Most would have originally been single family dwellings, run with the help of a large staff, and popular with retired surgeons, Indian Army officers and the like. By this date many had already been converted into hotels.

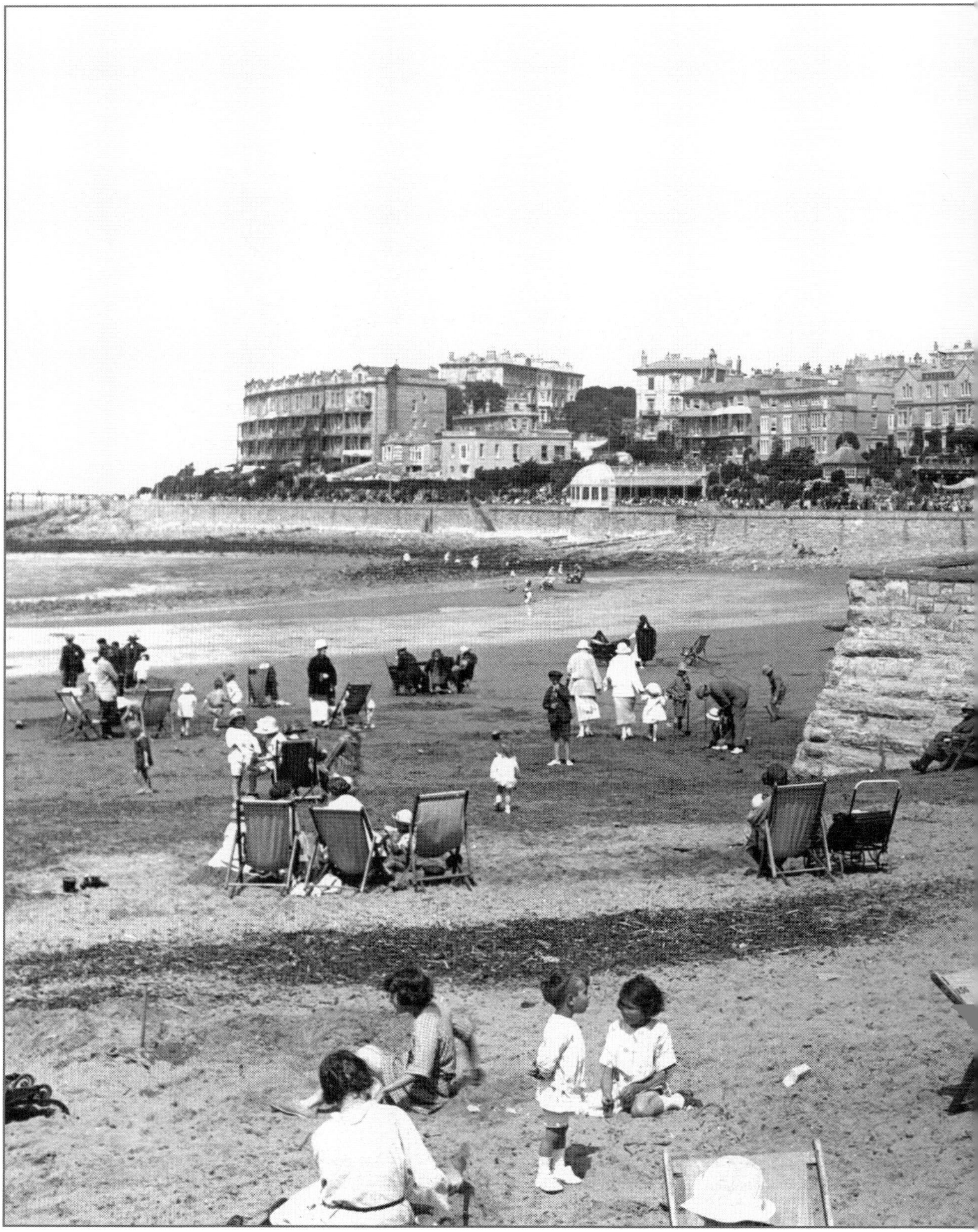

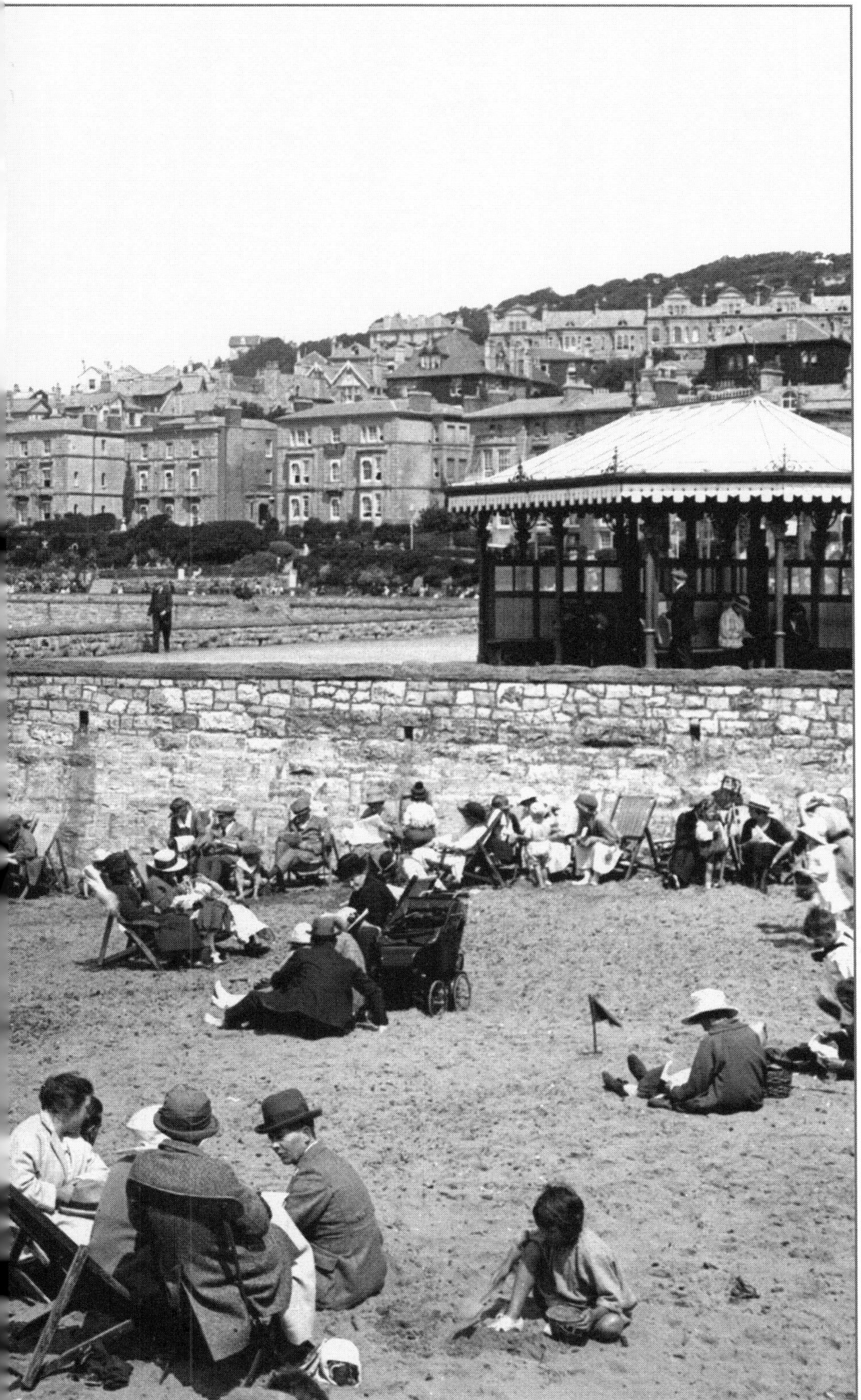

The Sands 1923 74022
Glentworth Bay is pictured just five years before the causeway was built, creating Marine Lake. In the far distance on the left you can just glimpse the low-water westward jetty of Birnbeck Pier. This was built so that steamers could berth at all states of the tide. It was demolished the same year that this picture was taken.

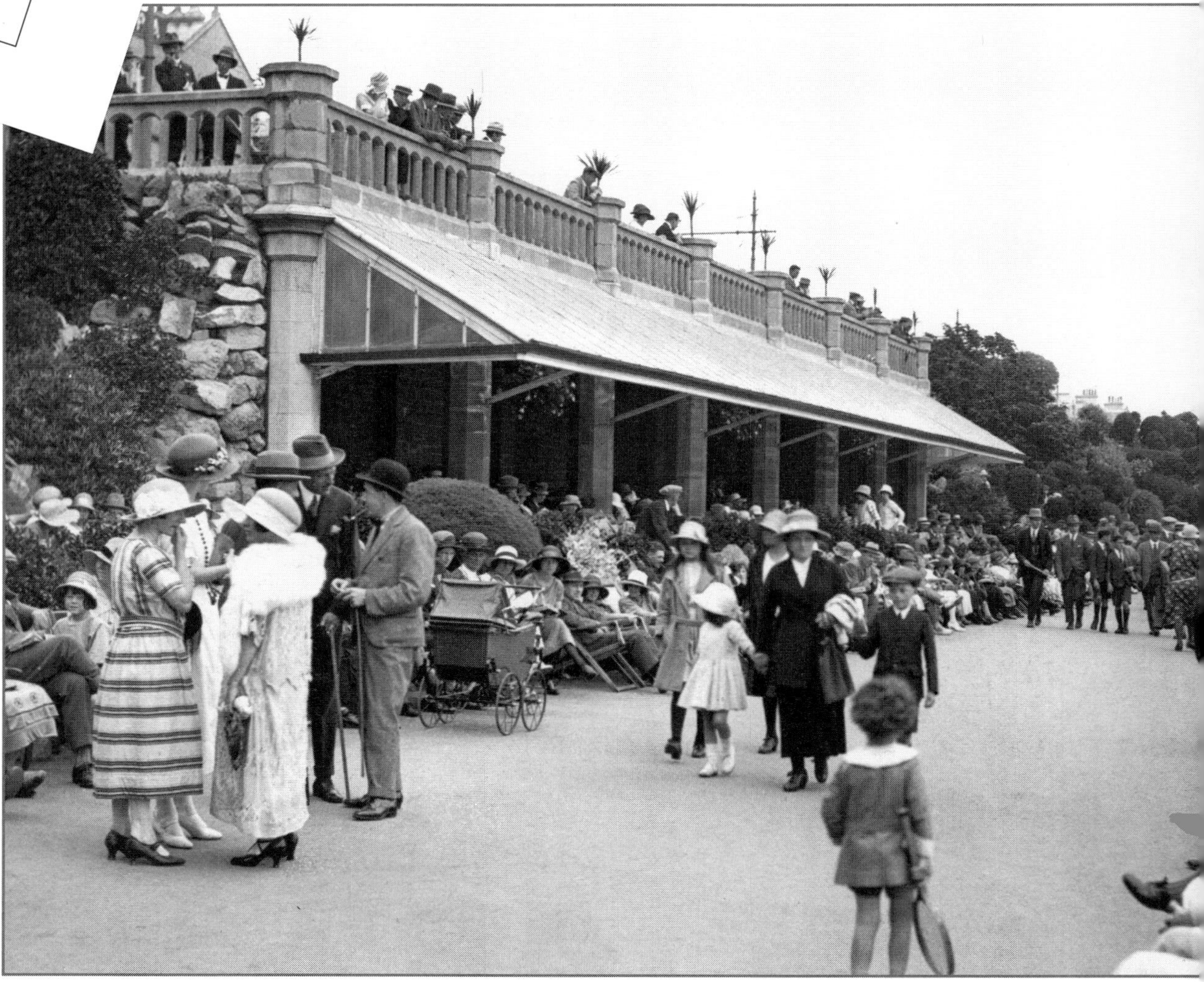

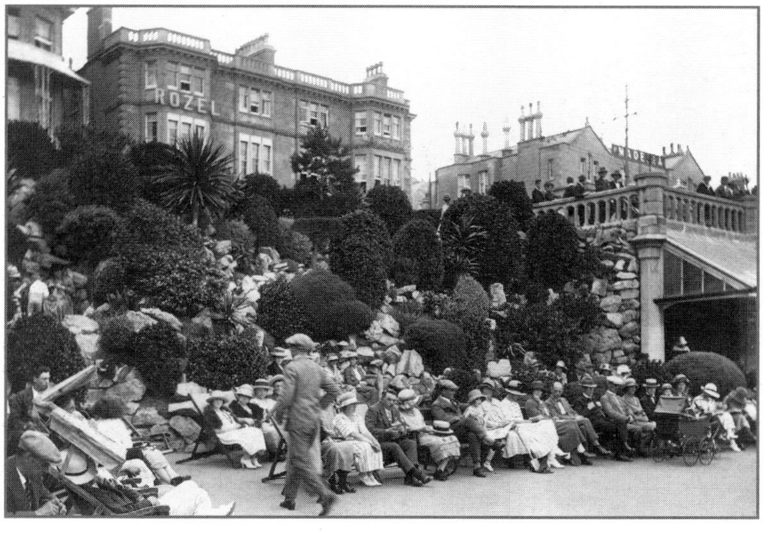

Madeira Cove 1923 74028A
This is a close-up view of the audience at the Dutch Oven bandstand. Most of the ladies are wearing light summer dresses, while some of the gentlemen have even discarded their headwear. In the road above, the hotels include the Rozel, Marlborough and Madeira.

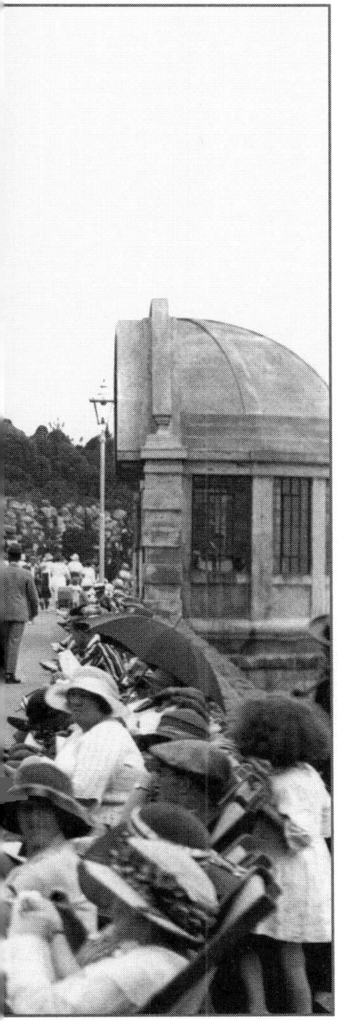

Madera Cove and the Bandstand 1923 74024

Further development in this area included the Dutch Oven Bandstand seen here on the right. This was built in 1920 and proved very popular with visitors. There was no charge to listen, but a collection was taken at the end of performances. However, it was not so popular with orchestras, as the conductor had to stand out in the open, even if it was raining.

Grand Parade 1887 20327A

In this picture the new promenade and sea wall provide plenty of space to walk, while the beach below gives a hint of what it looked like in its natural state. On the right in the distance are the Ladies' bathing machines, well separated from those used by men, which were at the southern end of the sands.

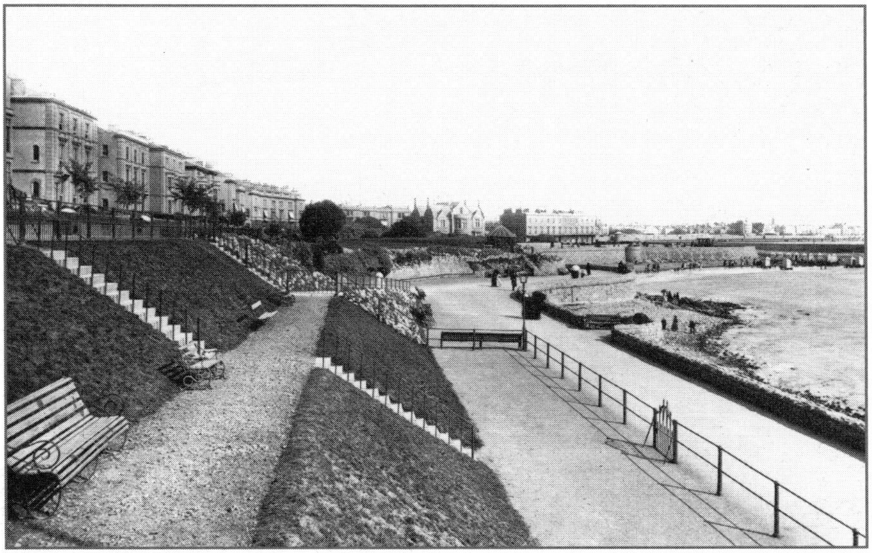

Madeira Cove 1913 65356

The seating terraces of the previous picture have been replaced by this concrete and glass shelter, built into the hillside. In the distance on the right is the shelter beside the Cove Pavilion. Notice how the ladies' skirts are gradually getting shorter and now show a glimpse of ankle!

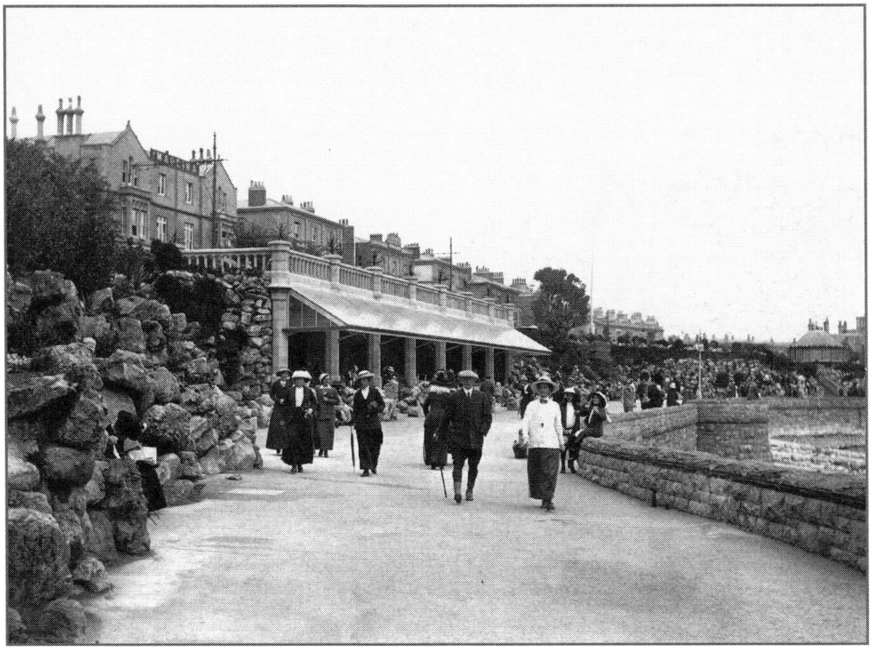

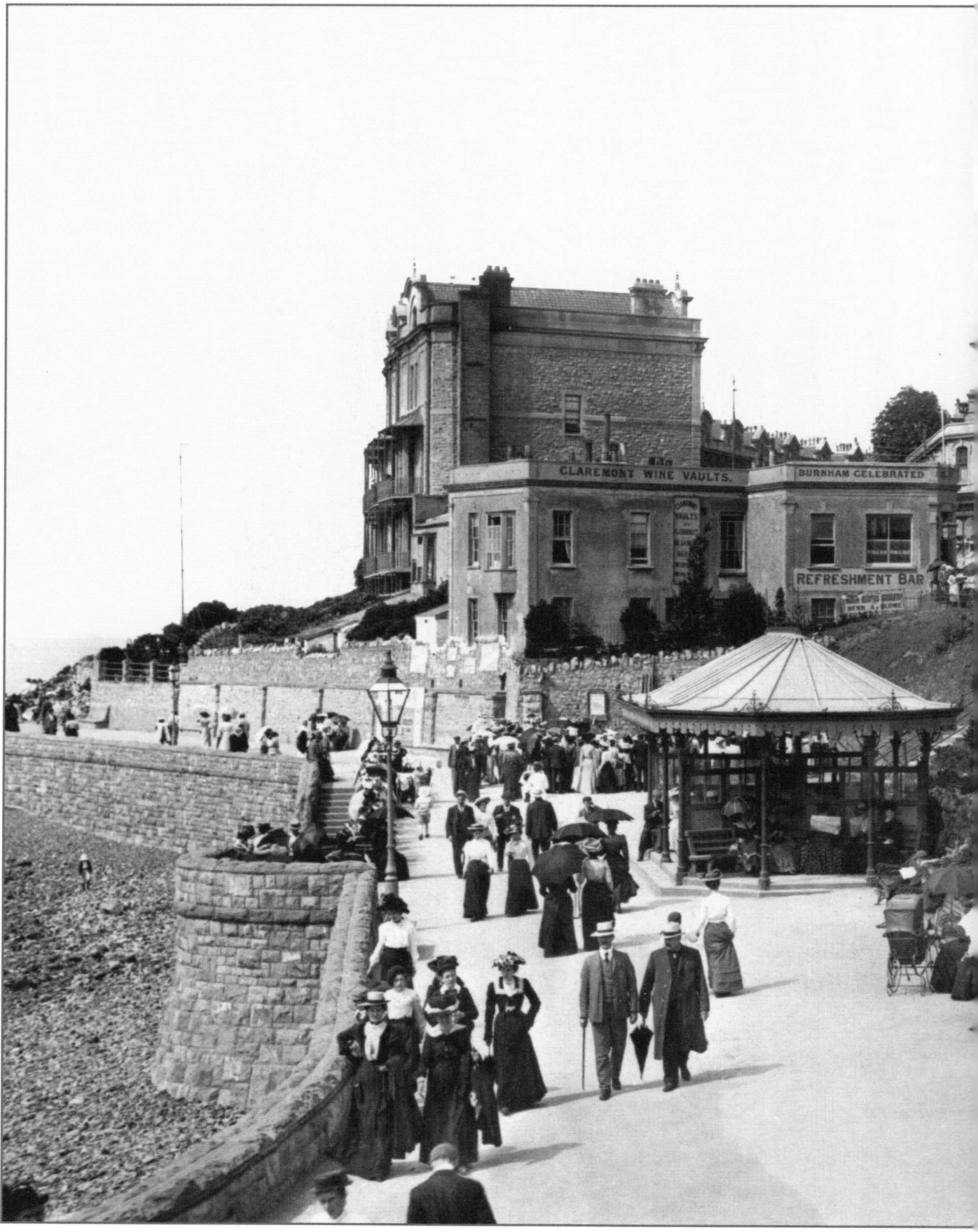
CLAREMONT WINE VAULTS.
BURNHAM CELEBRATED
REFRESHMENT BAR

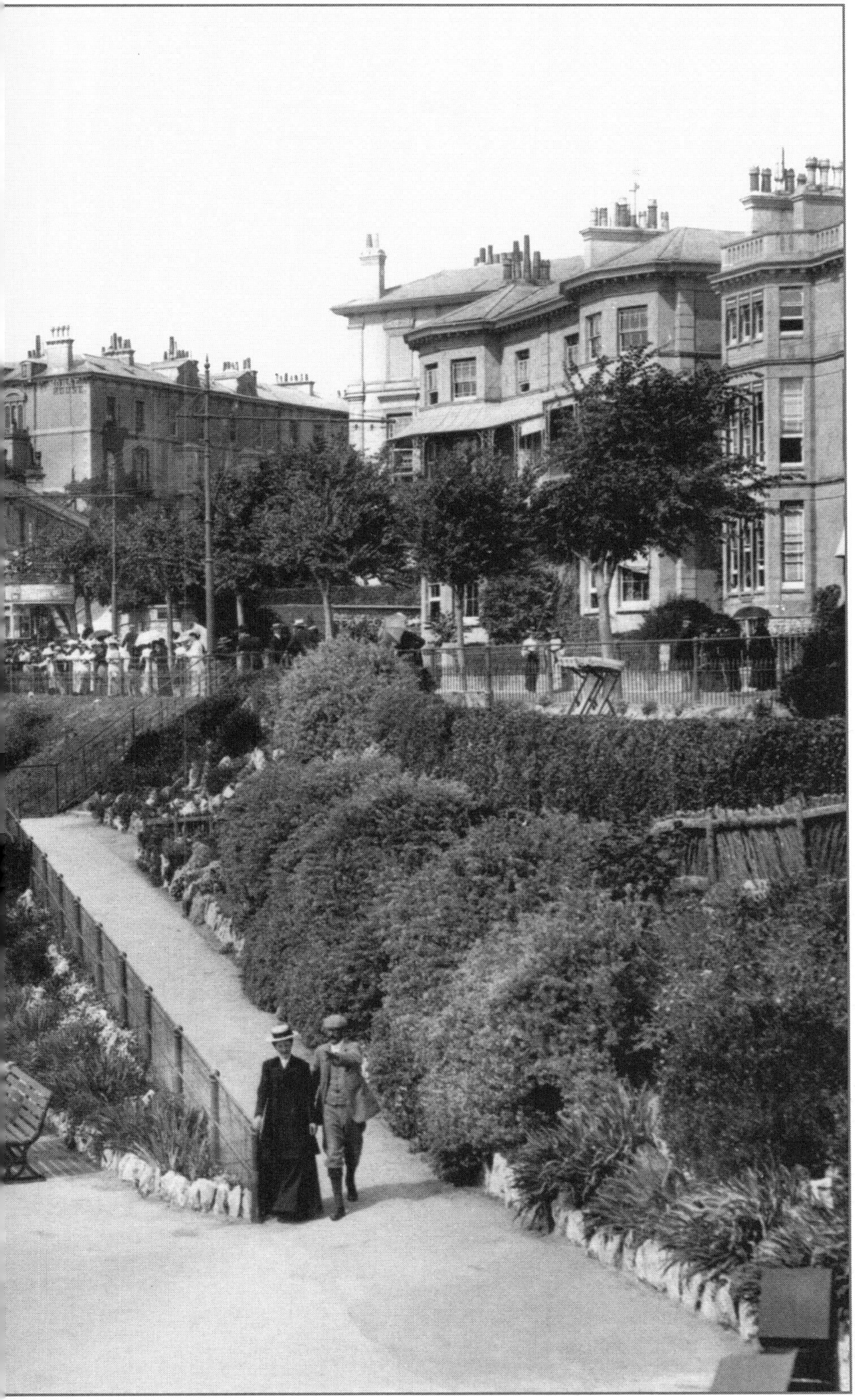

Madeira Cove 1902

48776

As the following pictures show, this part of the seafront underwent numerous changes over the next few years, gradually increasing the amount of entertainment on offer. Below the Claremont Wine Vaults, a meeting or show appears to be taking place. On the promenade above, a tram is heading for Birnbeck Pier.

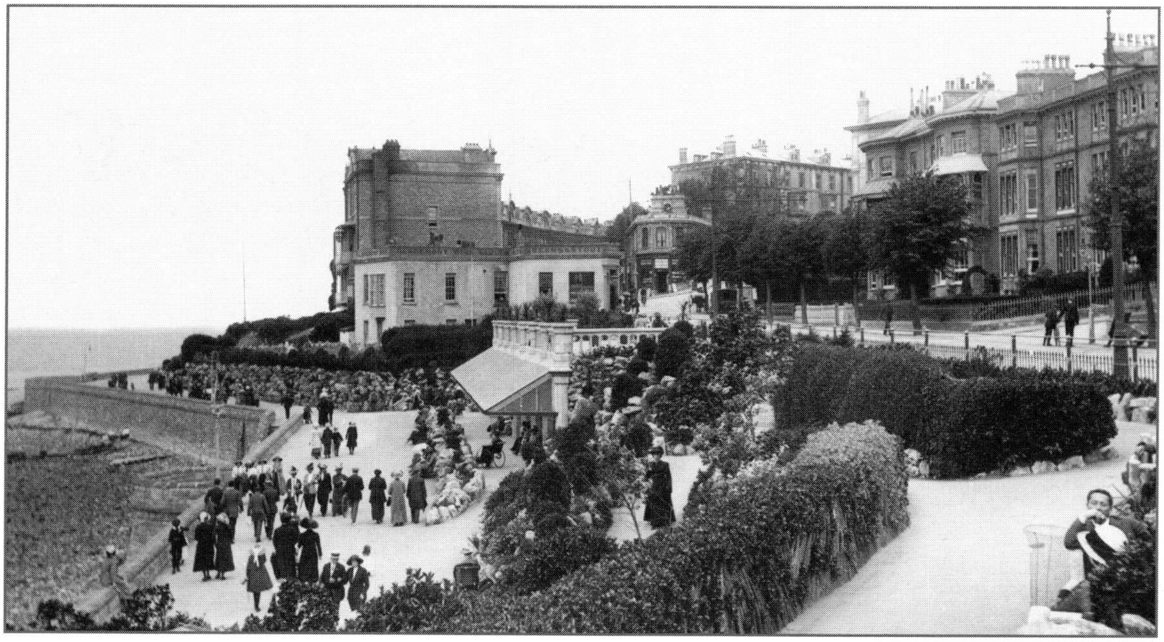

Madeira Cove 1913 65358
This view contrasts nicely with photograph 48776. The cast iron shelter has been replaced with a concrete and glass structure, built into the hillside with a seating platform forming the roof. The Claremont Wine Vaults have been given a coat of paint, and new planting and rockeries complete the scene.

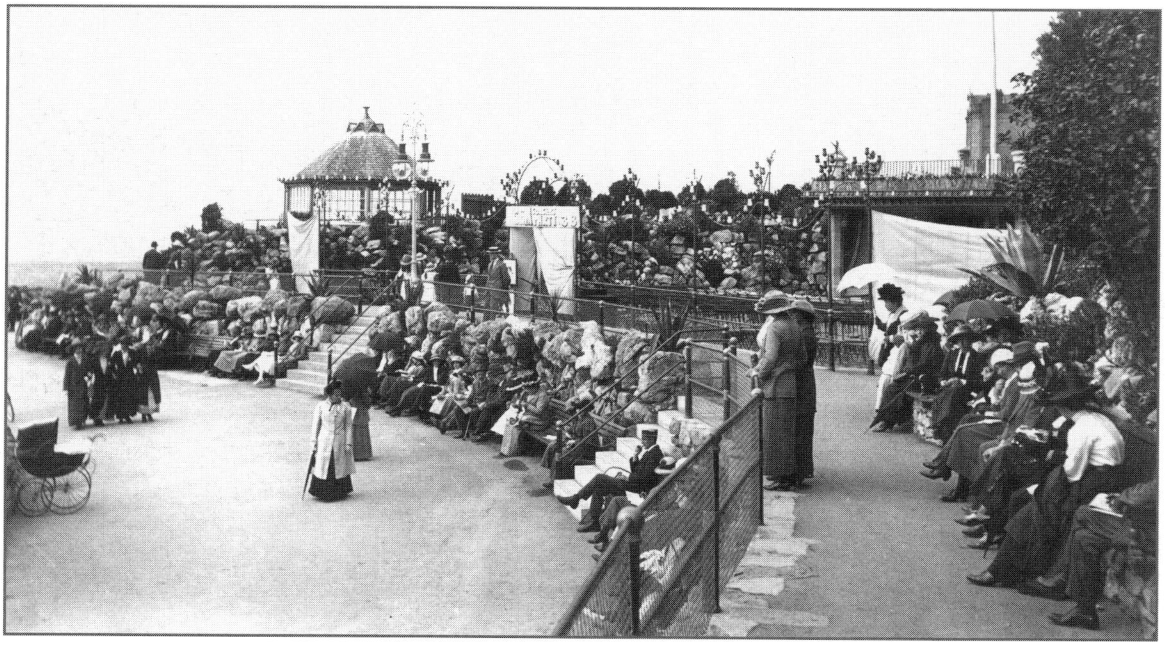

Madeira Cove 1913 65365
On the right is the original Cove Pavilion, the open-fronted shelter where the Gem Concert Party is here performing. Elaborate arrangements of glass fairy lights illuminate the scene at night. The baby's pram looks somewhat abandoned here. I wonder where its nanny or mother has gone?

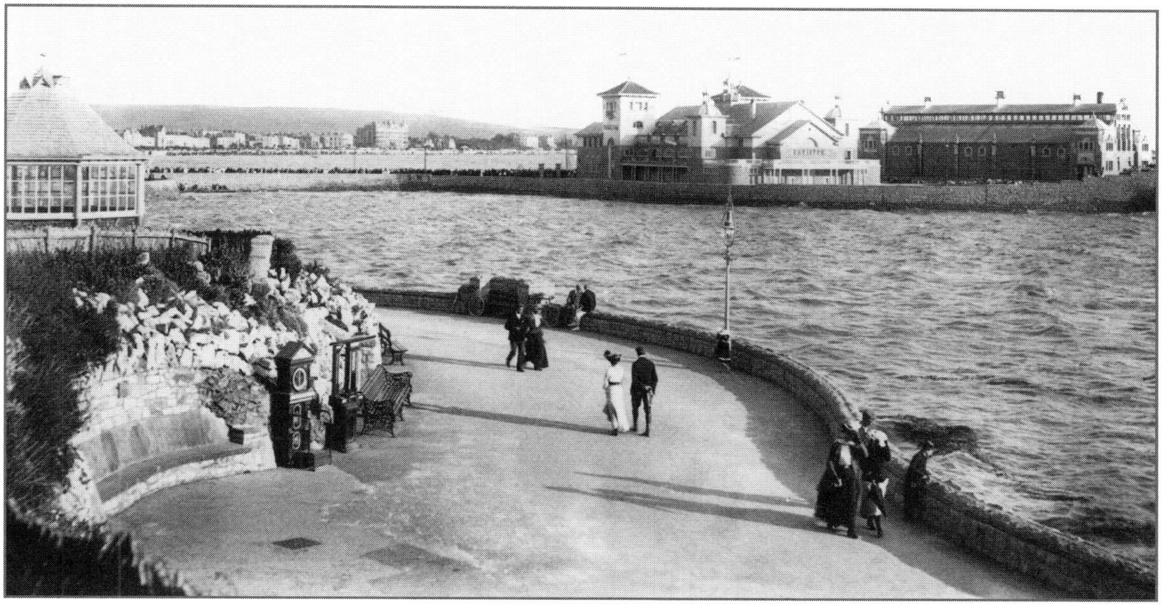

Knightstone Pavilion 1903 50112
Here is the newly-built Knightstone Pavilion to the left of the Baths. Both opened in 1902 to meet the changing needs of Edwardian visitors. The pavilion housed a fine theatre showing variety shows and theatrical productions. The baths were Weston's only indoor swimming facility and were in use until the 1980s when Hutton Moor Pool was opened. Note the weighing and test-your-strength machines on the promenade.

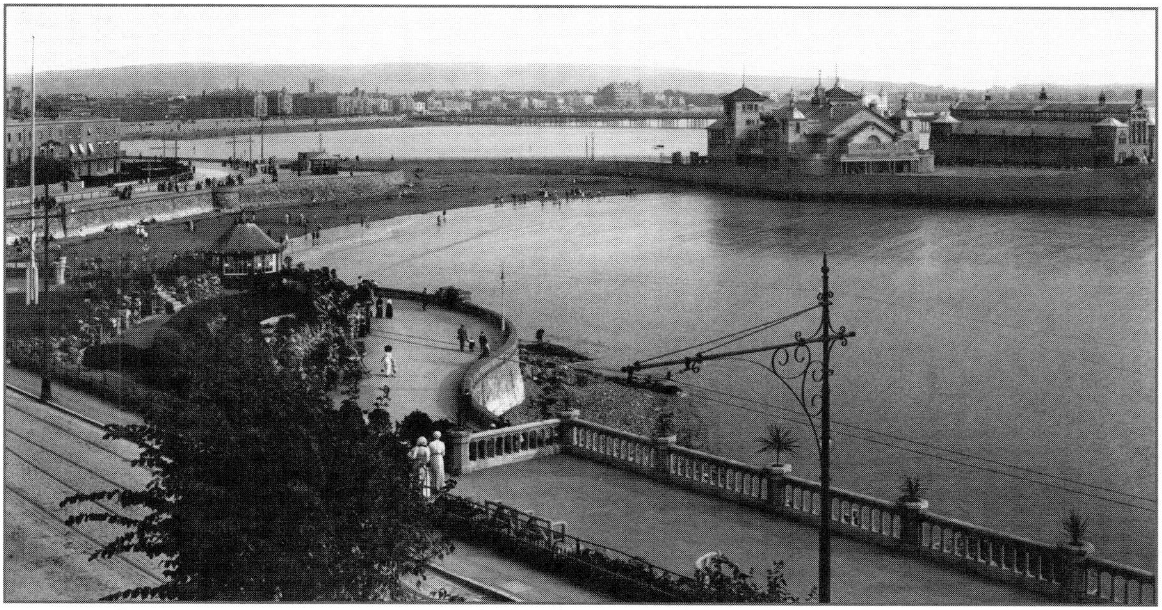

The Two Bays and Pavilion 1913 65161
This view is taken from the Rozel Hotel in Birnbeck Road. The twin tram tracks in the road indicate a passing loop, as most of the line was single track. In the distance the Grand Pier can be seen. If you follow its line, you can just see that it extends way beyond the Pavilion. In 1907 it was extended to make it nearly twice as long as it is today. The extra section was dismantled in 1916.

Madeira Cove 1923 74028

This is the sheltered area between the Rozel Bandstand and the Cove Pavilion. The gardens and rockeries create secluded little seating areas, while the winding path leads up to Birnbeck Road. Over the trees, the roof of Glentworth Hall is visible. At this date it was used by Hazelhurst School, becoming a hotel in 1926. It was demolished in the 1970s.

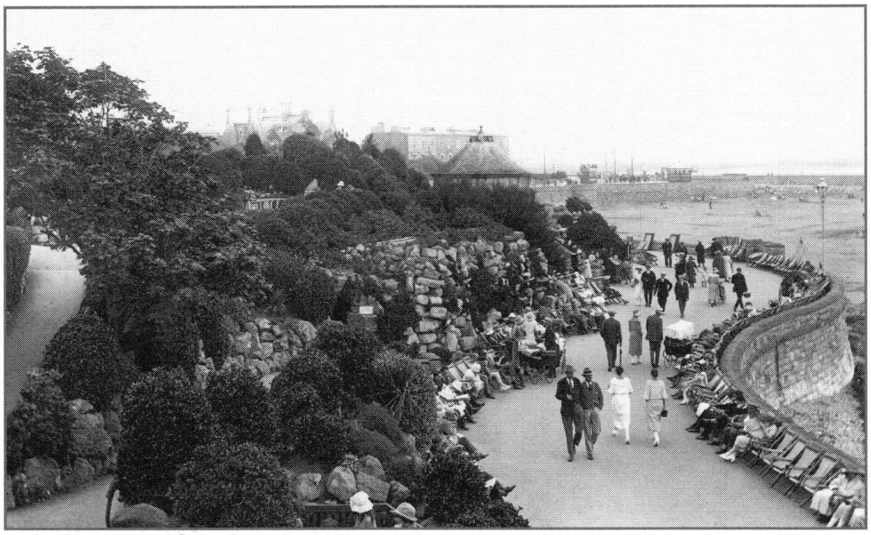

Marine Lake c1955 W69018

Marine Lake was created by building a causeway across Glentworth Bay in 1927. This gave a part of the beach where the tide was always in and where people could bathe whenever they liked. The colonnade was added a few years later, by widening the promenade on top. Rows of beach huts on Knightstone provided changing facilities.

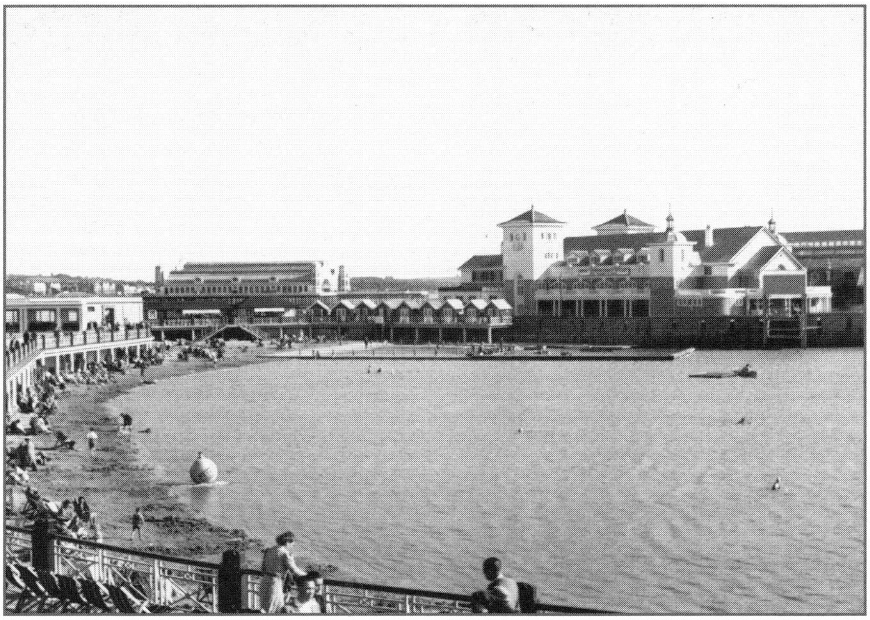

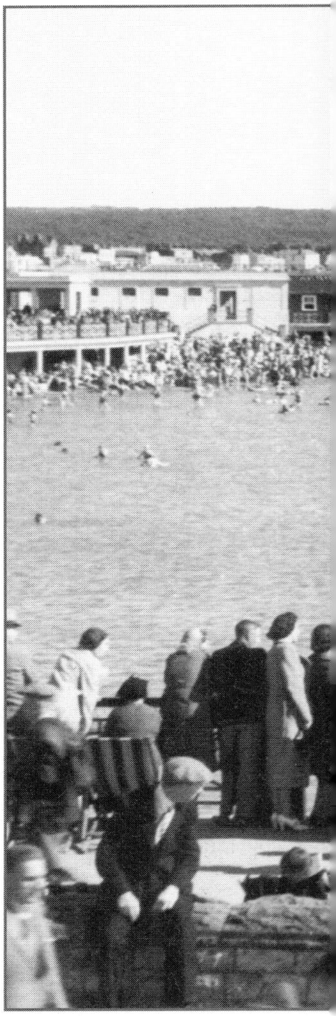

Marine Lake c1955 W69048

Two bathers are about to take the water chute into the lake, watched by crowds of visitors. Other facilities here included a children's play area, rowing and paddle boats. Banners on Knightstone Theatre advertise a Variety Show. The late Harry Secombe had his first professional appearance here and other performers included Morecambe and Wise (at the bottom of the bill!), Hutch and other top names.

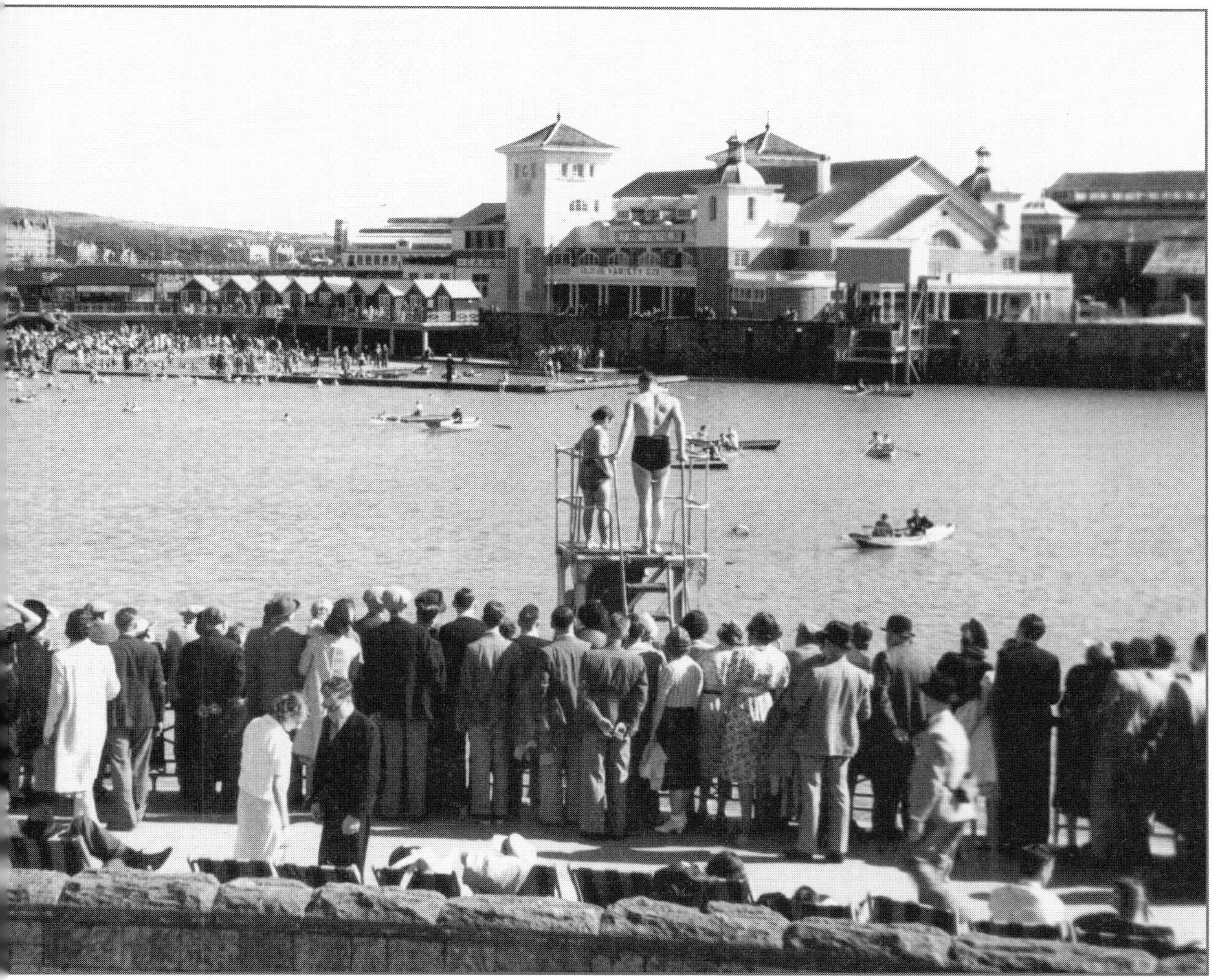

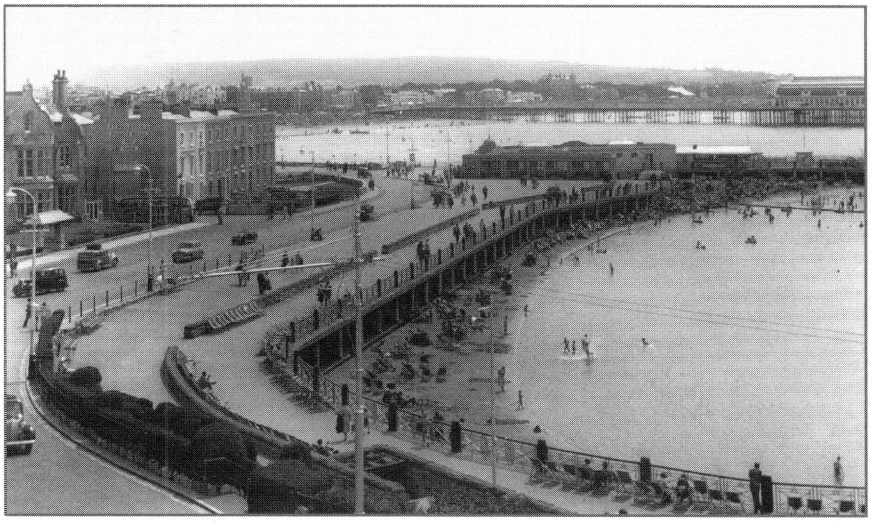

The Two Bays c1955

W69060

This view is taken from Manilla Crescent. You can clearly see where the promenade was widened to create the colonnade around Marine Lake. This area suffered badly in a big storm in 1981 and the colonnade had to be removed, together with the buildings at the entrance to Knightstone. These housed a small zoo and aquarium, as well as a café and public toilets.

Anchor Head

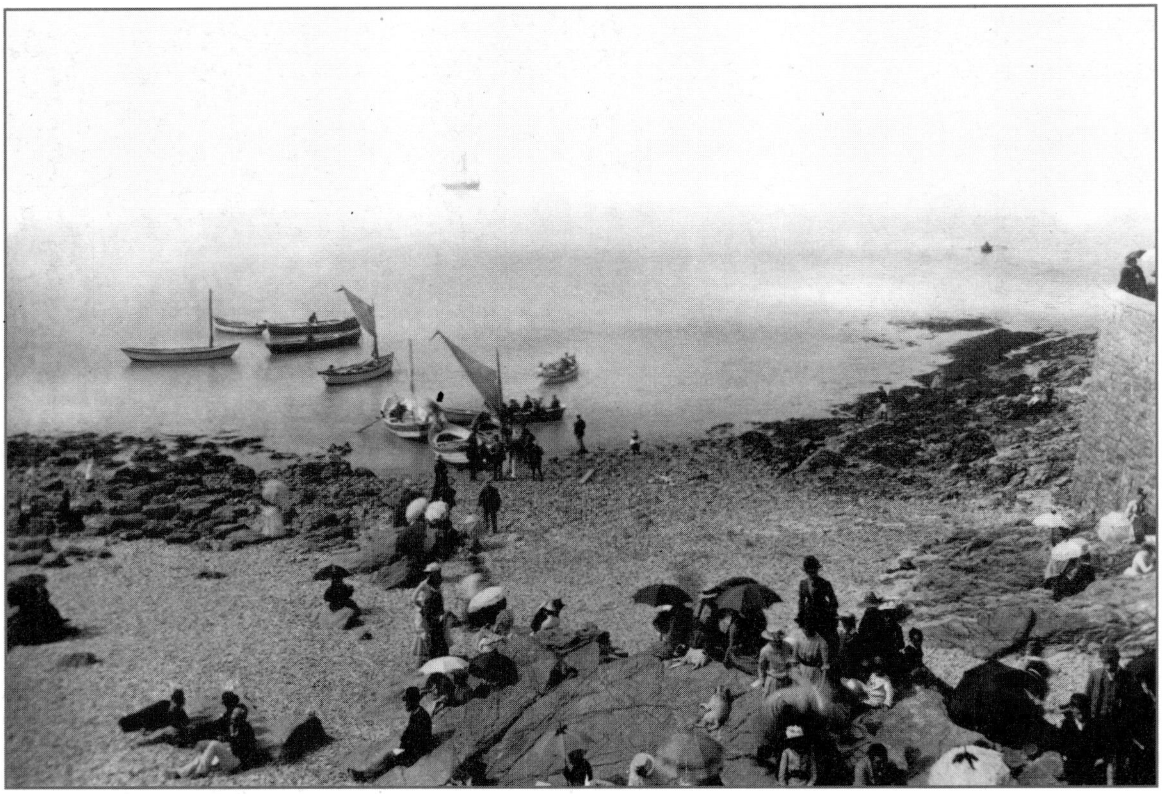

Anchor Head 1887 20335

This small cove was used as the Ladies' Bathing Place in the 1830s and 1840s. It is very secluded and private and was ideal for Weston's bathing woman, Betty Muggleworth, to attend to her customers. An old sail was spread across the rocks to provide privacy for ladies to change into bathing dresses before being escorted down to the water.

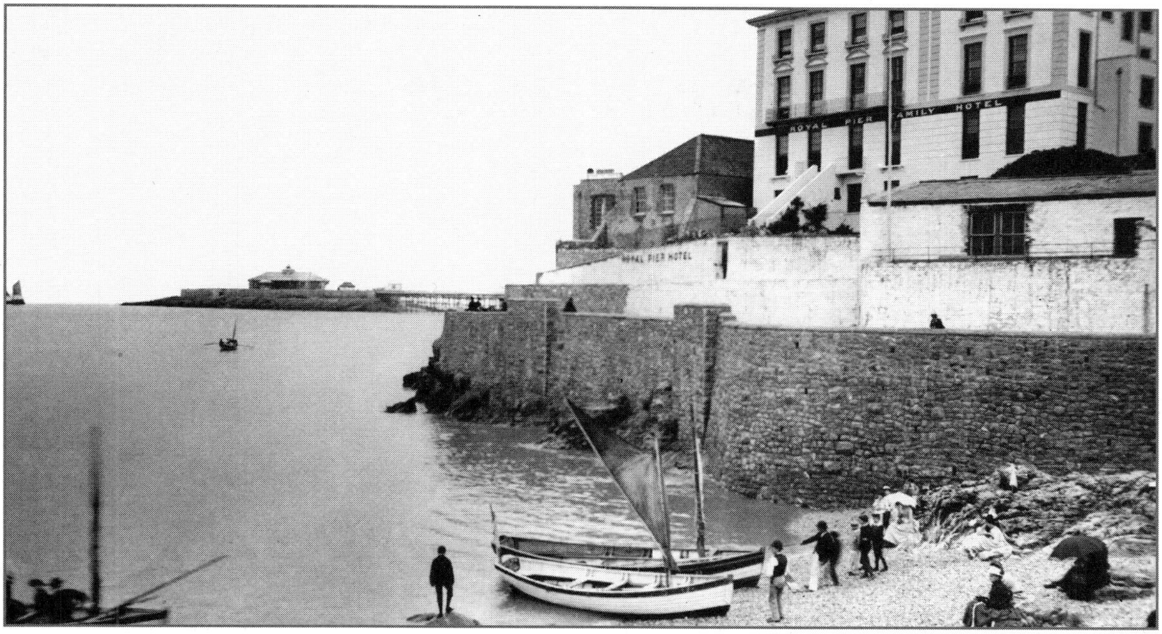

Anchor Head and Pier 1887 20336
This view shows two of the local fishing boats, or 'flatners', on the beach. Their owners used them in the summer to provide trips round the bay, reverting to their use for fishing for sprats and herring in the winter. In the distance is Birnbeck Pier.

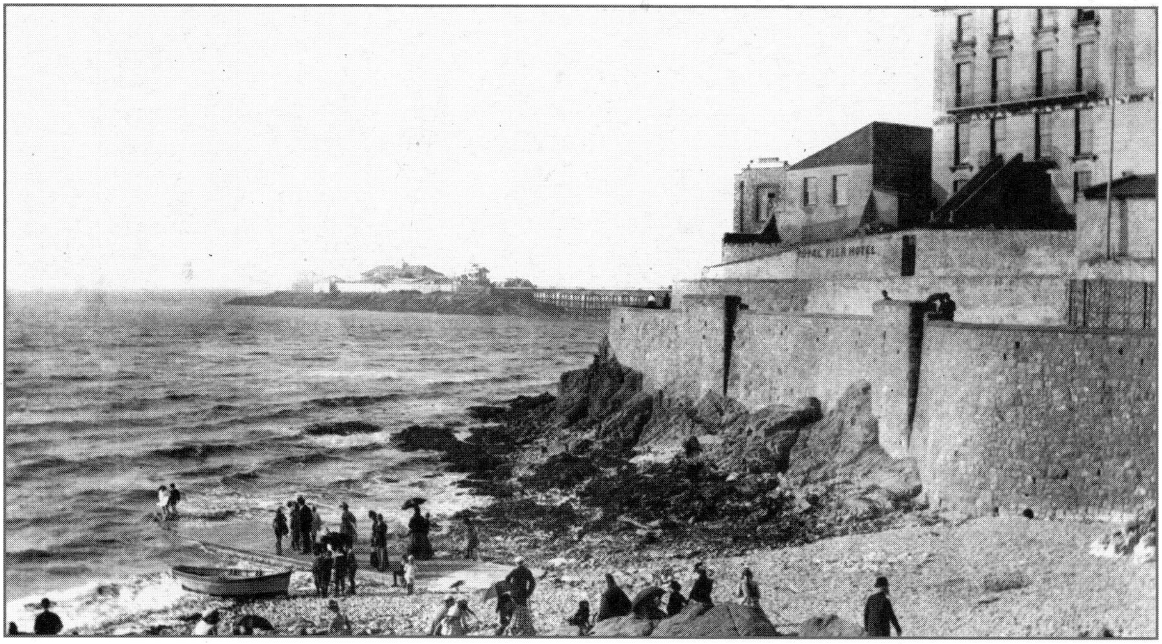

Anchor Head 1890 27886
This view shows a number of changes from the previous scene. On Birnbeck Pier, new amusements include a switchback railway. Note that there is no lifeboat slipway visible. This was not built until 1902. The Royal Pier Hotel opened in 1854 and was Weston's second purpose-built hotel after the Royal Hotel.

Anchor Head and Old Pier 1923 74026
This later view of Anchor Head shows yet more developments on Birnbeck, including the construction of the low-water westward jetty, which allowed steamers to berth at any time or state of the tide. The terraces and buildings in front of the Royal Pier Hotel have been demolished, and rockeries and shrubs planted. There is also a new extension on to the Claremont Hotel.

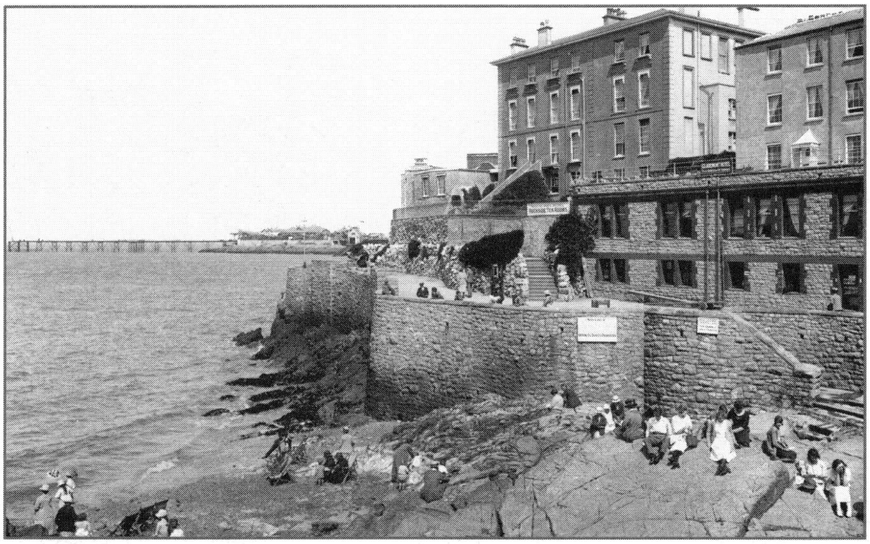

Anchor Head 1896 38453
With the building of the promenade in the 1880s, Anchor Head became easier to reach and was a poplar place to rest. The natural rocky outcrops and rockpools kept children busy, and it was from here that trips round the bay could be taken. Note the fine gas lamp on the wall in the centre.

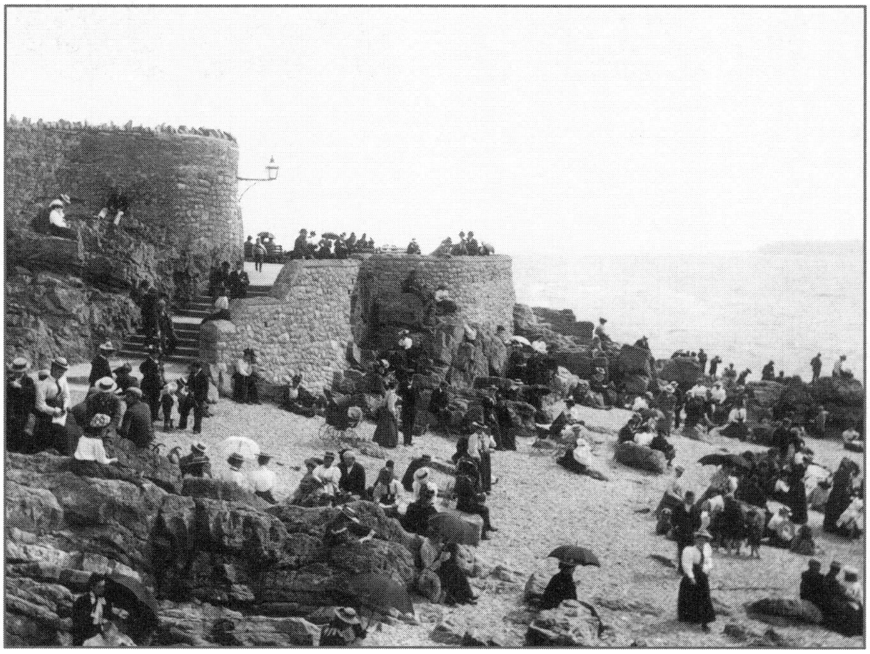

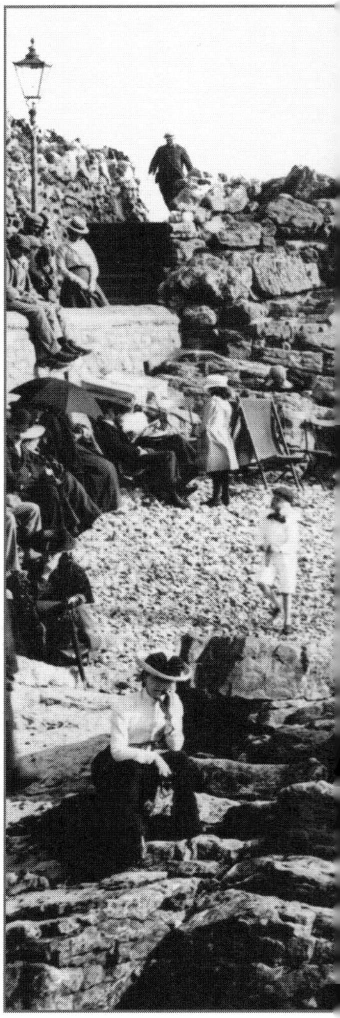

Anchor Head 1902 48779
This photograph shows the ladies' summer dresses and elaborate hats very clearly. Their long dresses don't seem to have prevented them clambering on to the rocks to find suitable seats. The wall-mounted gas light has been changed to a free-standing one and a flagpole has been erected in the circular enclosure.

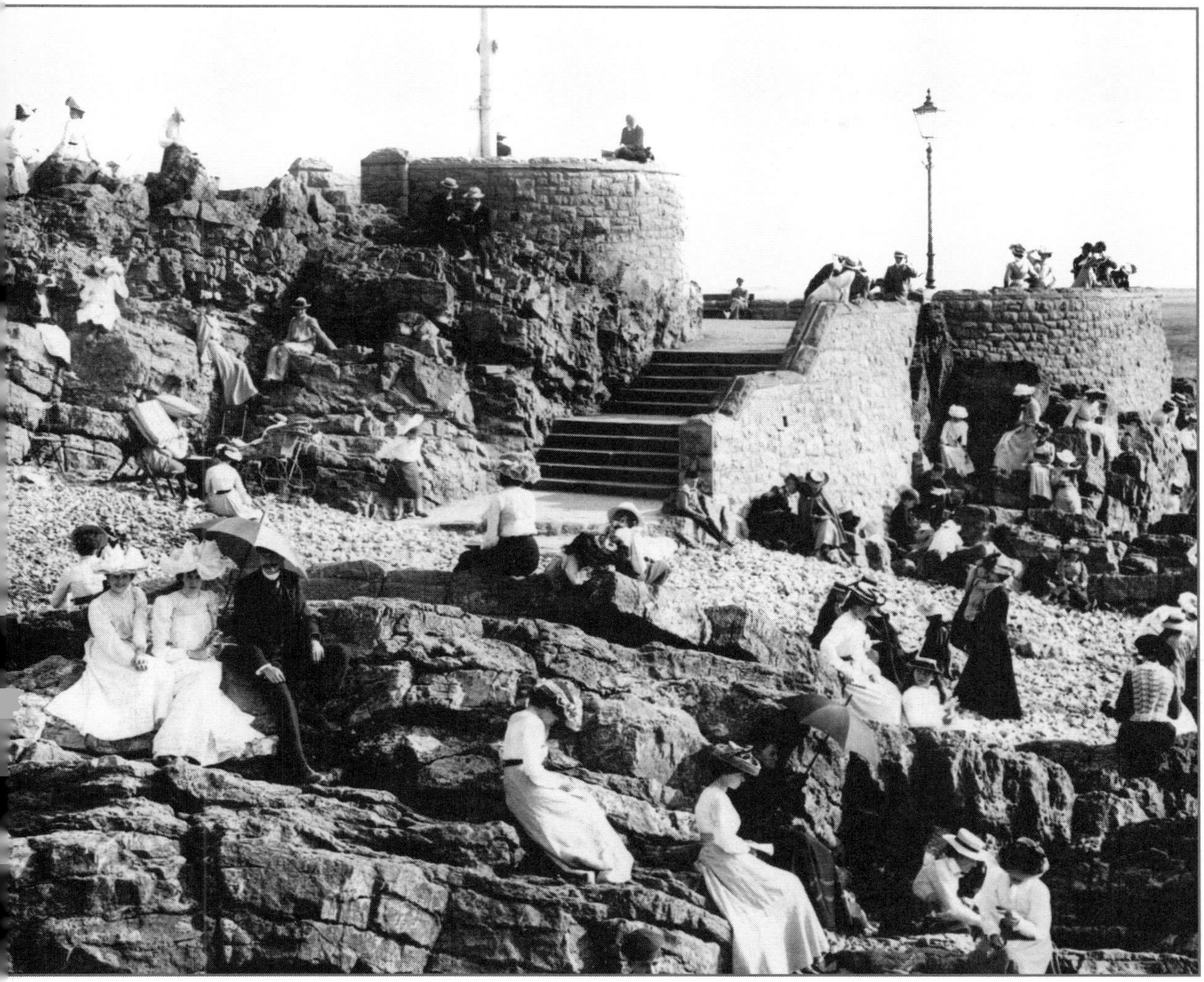

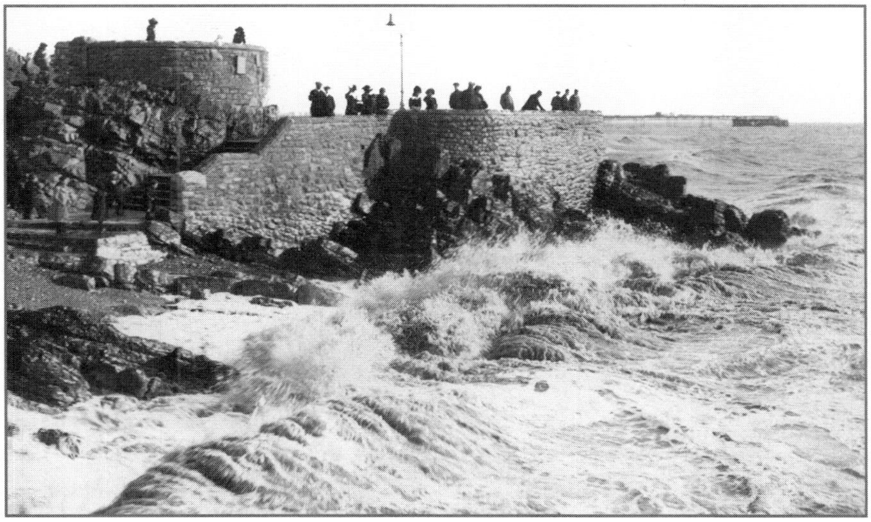

Anchor Head 1913 65360B
These waves crashing on to the rocks show the other side of the seaside. Aside from frequent minor damage, Weston has suffered two major storms, both made worse by very high tides and westerly winds. In 1903 and again in 1981 areas of the promenade were wrecked and damage amounted to thousands of pounds worth. In the distance the end of the Grand Pier extension can be seen.

Birnbeck Pier, Woods & Toll Road

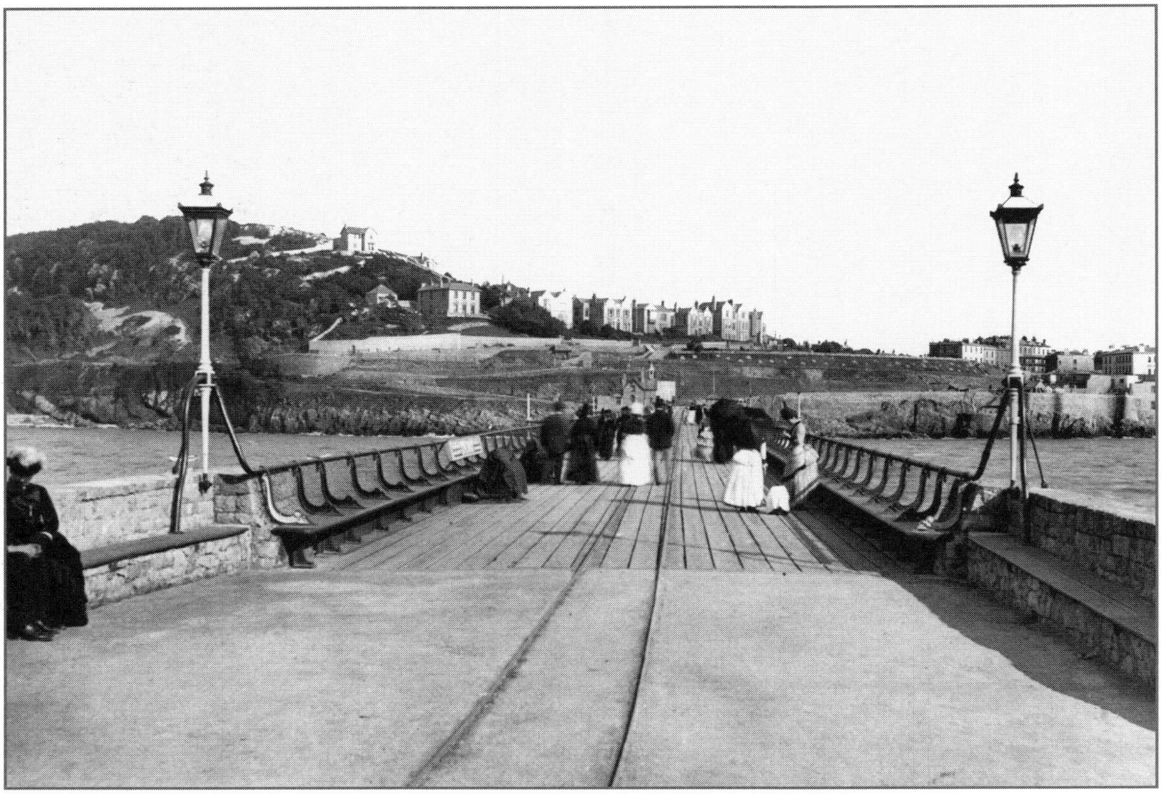

The View from the Pier 1887 20330
To the left, the stone ramparts of Worlebury Iron Age Hillfort can be seen on the very top of the hill. Prince Consort Gardens have yet to be built and a number of terraces lead up to what was then called Flagstaff Hill. On the pier itself, you can see the iron seat brackets shaped liked dolphins and the junction where the pier meets the island.

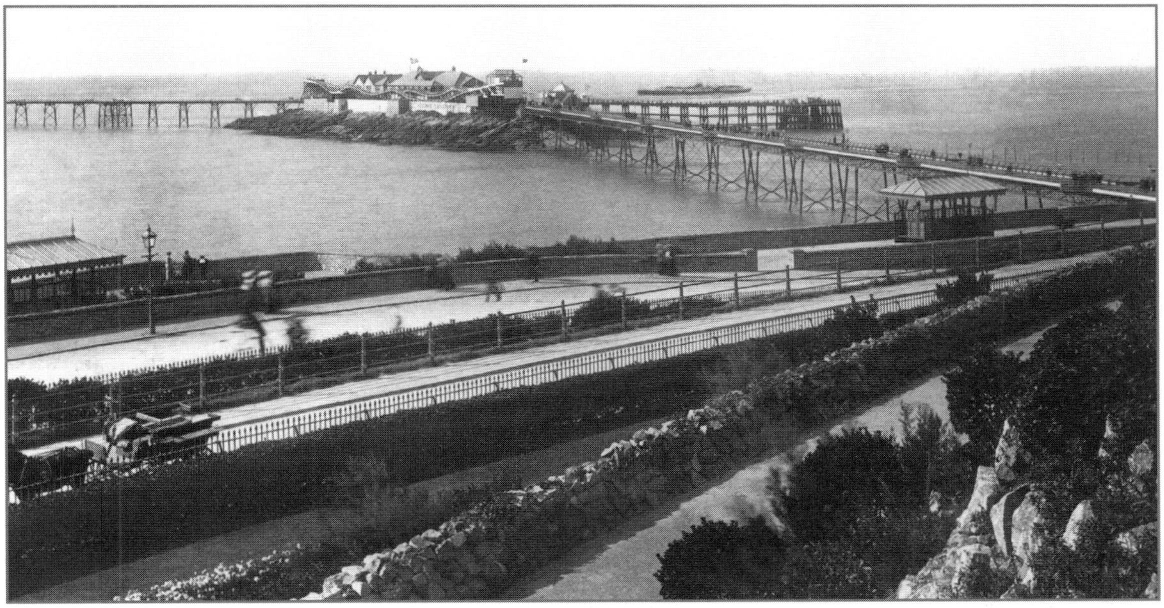

The Pier 1901 47877
Three years before the Grand Pier was built, the Pier is still sufficient description for Birnbeck. Both landing jetties can be seen, with a steamer just leaving the northern one. The switchback railway undulates along the side of the island. The wooden stakes in the water, just to the right of the main pier, supported the fishermen's stow nets, used to catch sprats and other local fish.

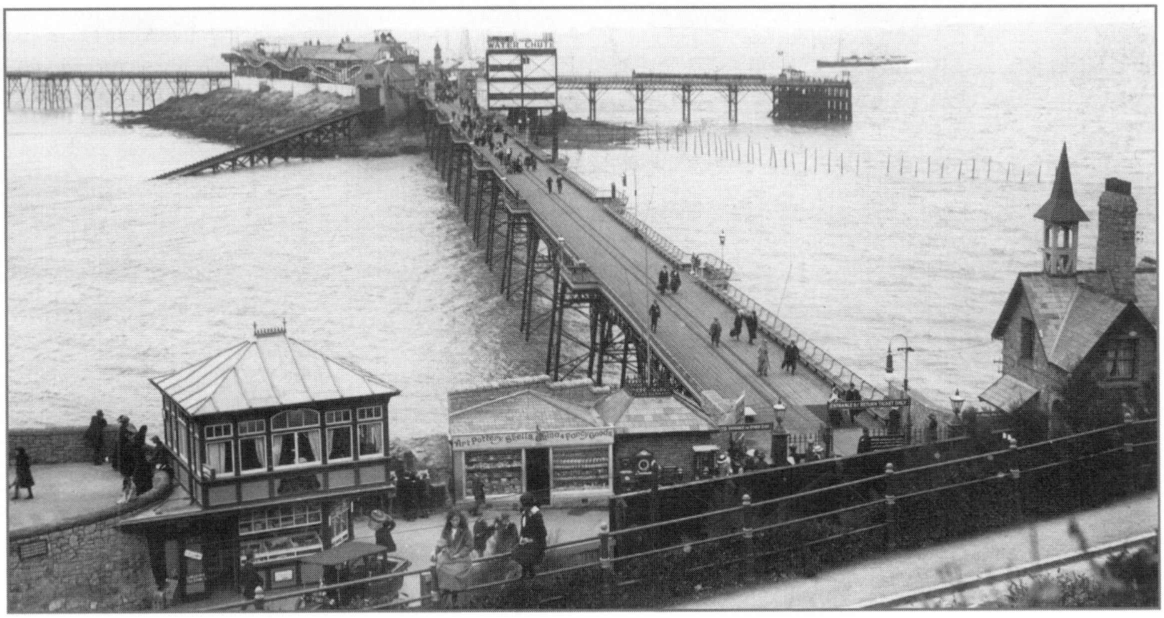

The Old Pier 1913 65354A
This period was perhaps the heyday of the pier, now named the Old Pier. Amusements included the Flying Machine or Airships, Helter Skelter, Maze, Bioscope, Waterchute, Switchback, Cake Walk, Zig Zag Slide, Shooting Jungle, Motor and Bicycle racing, Darts, Ping Pong, Coconut Shies and Aunt Sally. At the entrance, souvenirs, art pottery and seashells were on sale, whilst automatic machines spoke your weight or delivered chocolate bars.

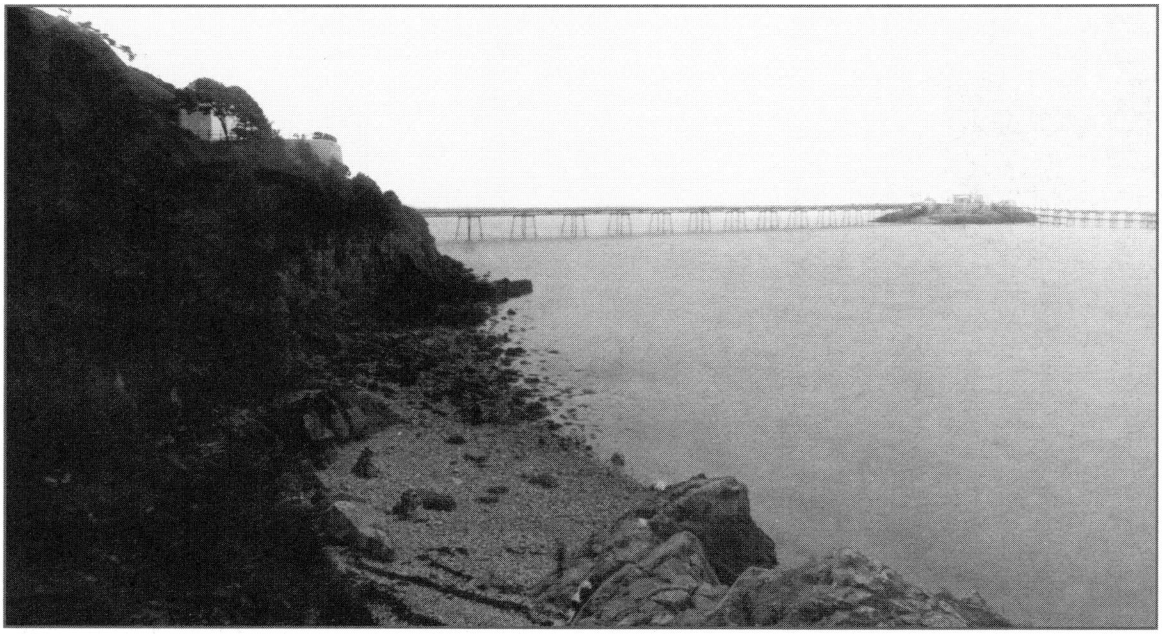

The Pier from Spring Cove 1887 20333
Once a little landing place, Spring Cove takes its name from a freshwater spring that trickled out of the rocks inside a sea-cave. The cave collapsed in a storm in 1861, but the spring still functions. Students of geology travel from far afield to study the volcanic rocks that form the cliff just below the tree on the left.

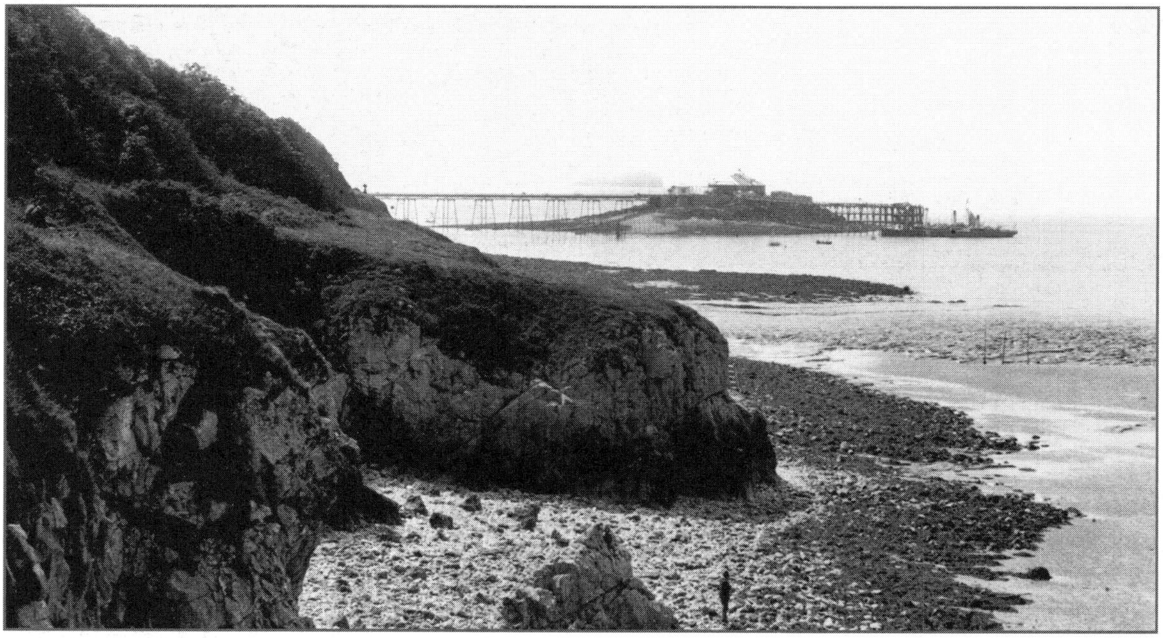

The Pier and Steep Holm 1887 20334
This sheltered cove below the Toll Road clearly shows the Carboniferous limestone that forms Worle Hill. In the foreground is a 'stack', a pillar of rock isolated from the cliff by erosion. On the spur of rock a wooden ladder can just be seen. This gave access to the cove for bathers. In the distance, a paddle steamer leaves Birnbeck Pier jetty.

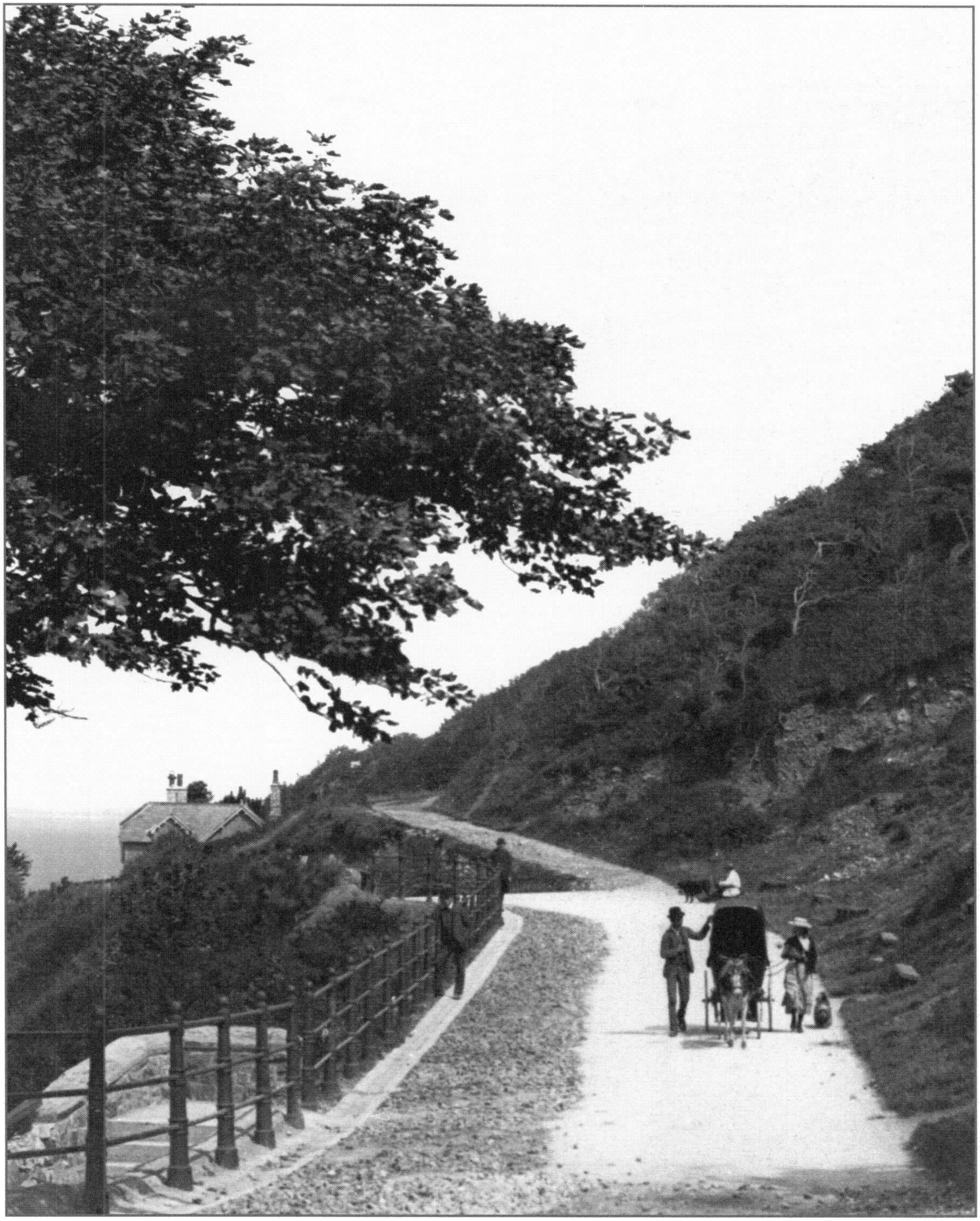

On the Kewstoke Road 1887 20337
The Toll Road was constructed as a private drive in 1848 by the local Lord of the Manor through his game reserve. There was a lodge and gate at each end, the roof of one of which can be seen under the tree. In 1848 tolls were 6d (2½p) for a carriage, 3d (1½p)for a horse and 1d (½p) for a donkey chair as pictured here.

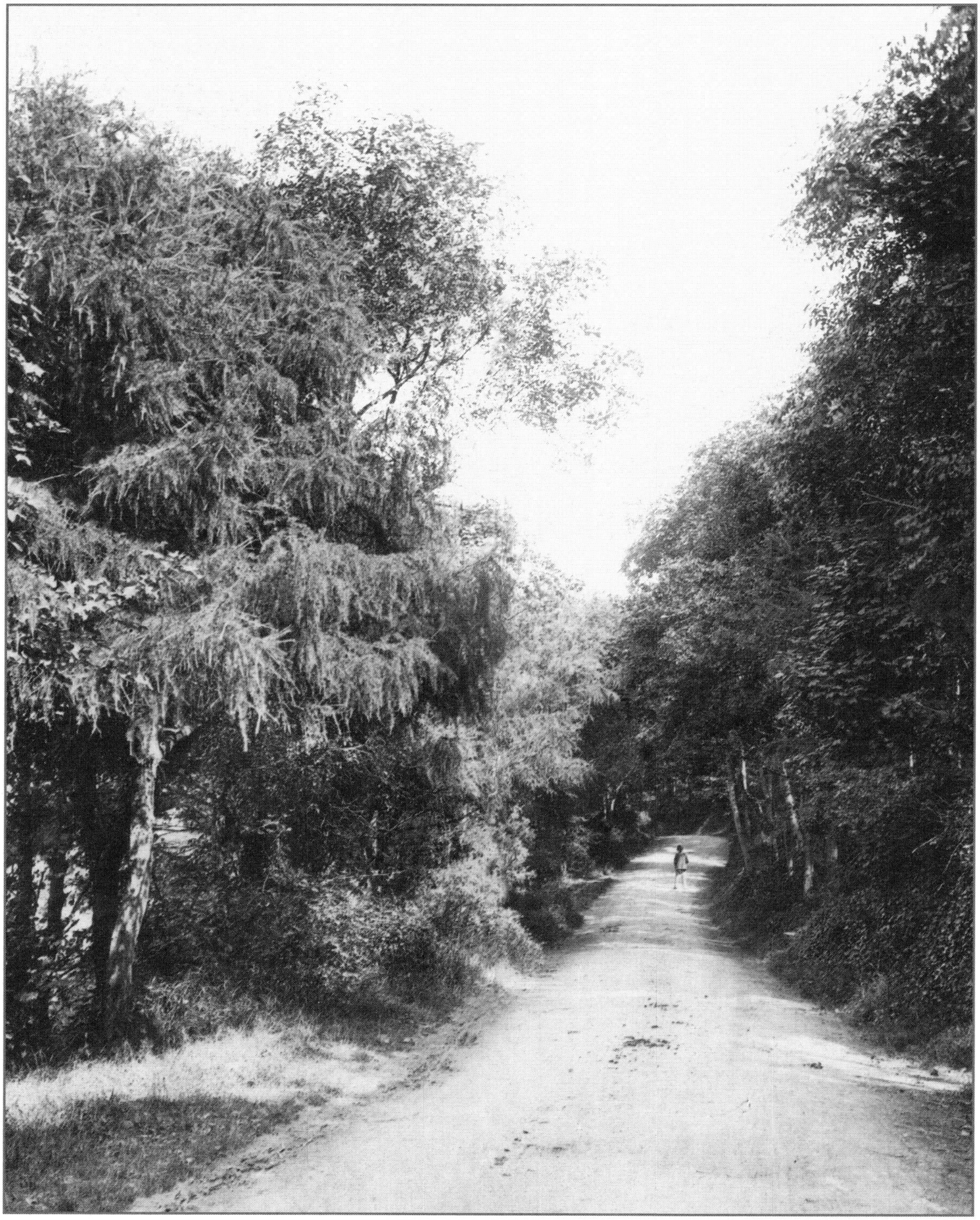

On the Kewstoke Road 1887 20346
There has never been a charge for pedestrians on the Toll Road as it was originally a public footpath called Black Rock Path. The road has been called Channel Road, North Road and Kewstoke Road as here, but Toll Road seems to stick.

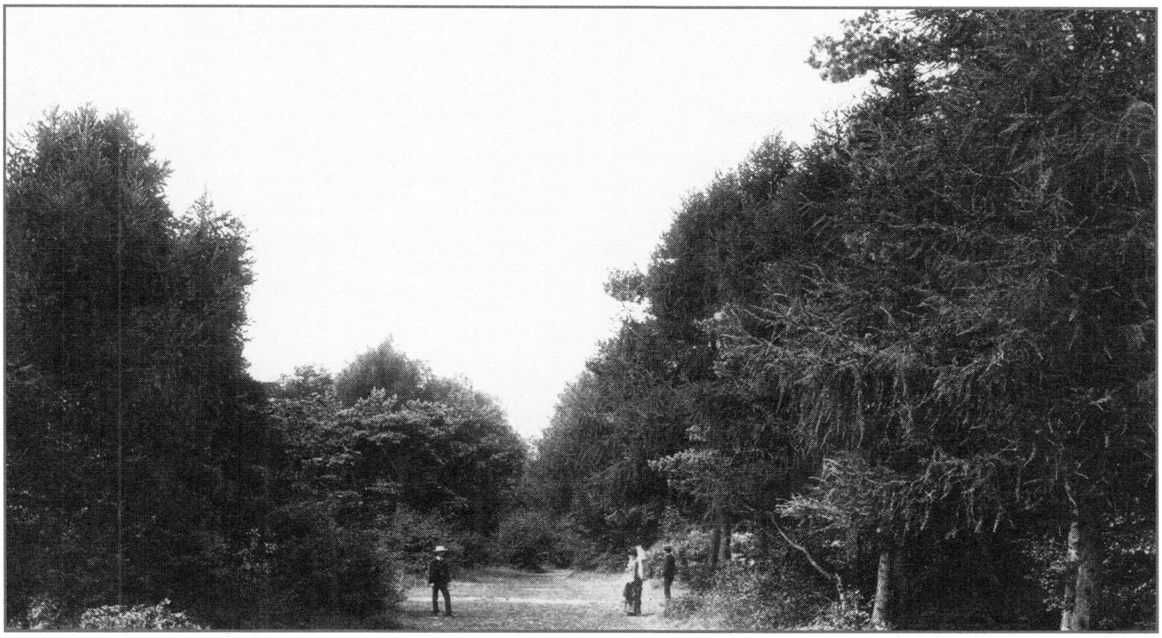

In the Woods 1887 20344
In its natural state, the hilltop was flat grazing land as the neighbouring hills of Sand Point and Brean Down are today. The woods were planted in 1823 by the Lord of the Manor, to create a private game reserve. Before the thinning and clear felling during World War One, the Woods were much more coniferous, as this picture shows.

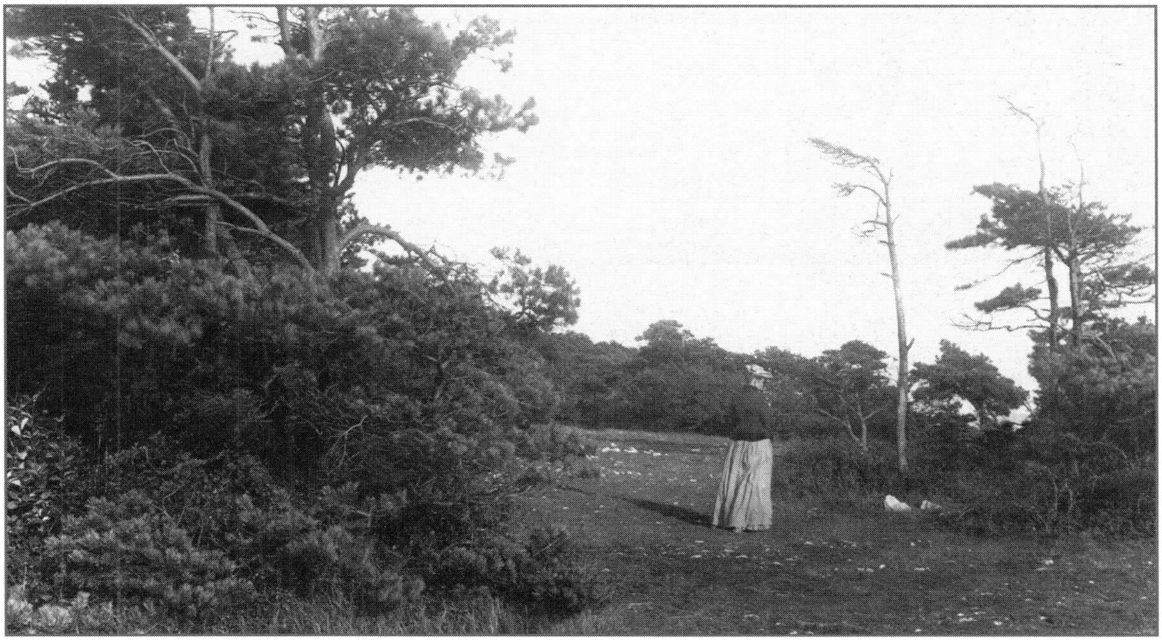

View of the Encampment 1890 27895
This photograph is taken inside the walls of the Iron Age hillfort of Worlebury. The lady is looking into one of the numerous prehistoric crop storage pits that had been excavated by the antiquarian C W Dymond a few years previously. The hillfort is one of the best preserved in the country.

Around Weston-super-Mare

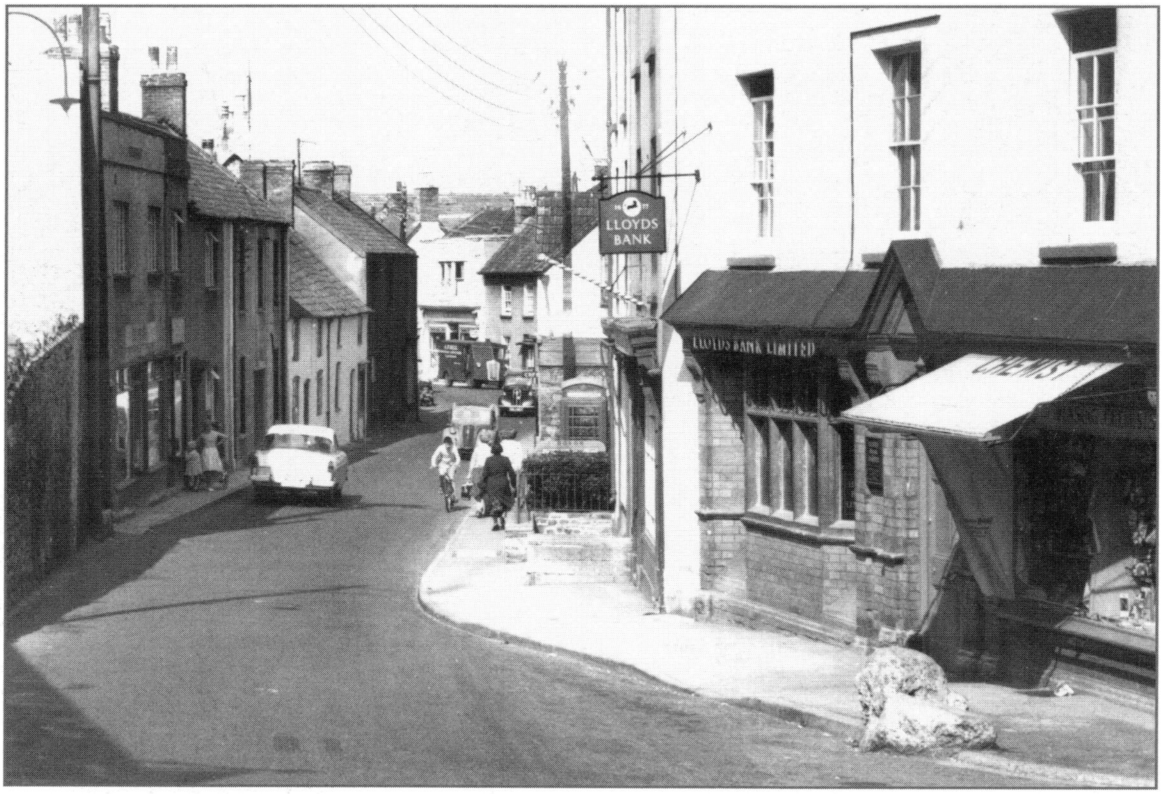

Banwell, West Street c1960 B307018
Banwell is one of the most picturesque villages in the area, retaining many of its old buildings. Just under the chemist's blind on the right of this view is a reminder of a much more leisurely age in the form of the stone mounting block. It is outside Butstone House, which in earlier times housed Mr Hollyman's Saddlery shop; it is now the library.

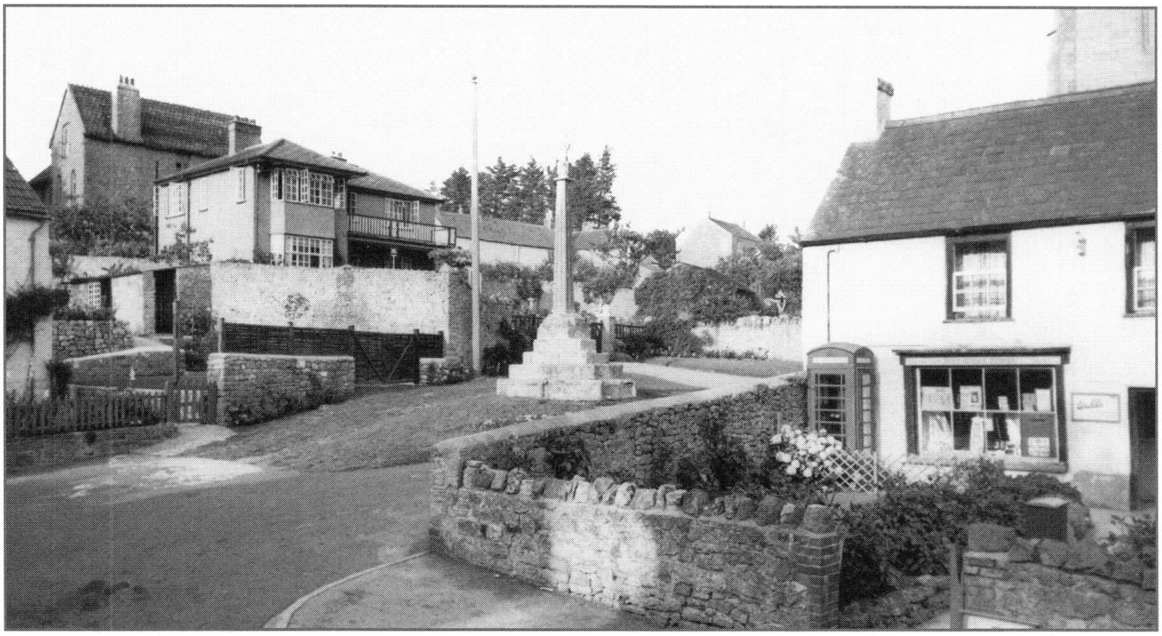

Bleadon, The Village and Post Office c1960 B313016
Surprisingly, this view is little changed today. The medieval village cross, which once stood within the churchyard itself, still stands sentry outside the gate to the 14th-century church of St Peter and St Paul, the tower of which can just be glimpsed behind the post office on the right.

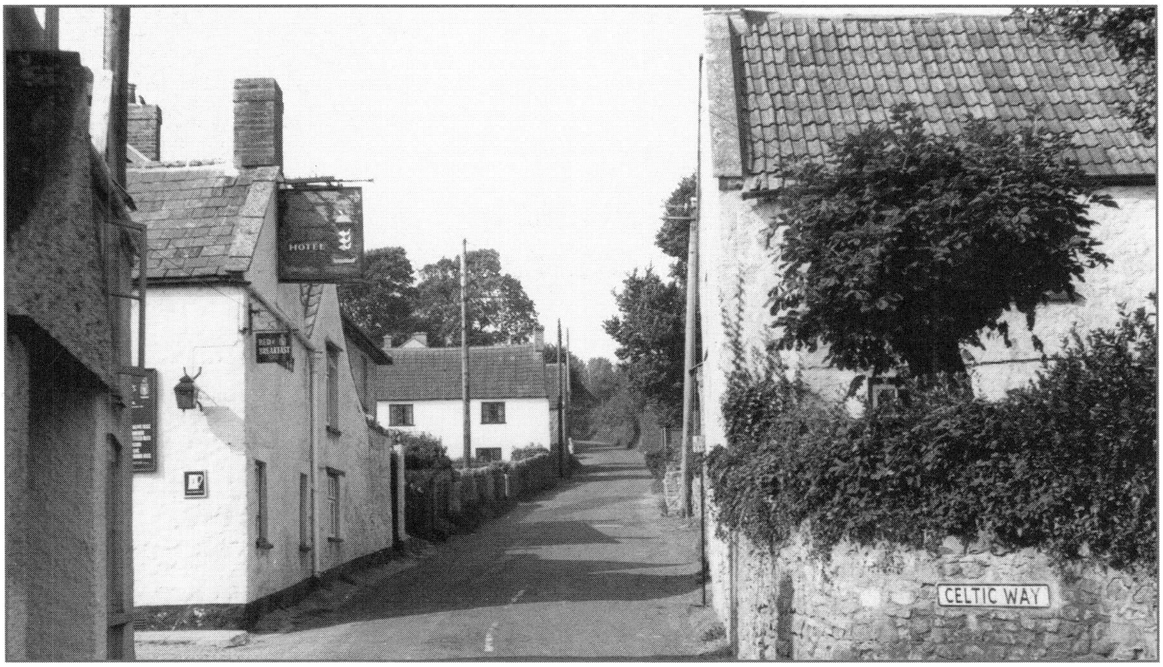

Bleadon, Celtic Way c1965 B313035
Celtic Way is the main road through the village; it leads up to Bleadon Hill. On the left is the Queens Arms Hotel. The road to the right leads to Christon and Loxton.

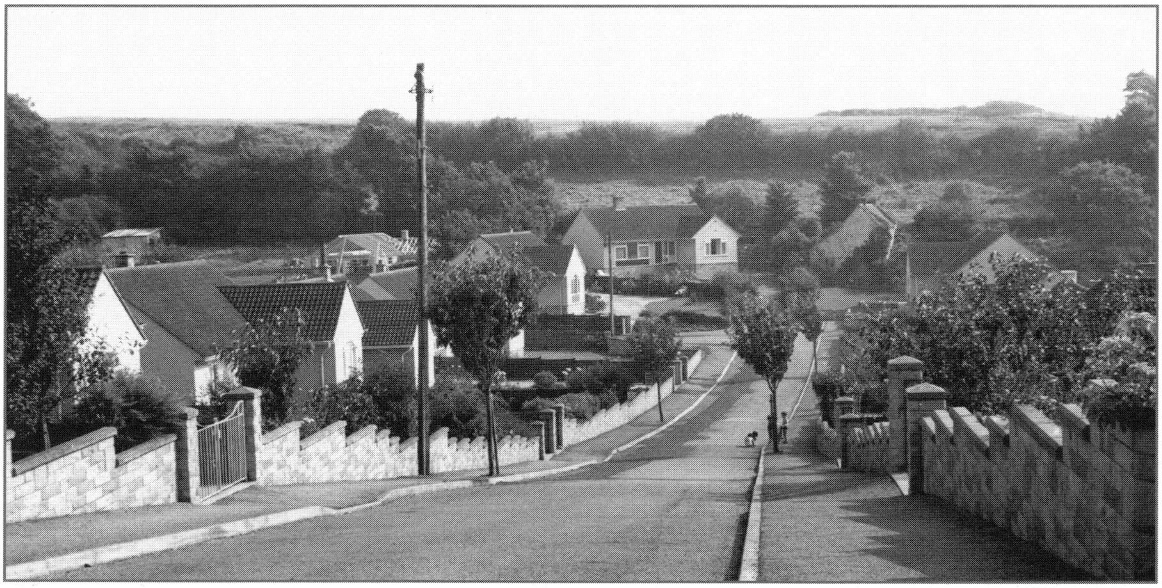

Bleadon, Birch Avenue c1965 B313038
The bungalows are overlooked by the flat summit of South Hill, which is covered in prehistoric field systems. The estate is built on what was the site of the arable East Field of the Middle Ages. The bank on the skyline surrounds Bleadon Quarry and marks an attempt to extend the workings over 40 years ago.

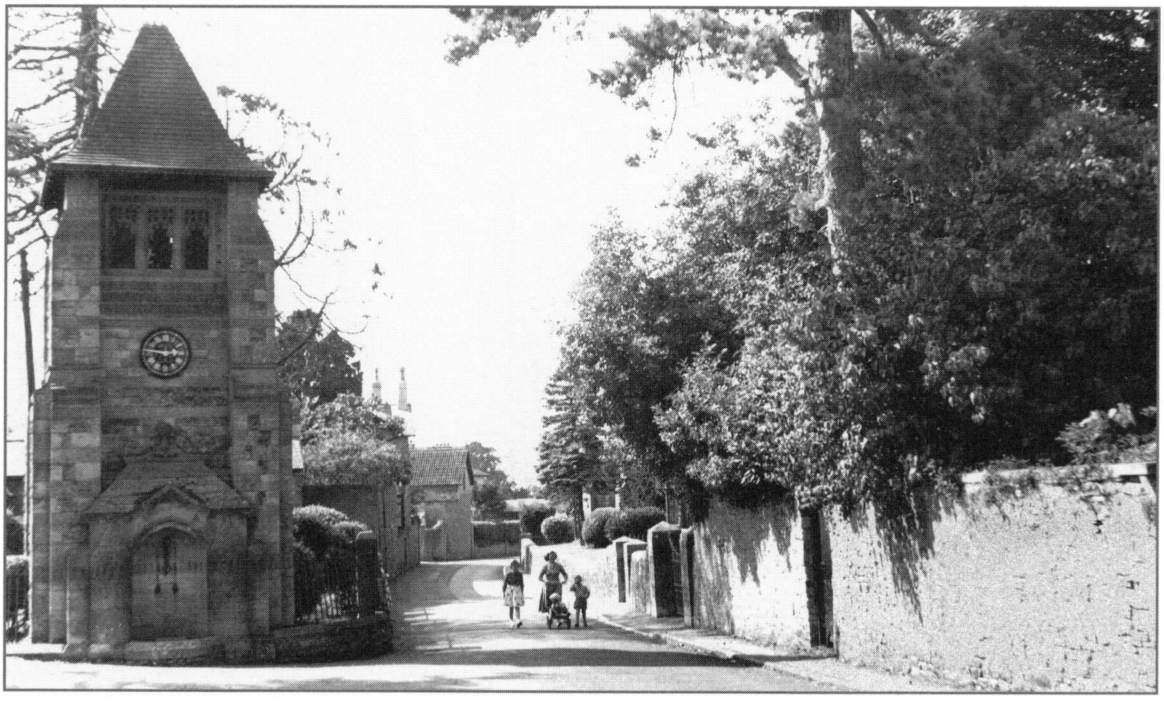

Churchill, Clock Tower c1955 C231022
This fine clock tower was built to mark the Diamond Jubilee of Queen Victoria in 1897. It was erected by Sidney Hill, a local benefactor who also provided several almshouses for the elderly in the village. Amongst the stone used in its construction is a local pudding stone (or conglomerate) that creates an interesting mottled effect.

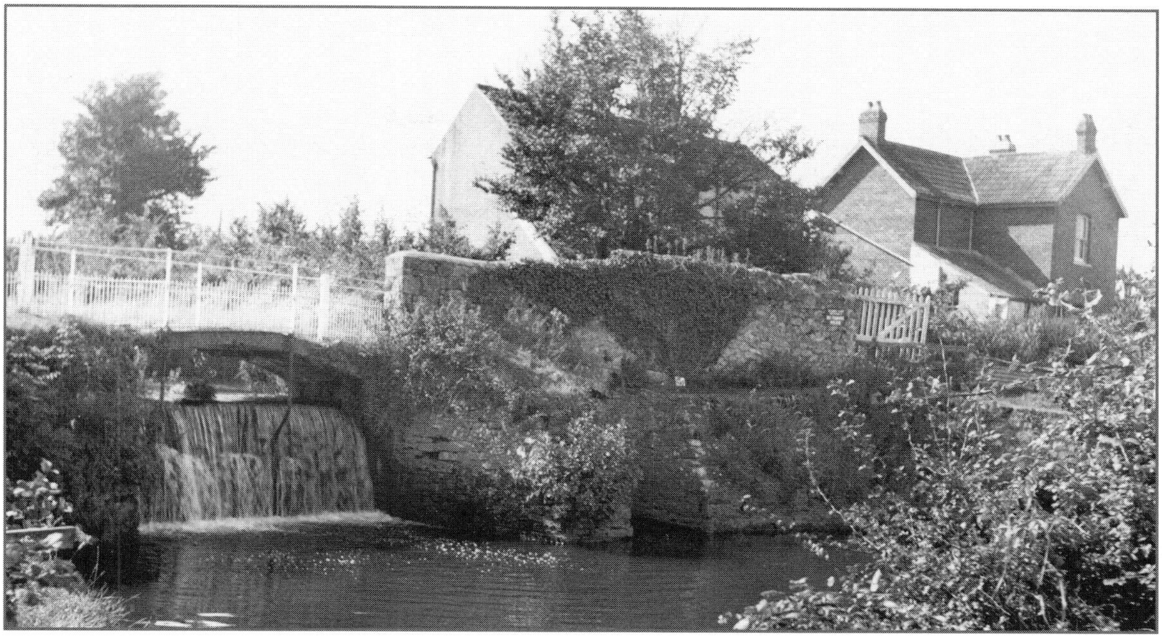

Congresbury, The Waterfall c1965 C234011
This weir on the River Yeo was originally known as the Tumbling Weir and was close to the site of one of Congresbury's mills. In the mid-18th century this mill produced rods from iron bars for use in the nail-making industry. The river is tidal to this point.

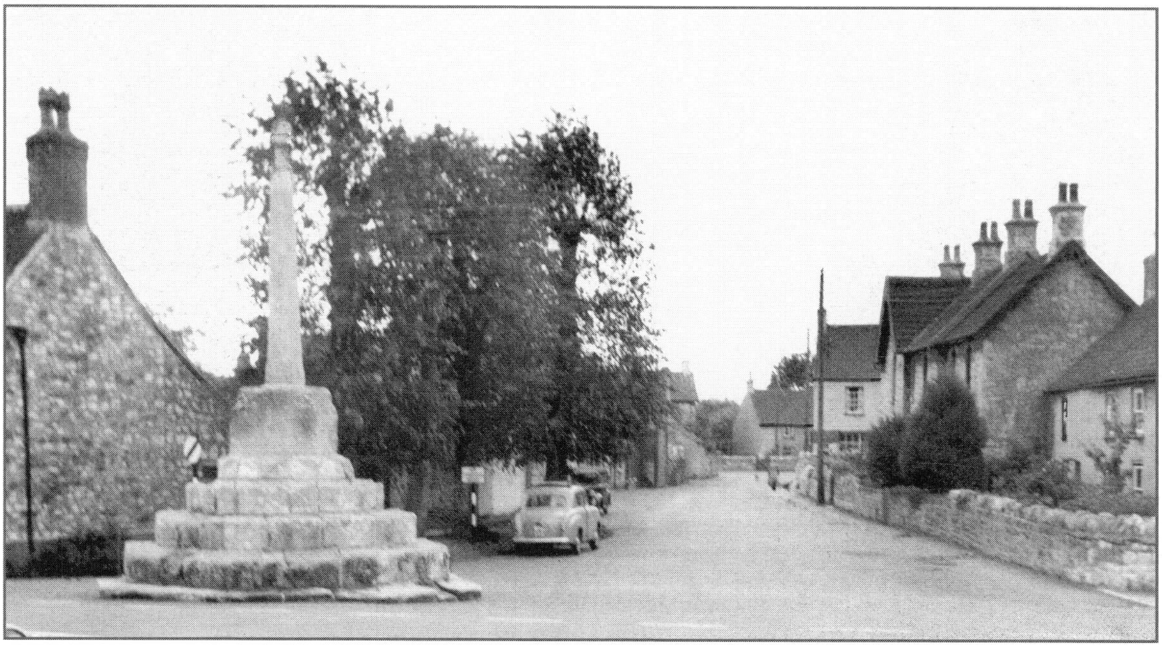

Congresbury, The Village c1965 C234022
This 15th-century market cross stands in the centre of the village. The right to hold a weekly market and an annual fair was granted in 1227. These continued to be held until the 1960s. This view is looking toward Broad Street with the road to Weston-super-Mare on the right.

Hutton, The Village c1945 H166001
This view looks west along Main Road. In the distance a lorry is being loaded with milk churns from Old Post Office Farm. In 1900 there were twelve farms in the village, all with dairy herds. Now just three are left.

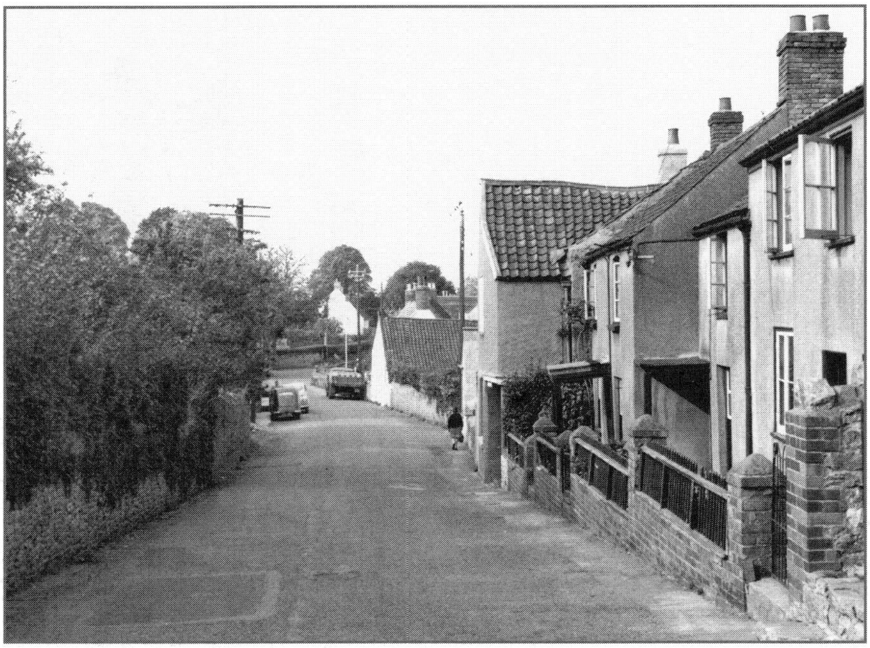

Hutton, The Village c1945 H166002
The Old Farm Stores and Post Office, on the left, was originally a domestic house. By 1834 it had become the farmhouse for Hutton Farm. It closed down as a shop and post office in the late 1970s. The YHA sign on the right points to the youth hostel that used to be at the end of Eastfield Road.

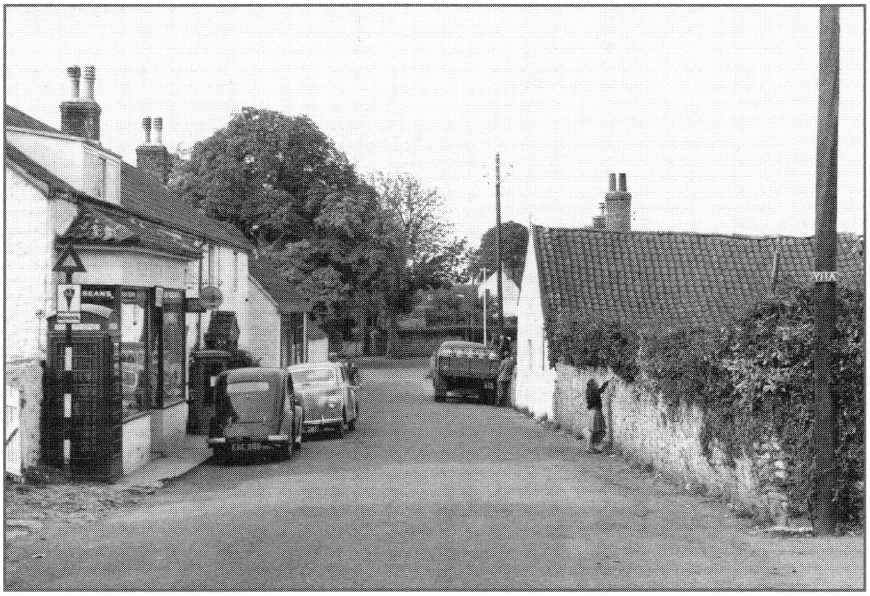

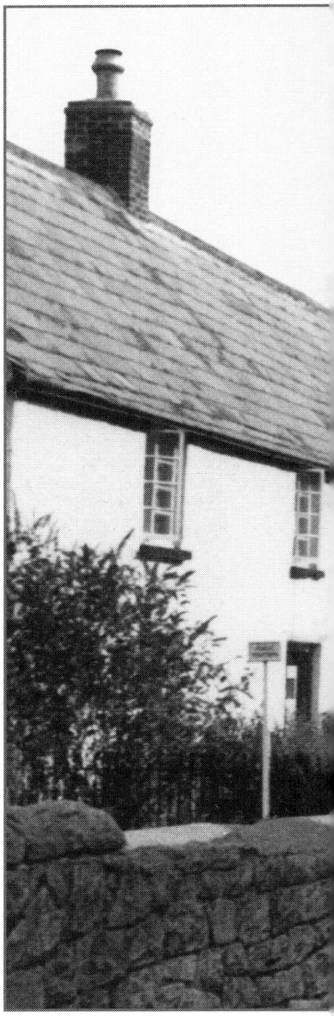

Hutton, The Village c1945 H166008
This is the main road through the village looking towards Hutton Hill. The white cottage on the left used to be the Post Office, before it was moved to the other side of the road in the 1930s.

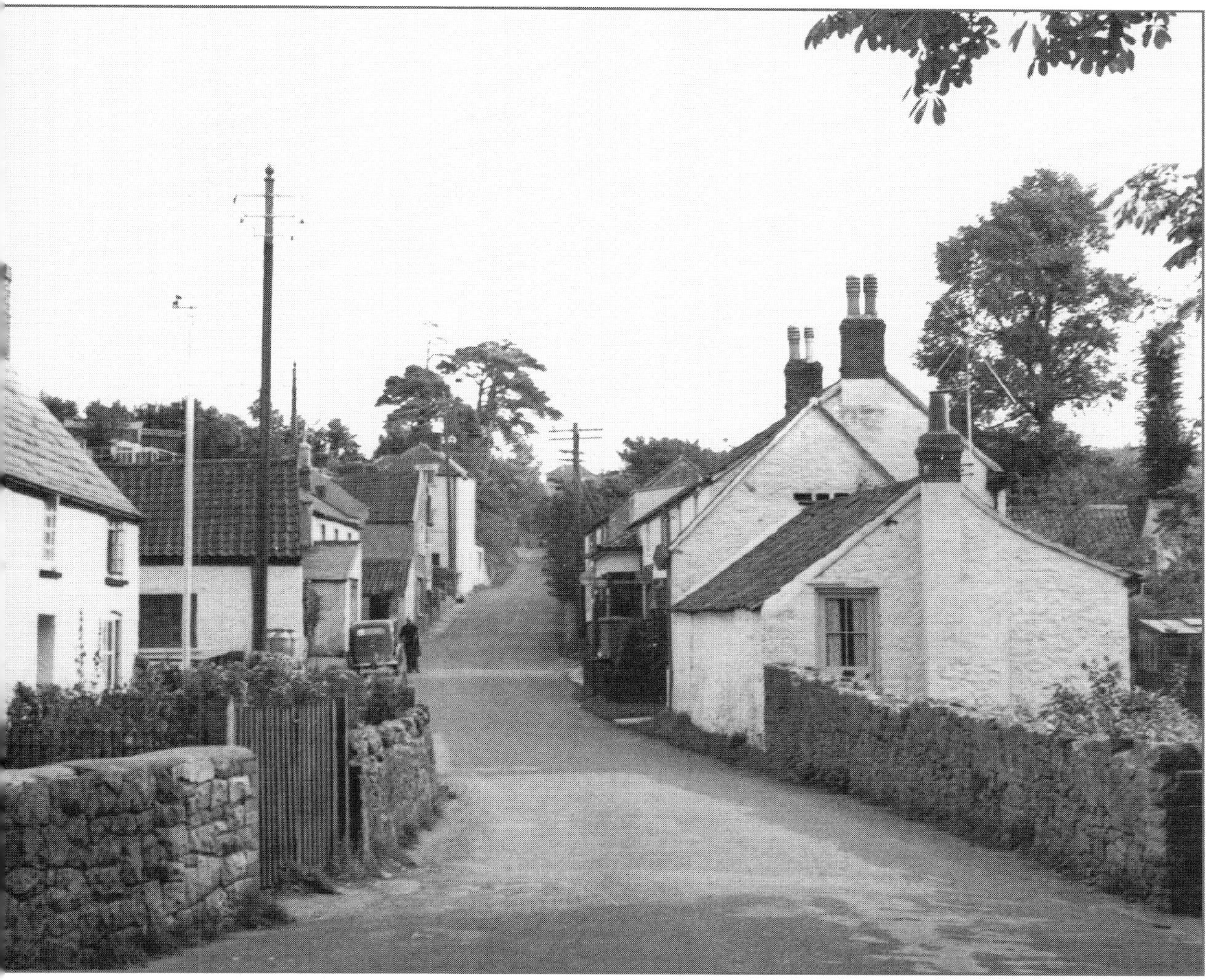

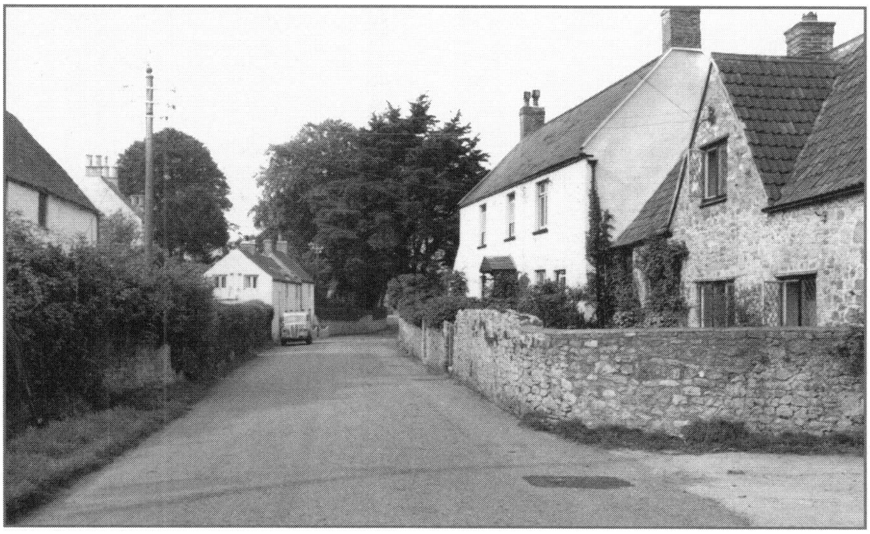

Hutton, The Village c1945
H166009
The buildings on the right were once part of Middle Farm and date back to Tudor times. The right-hand house, converted from an old barn, bears the coat of arms of Christopher Kenn over the doorway. The other buildings in this photograph are 16th- and 17th-century in date.

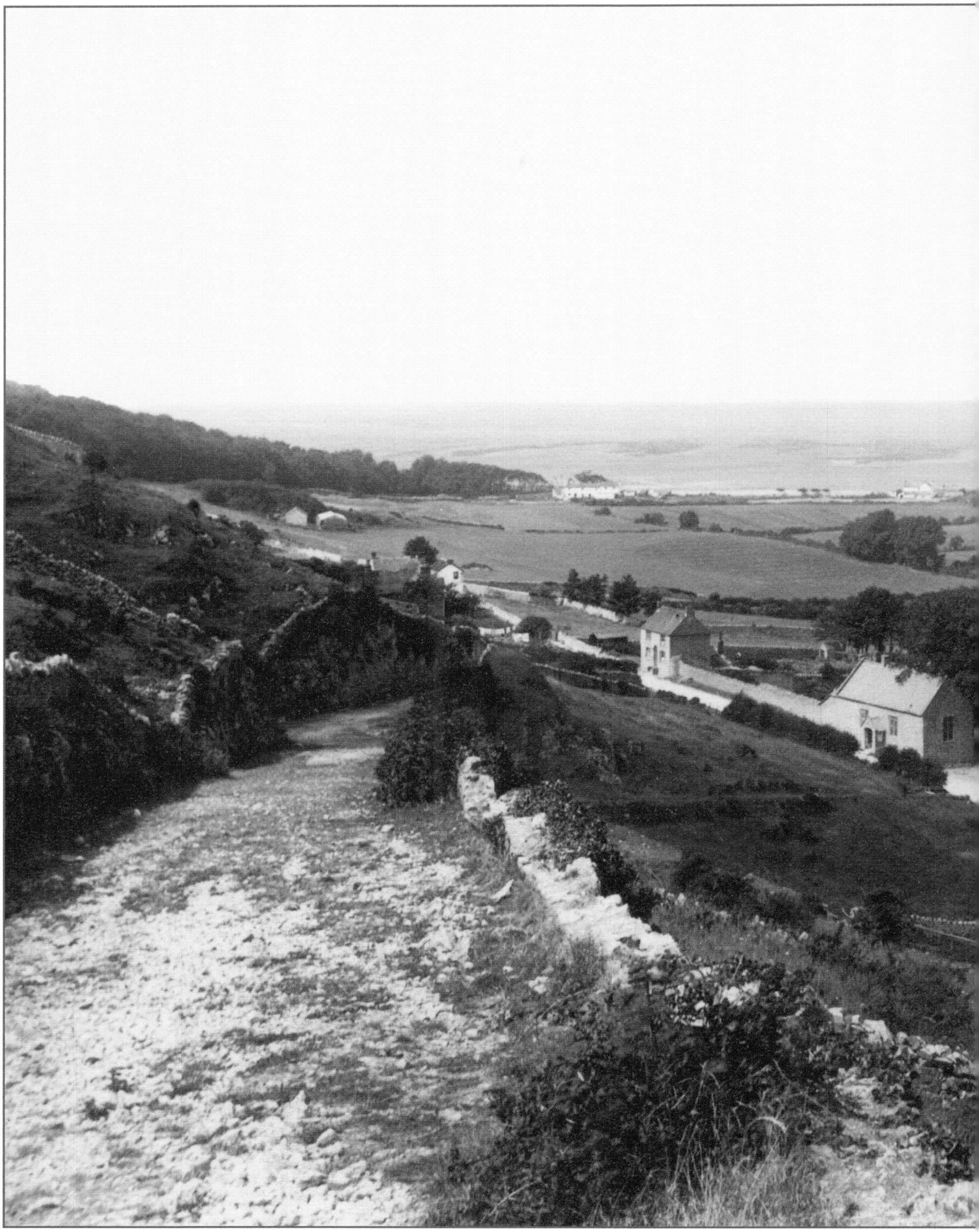

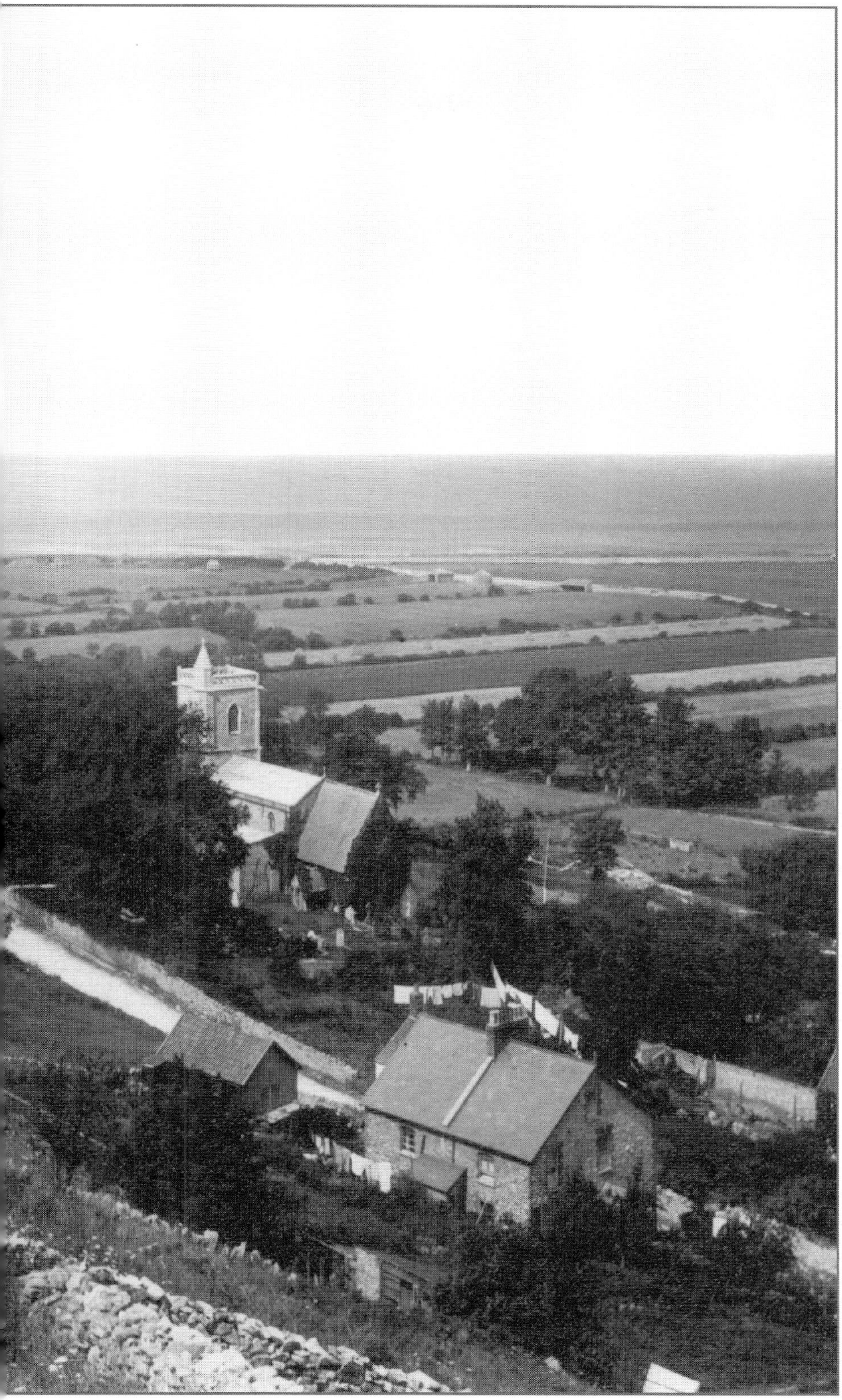

Kewstoke, The Village 1896 38454
The photographer is standing on Monks Hill, looking down the winding road that leads to the centre of the original village. The Church stands surrounded by trees, whilst in the distance is Sand Bay. The small building to the left of the church was once used as a Poorhouse but was converted for use as Kewstoke's first schoolroom in 1840.

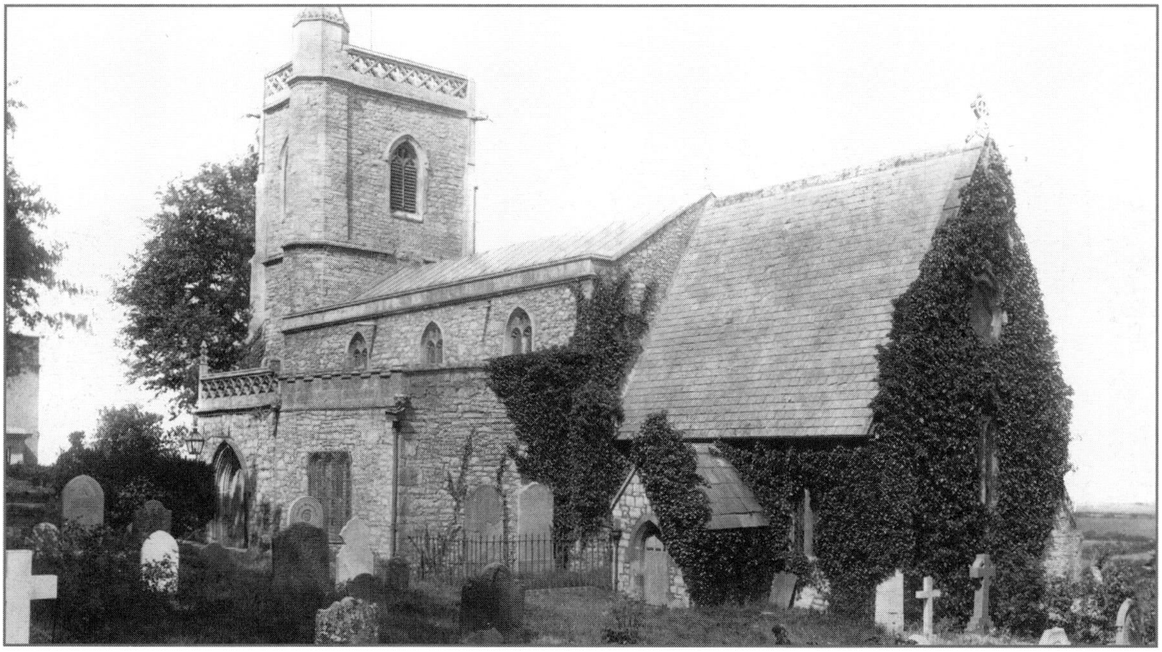

Kewstoke, The Church 1896 38455
Dedicated to St Paul, the church is mainly 13th-century with later alterations. Its earlier foundation is revealed, however, by the superb Norman doorway that survives today. In 1849, during building work, an ancient stone reliquary was found together with part of a wooden cup. The cup was stained with blood, said to be that of St Thomas à Becket.

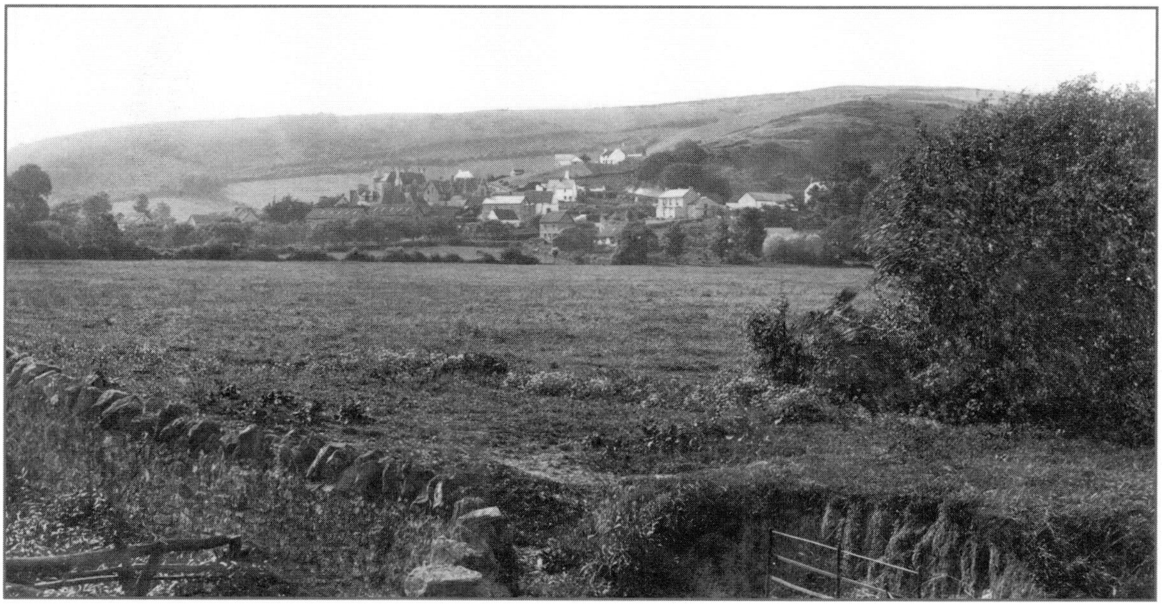

Loxton, The Village 1907 58722
Situated in the Lox Yeo valley, this village enjoyed one of the finest views of the Mendip Hills. There is a charming 13th-century church with a Norman doorway and one of the superb carved medieval pulpits that adorn many of the village churches of this area.

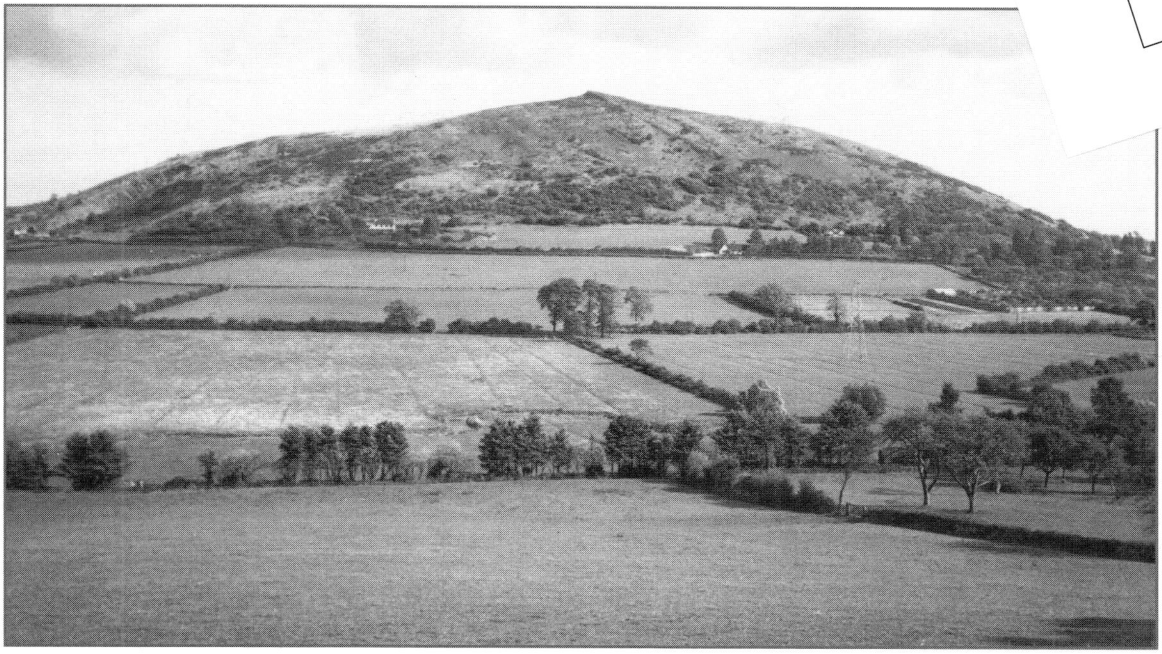

Loxton, Crook Peak c1965 L149002
This tranquil scene was changed forever in 1970 when huge earth-moving vehicles were brought in to construct the M5 motorway right through the middle of these fields. In the distance is Crook Peak, not the highest point on Mendip but one of the most conspicuous. In the foreground is the Lox Yeo river, once a minor trout stream, that rises from springs around Winscombe.

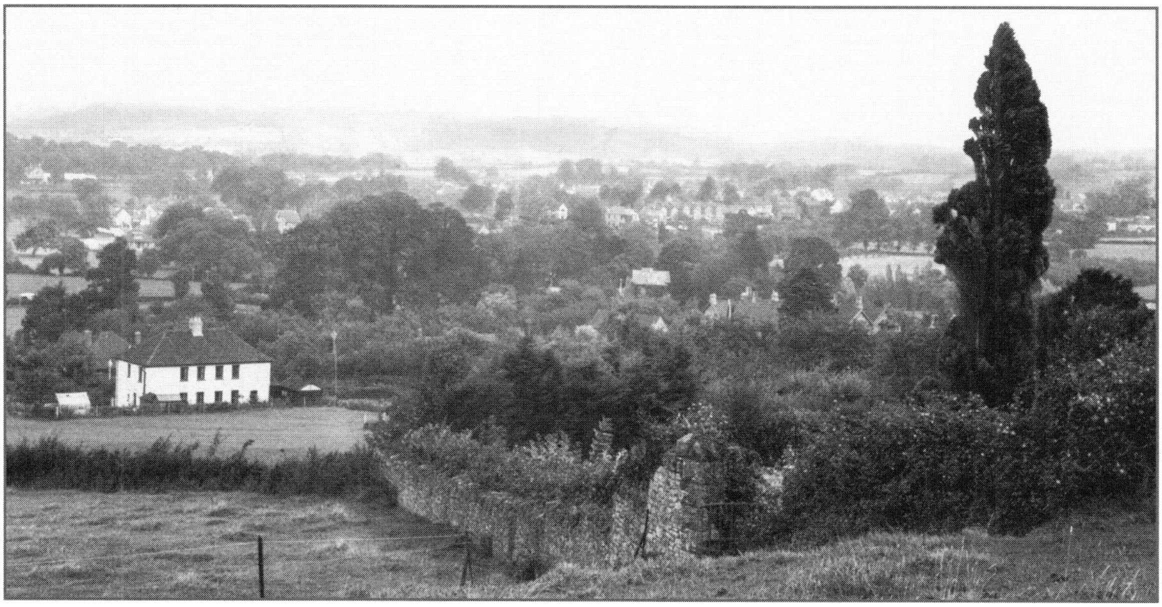

Winscombe, Sandford Hill c1965 W183011
This picture was taken from just outside the parish churchyard looking north towards Sandford Hill. The white building on the left is Jubilee Cottages, built in 1935. Despite modern development, much remains of the old Winscombe immortalised in Theodore Compton's 'A Mendip Valley' of 1892.

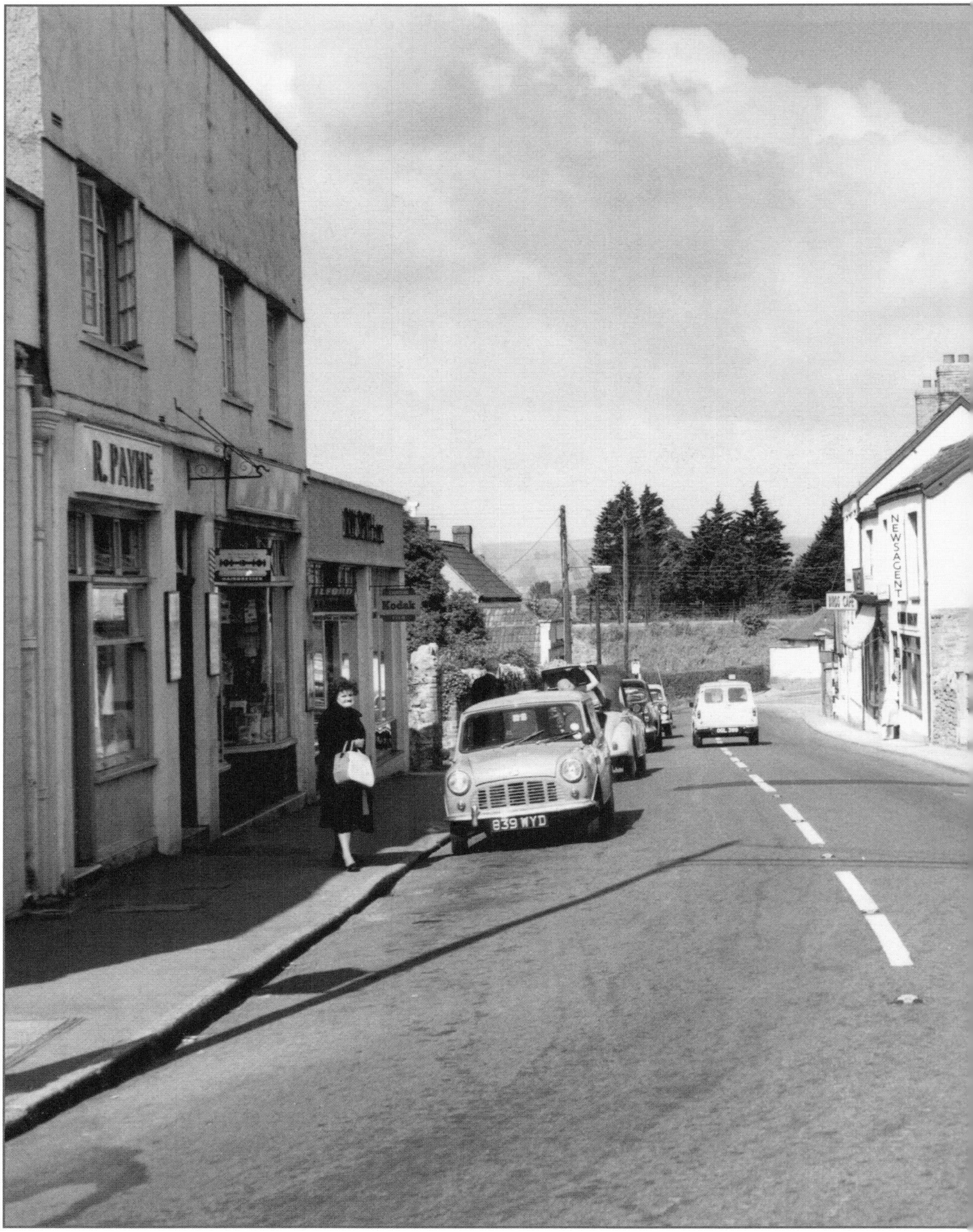
R. PAYNE
Kodak
NEWSAGENT
839 WYD

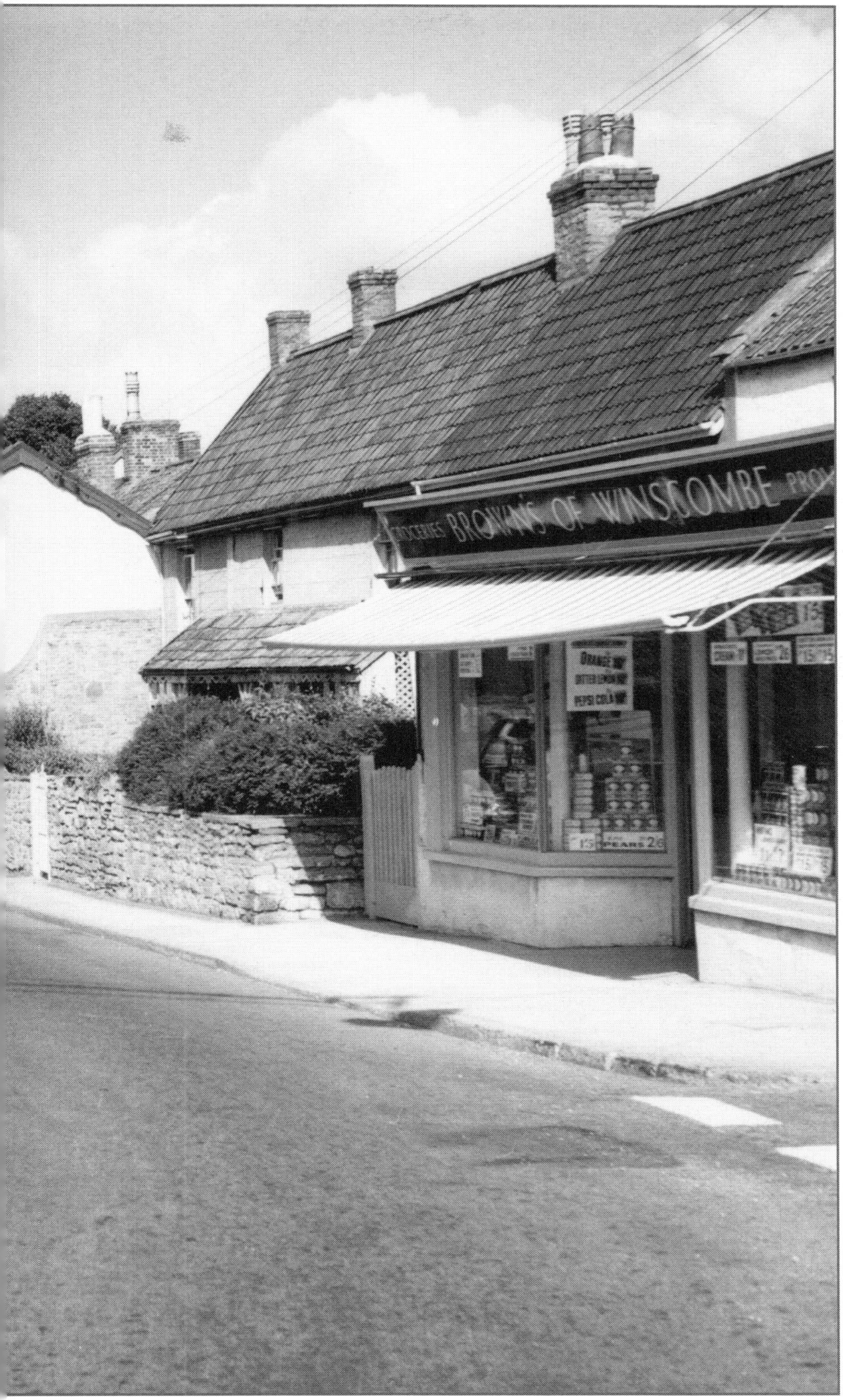

Winscombe Woodborough Road c1965 W183034
Woodborough was originally a separate hamlet in its own right until it became part of Winscombe. At the end of this main road you can see the embankment of the Cheddar Valley Railway, closed in 1963. It is hard to imagine now that lead-ore and calamine mines were once worked here.

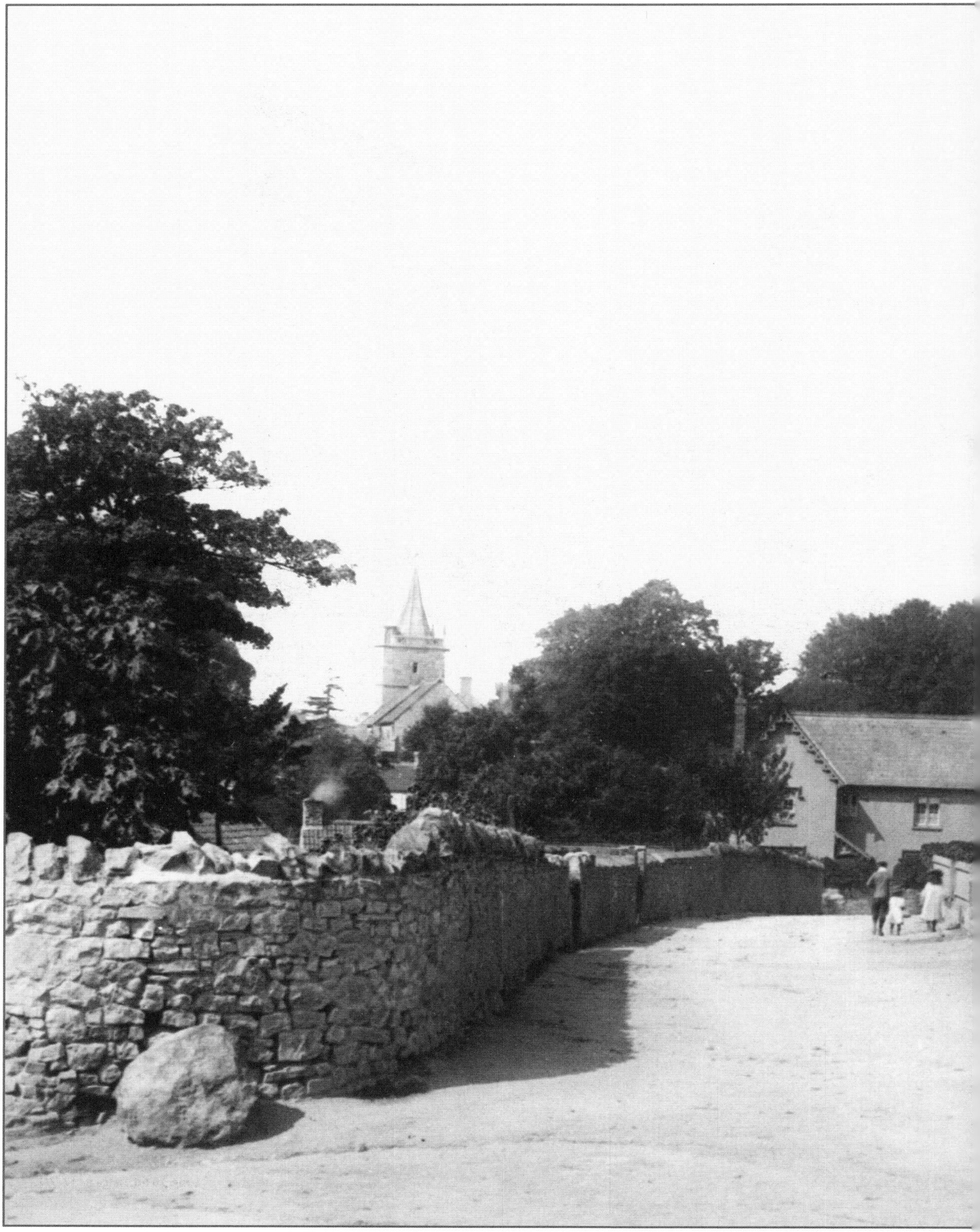

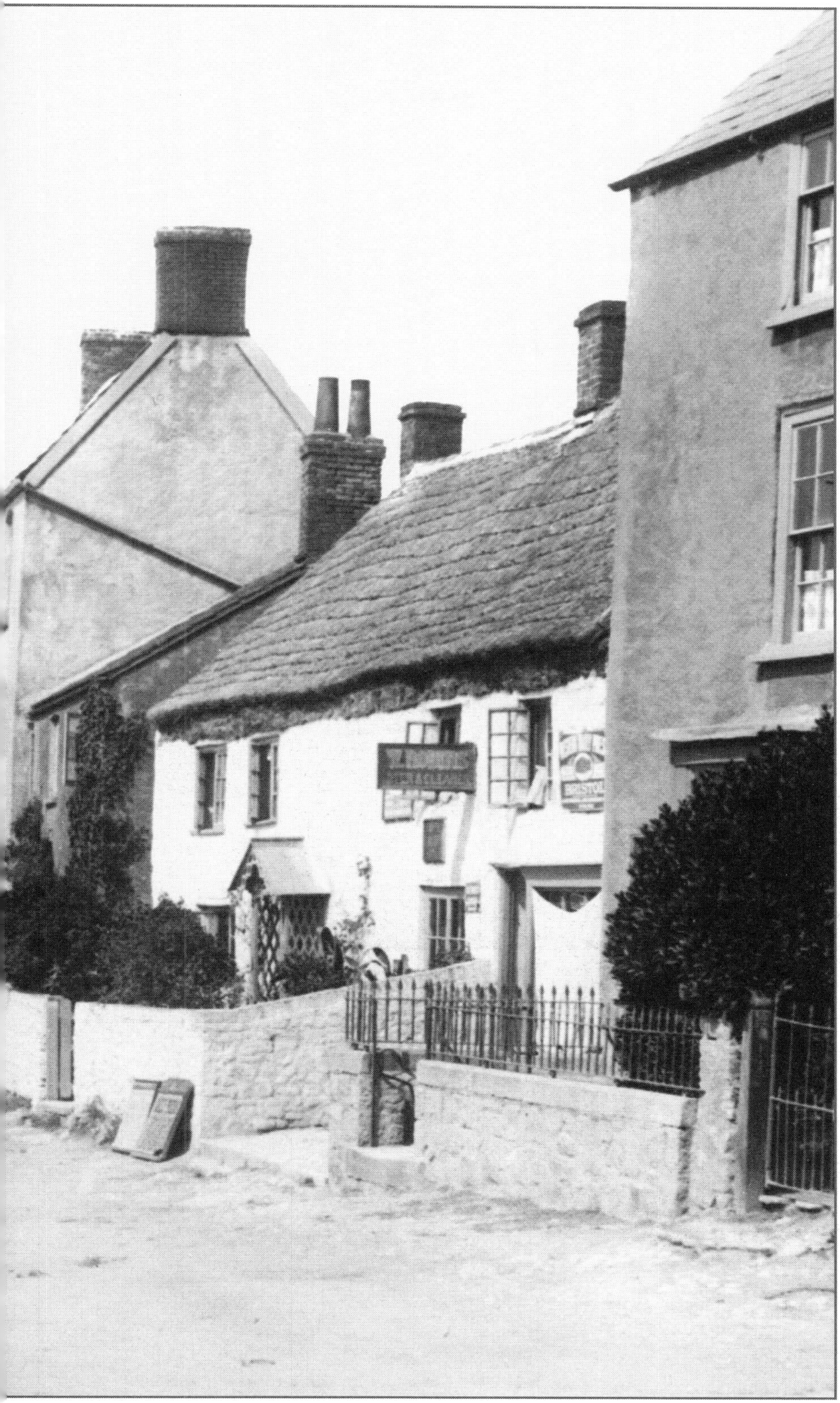

Worle, The Village 1896 38460

This is the oldest part of the village, with some properties dating back to medieval times. The shop with the thatched roof, here belonging to Mr Rollins, a dyer and cleaner, used to be a bakery. It was converted into cottages in 1931, when the thatch was replaced by tiles. The three-storey building in the centre used to be the Valiant Soldier Inn and was built about 1670. Note the stone mounting block by the wall.

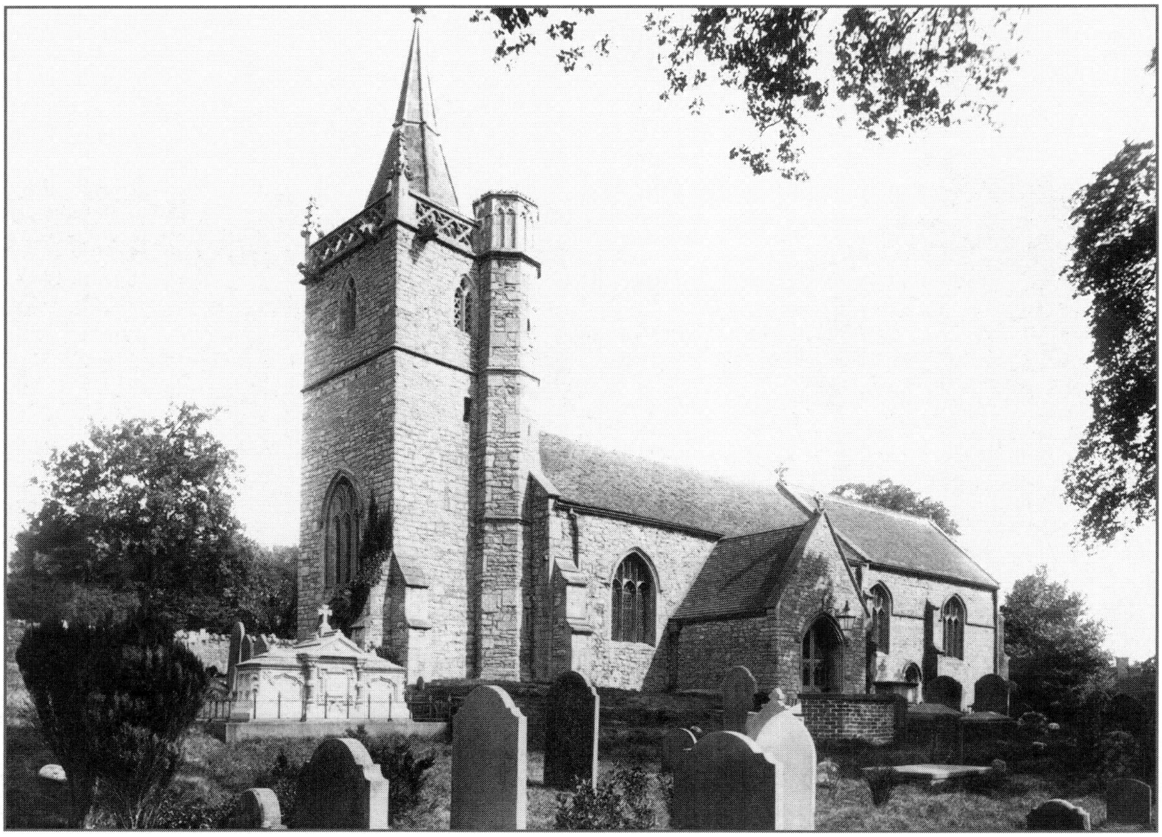

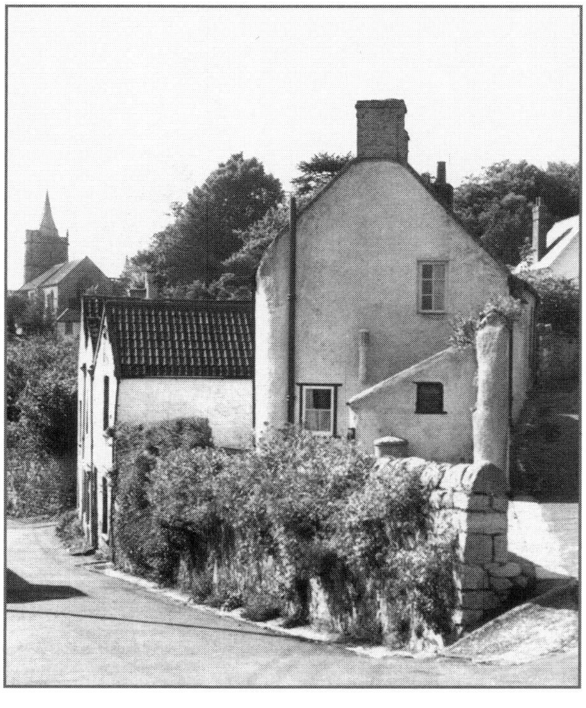

Worle, The Church 1896 38459
St Martin's Church at Worle is mostly 12th-century, although it was largely restored in 1870. The south porch, in this picture, contains the original Norman arch of about 1125. The large tomb by the tower is for members of the Caple family of Worle and was designed by Weston architect, Sidney Wilde.

Worle, The Village c1955 W184005
In this view of Lawrence Road, Rock Cottage is in the centre. In the distance is St Martin's Church with its 12th-century tower. The two cottages left of Rock Cottage have now been demolished, but otherwise the view is little changed today.

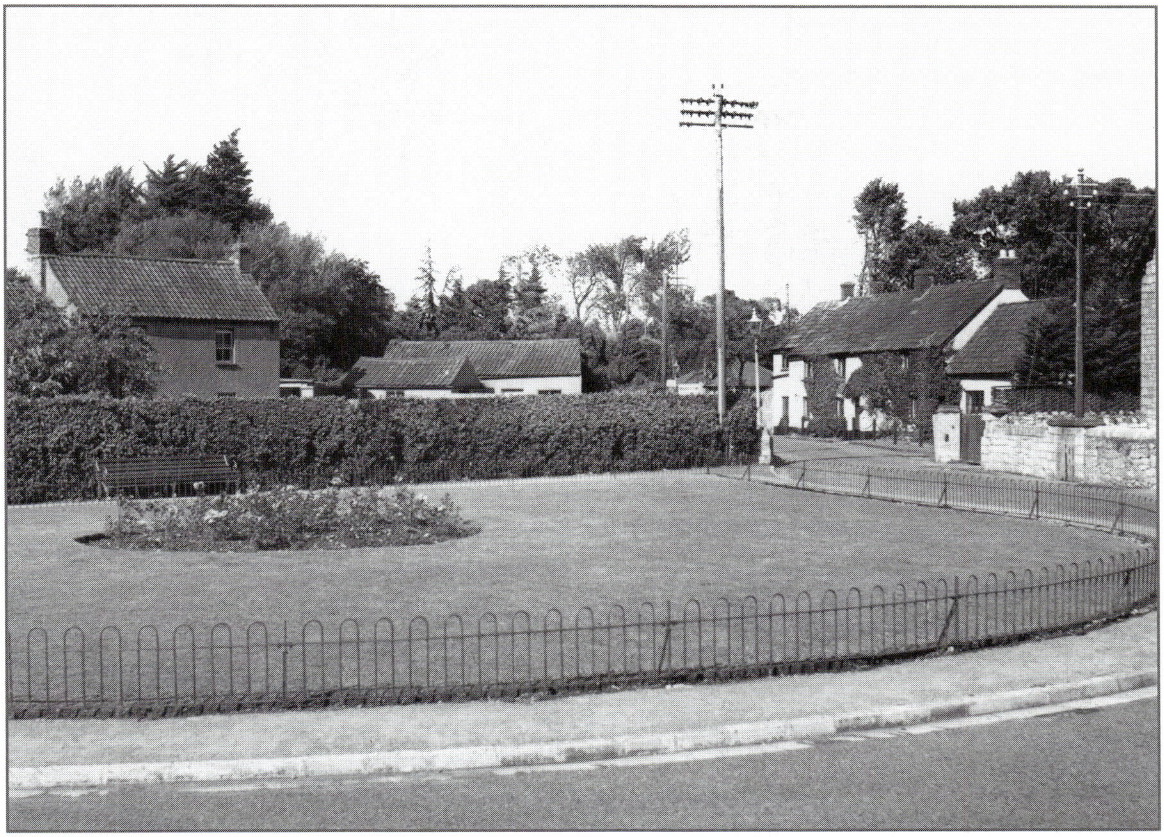

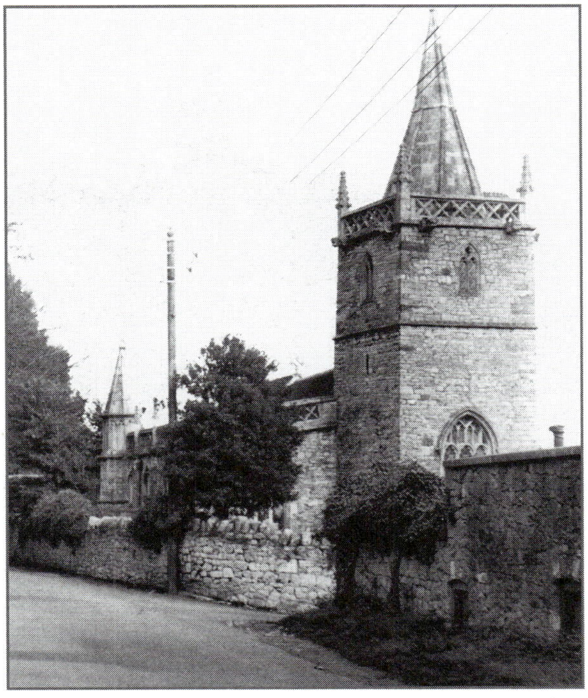

Worle, Ebdon Road c1960 W184006
This municipal flower bed and lawn contrasts with the old cottages surrounding it. Note the old gas lamp next to the telegraph pole. Ebdon Road leads out to Wick St Lawrence. At the time of this photograph, you would soon be amongst open fields. Now, however, new housing estates line most of the road beyond this point.

Worle, Church Road c1955 W184013
The road on the right leading down is Hill Road with St Martin's Church on the corner. The church contains many interesting features, including a sedilia, a pair of stone seats in the chancel, misericords and a squint. A 'squint' was a window cut into one of the columns so that all members of the congregation could see the altar.

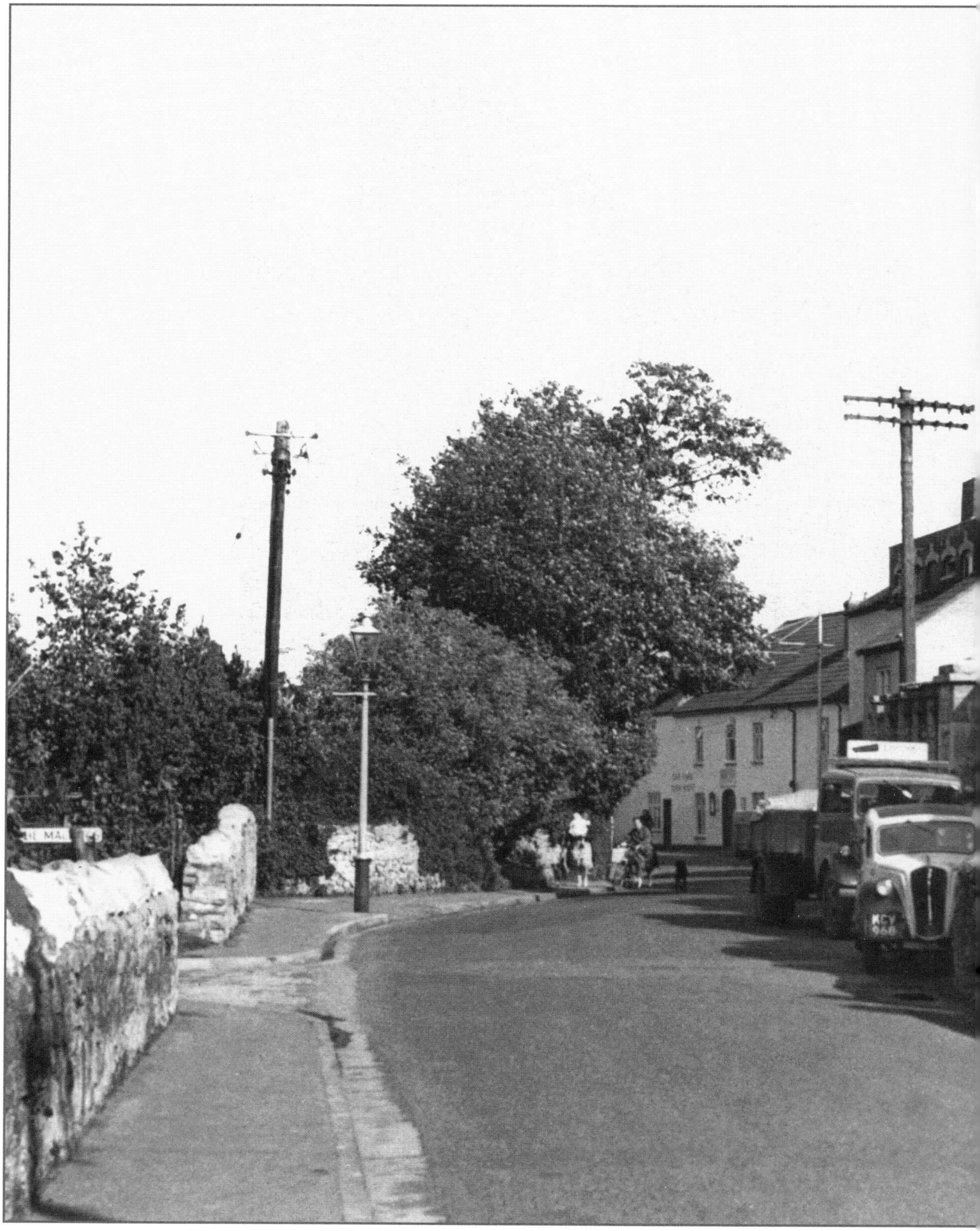

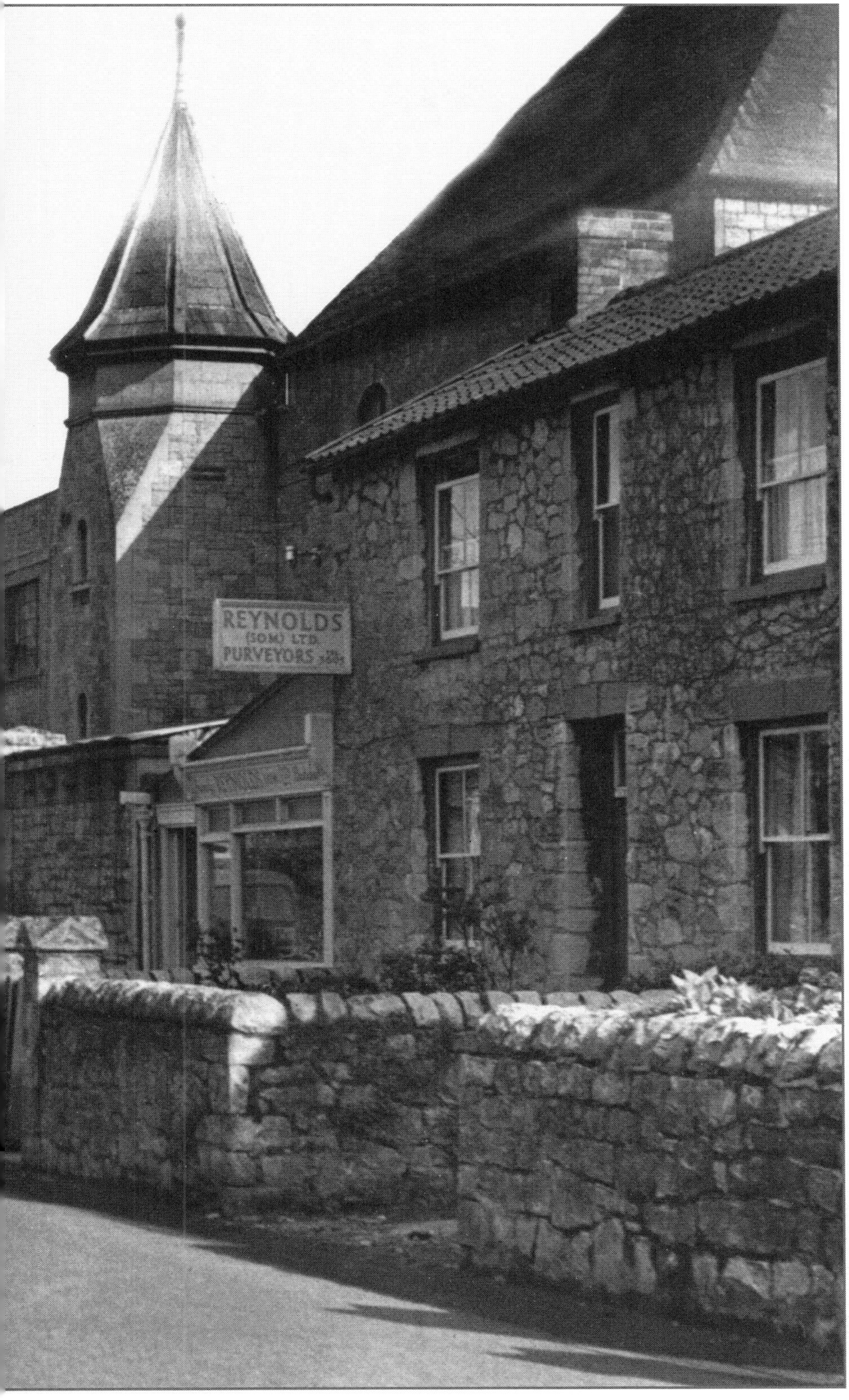

Worle, High Street c1955 W184010
Worle at this time still retained a village feel, even down to its gas lamps, seen next to the telegraph pole. On the right are the laundry and the malthouse. In the distance is the New Inn, an old coaching inn, now renamed The Woodspring. By the 1970s, Worle's population grew rapidly due to the development of new housing. The High Street was redeveloped with new shops and facilities.

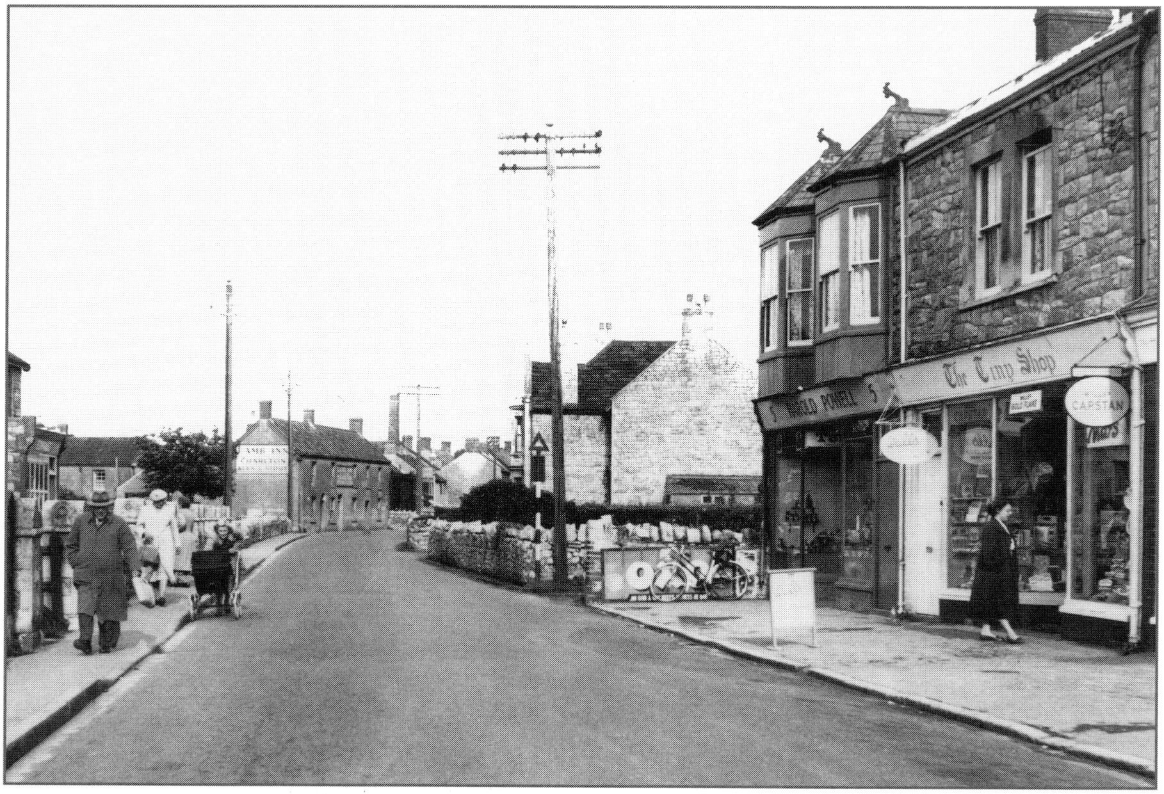

Worle, High Street 1954 W184020
On the right is the Parade, a Victorian terrace of shops. Note the bicycle leaning against an enamel sign advertising Oxo. In the distance is the Lamb Inn, one of Worle's four pubs. While these buildings can still be seen today, most of the open land here has been infilled with supermarkets and other shops.

Index

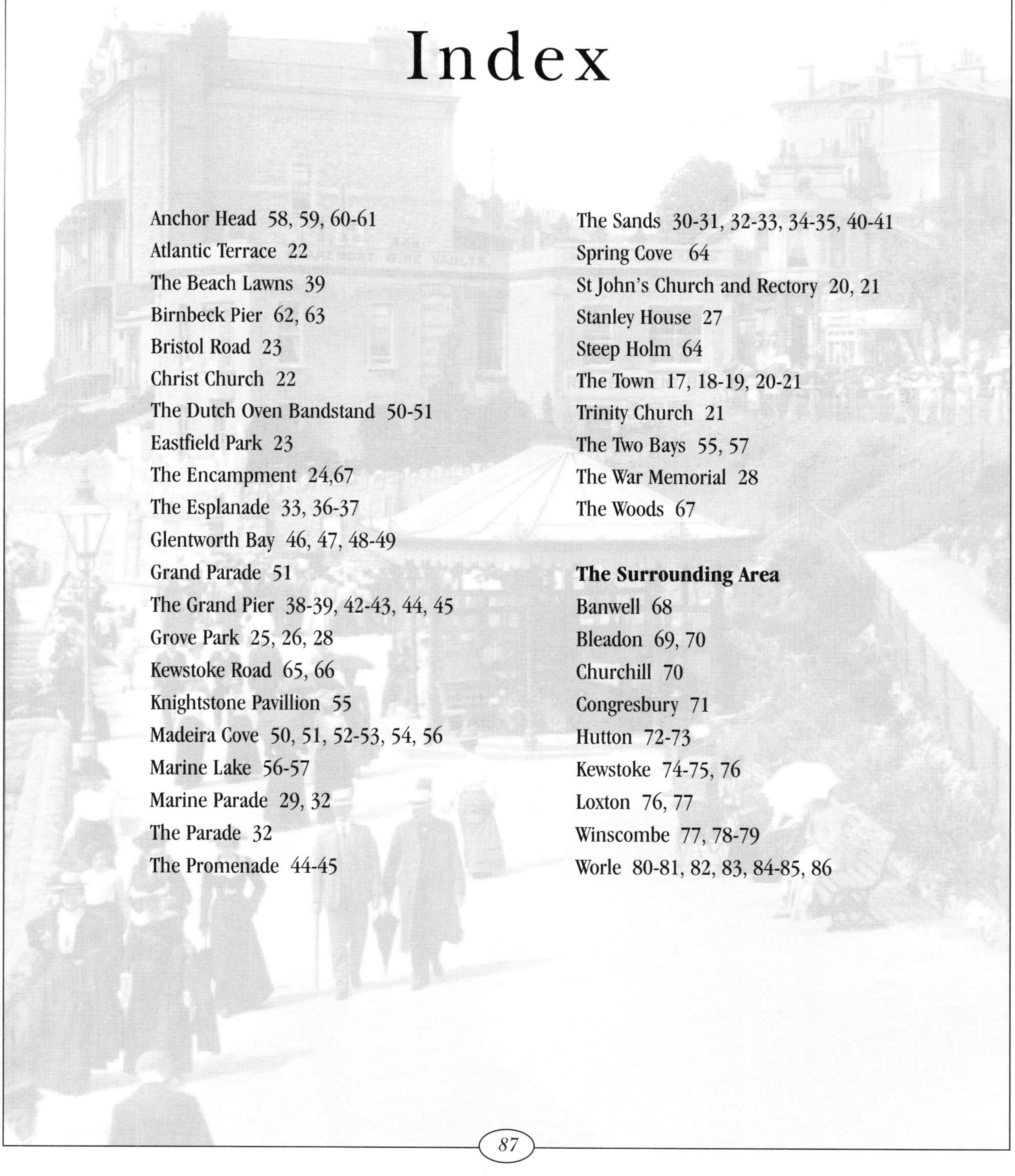

Anchor Head 58, 59, 60-61
Atlantic Terrace 22
The Beach Lawns 39
Birnbeck Pier 62, 63
Bristol Road 23
Christ Church 22
The Dutch Oven Bandstand 50-51
Eastfield Park 23
The Encampment 24,67
The Esplanade 33, 36-37
Glentworth Bay 46, 47, 48-49
Grand Parade 51
The Grand Pier 38-39, 42-43, 44, 45
Grove Park 25, 26, 28
Kewstoke Road 65, 66
Knightstone Pavillion 55
Madeira Cove 50, 51, 52-53, 54, 56
Marine Lake 56-57
Marine Parade 29, 32
The Parade 32
The Promenade 44-45
The Sands 30-31, 32-33, 34-35, 40-41
Spring Cove 64
St John's Church and Rectory 20, 21
Stanley House 27
Steep Holm 64
The Town 17, 18-19, 20-21
Trinity Church 21
The Two Bays 55, 57
The War Memorial 28
The Woods 67

The Surrounding Area

Banwell 68
Bleadon 69, 70
Churchill 70
Congresbury 71
Hutton 72-73
Kewstoke 74-75, 76
Loxton 76, 77
Winscombe 77, 78-79
Worle 80-81, 82, 83, 84-85, 86

Frith Book Co Titles

www.francisfrith.co.uk

The Frith Book Company publishes over 100 new titles each year. A selection of those currently available is listed below. For latest catalogue please contact Frith Book Co.

Town Books 96 pages, approximately 100 photos. ***County and Themed Books*** 128 pages, approximately 150 photos (unless specified). All titles hardback with laminated case and jacket, except those indicated pb (paperback)

Amersham, Chesham & Rickmansworth (pb)	1-85937-340-2	£9.99
Andover (pb)	1-85937-292-9	£9.99
Aylesbury (pb)	1-85937-227-9	£9.99
Barnstaple (pb)	1-85937-300-3	£9.99
Basildon Living Memories (pb)	1-85937-515-4	£9.99
Bath (pb)	1-85937-419-0	£9.99
Bedford (pb)	1-85937-205-8	£9.99
Bedfordshire Living Memories	1-85937-513-8	£14.99
Belfast (pb)	1-85937-303-8	£9.99
Berkshire (pb)	1-85937-191-4	£9.99
Berkshire Churches	1-85937-170-1	£17.99
Berkshire Living Memories	1-85937-332-1	£14.99
Black Country	1-85937-497-2	£12.99
Blackpool (pb)	1-85937-393-3	£9.99
Bognor Regis (pb)	1-85937-431-x	£9.99
Bournemouth (pb)	1-85937-545-6	£9.99
Bradford (pb)	1-85937-204-x	£9.99
Bridgend (pb)	1-85937-386-0	£7.99
Bridgwater (pb)	1-85937-305-4	£9.99
Bridport (pb)	1-85937-327-5	£9.99
Brighton (pb)	1-85937-192-2	£8.99
Bristol (pb)	1-85937-264-3	£9.99
British Life A Century Ago (pb)	1-85937-213-9	£9.99
Buckinghamshire (pb)	1-85937-200-7	£9.99
Camberley (pb)	1-85937-222-8	£9.99
Cambridge (pb)	1-85937-422-0	£9.99
Cambridgeshire (pb)	1-85937-420-4	£9.99
Cambridgeshire Villages	1-85937-523-5	£14.99
Canals And Waterways (pb)	1-85937-291-0	£9.99
Canterbury Cathedral (pb)	1-85937-179-5	£9.99
Cardiff (pb)	1-85937-093-4	£9.99
Carmarthenshire (pb)	1-85937-604-5	£9.99
Chelmsford (pb)	1-85937-310-0	£9.99
Cheltenham (pb)	1-85937-095-0	£9.99
Cheshire (pb)	1-85937-271-6	£9.99
Chester (pb)	1-85937-382 8	£9.99
Chesterfield (pb)	1-85937-378-x	£9.99
Chichester (pb)	1-85937-228-7	£9.99
Churches of East Cornwall (pb)	1-85937-249-x	£9.99
Churches of Hampshire (pb)	1-85937-207-4	£9.99
Cinque Ports & Two Ancient Towns	1-85937-492-1	£14.99
Colchester (pb)	1-85937-188-4	£8.99
Cornwall (pb)	1-85937-229-5	£9.99
Cornwall Living Memories	1-85937-248-1	£14.99
Cotswolds (pb)	1-85937-230-9	£9.99
Cotswolds Living Memories	1-85937-255-4	£14.99
County Durham (pb)	1-85937-398-4	£9.99
Croydon Living Memories (pb)	1-85937-162-0	£9.99
Cumbria (pb)	1-85937-621-5	£9.99
Derby (pb)	1-85937-367-4	£9.99
Derbyshire (pb)	1-85937-196-5	£9.99
Derbyshire Living Memories	1-85937-330-5	£14.99
Devon (pb)	1-85937-297-x	£9.99
Devon Churches (pb)	1-85937-250-3	£9.99
Dorchester (pb)	1-85937-307-0	£9.99
Dorset (pb)	1-85937-269-4	£9.99
Dorset Coast (pb)	1-85937-299-6	£9.99
Dorset Living Memories (pb)	1-85937-584-7	£9.99
Down the Severn (pb)	1-85937-560-x	£9.99
Down The Thames (pb)	1-85937-278-3	£9.99
Down the Trent	1-85937-311-9	£14.99
East Anglia (pb)	1-85937-265-1	£9.99
East Grinstead (pb)	1-85937-138-8	£9.99
East London	1-85937-080-2	£14.99
East Sussex (pb)	1-85937-606-1	£9.99
Eastbourne (pb)	1-85937-399-2	£9.99
Edinburgh (pb)	1-85937-193-0	£8.99
England In The 1880s	1-85937-331-3	£17.99
Essex - Second Selection	1-85937-456-5	£14.99
Essex (pb)	1-85937-270-8	£9.99
Essex Coast	1-85937-342-9	£14.99
Essex Living Memories	1-85937-490-5	£14.99
Exeter	1-85937-539-1	£9.99
Exmoor (pb)	1-85937-608-8	£9.99
Falmouth (pb)	1-85937-594-4	£9.99
Folkestone (pb)	1-85937-124-8	£9.99
Frome (pb)	1-85937-317-8	£9.99
Glamorgan	1-85937-488-3	£14.99
Glasgow (pb)	1-85937-190-6	£9.99
Glastonbury (pb)	1-85937-338-0	£7.99
Gloucester (pb)	1-85937-232-5	£9.99
Gloucestershire (pb)	1-85937-561-8	£9.99
Great Yarmouth (pb)	1-85937-426-3	£9.99
Greater Manchester (pb)	1-85937-266-x	£9.99
Guildford (pb)	1-85937-410-7	£9.99
Hampshire (pb)	1-85937-279-1	£9.99
Harrogate (pb)	1-85937-423-9	£9.99
Hastings and Bexhill (pb)	1-85937-131-0	£9.99
Heart of Lancashire (pb)	1-85937-197-3	£9.99
Helston (pb)	1-85937-214-7	£9.99
Hereford (pb)	1-85937-175-2	£9.99
Herefordshire (pb)	1-85937-567-7	£9.99
Herefordshire Living Memories	1-85937-514-6	£14.99
Hertfordshire (pb)	1-85937-247-3	£9.99
Horsham (pb)	1-85937-432-8	£9.99
Humberside (pb)	1-85937-605-3	£9.99
Hythe, Romney Marsh, Ashford (pb)	1-85937-256-2	£9.99
Ipswich (pb)	1-85937-424-7	£9.99
Isle of Man (pb)	1-85937-268-6	£9.99
Isle of Wight (pb)	1-85937-429-8	£9.99
Isle of Wight Living Memories	1-85937-304-6	£14.99
Kent (pb)	1-85937-189-2	£9.99
Kent Living Memories(pb)	1-85937-401-8	£9.99
Kings Lynn (pb)	1-85937-334-8	£9.99

Available from your local bookshop or from the publisher

Frith Book Co Titles (continued)

Lake District (pb)	1-85937-275-9	£9.99
Lancashire Living Memories	1-85937-335-6	£14.99
Lancaster, Morecambe, Heysham (pb)	1-85937-233-3	£9.99
Leeds (pb)	1-85937-202-3	£9.99
Leicester (pb)	1-85937-381-x	£9.99
Leicestershire & Rutland Living Memories	1-85937-500-6	£12.99
Leicestershire (pb)	1-85937-185-x	£9.99
Lighthouses	1-85937-257-0	£9.99
Lincoln (pb)	1-85937-380-1	£9.99
Lincolnshire (pb)	1-85937-433-6	£9.99
Liverpool and Merseyside (pb)	1-85937-234-1	£9.99
London (pb)	1-85937-183-3	£9.99
London Living Memories	1-85937-454-9	£14.99
Ludlow (pb)	1-85937-176-0	£9.99
Luton (pb)	1-85937-235-x	£9.99
Maidenhead (pb)	1-85937-339-9	£9.99
Maidstone (pb)	1-85937-391-7	£9.99
Manchester (pb)	1-85937-198-1	£9.99
Marlborough (pb)	1-85937-336-4	£9.99
Middlesex	1-85937-158-2	£14.99
Monmouthshire	1-85937-532-4	£14.99
New Forest (pb)	1-85937-390-9	£9.99
Newark (pb)	1-85937-366-6	£9.99
Newport, Wales (pb)	1-85937-258-9	£9.99
Newquay (pb)	1-85937-421-2	£9.99
Norfolk (pb)	1-85937-195-7	£9.99
Norfolk Broads	1-85937-486-7	£14.99
Norfolk Living Memories (pb)	1-85937-402-6	£9.99
North Buckinghamshire	1-85937-626-6	£14.99
North Devon Living Memories	1-85937-261-9	£14.99
North Hertfordshire	1-85937-547-2	£14.99
North London (pb)	1-85937-403-4	£9.99
North Somerset	1-85937-302-x	£14.99
North Wales (pb)	1-85937-298-8	£9.99
North Yorkshire (pb)	1-85937-236-8	£9.99
Northamptonshire Living Memories	1-85937-529-4	£14.99
Northamptonshire	1-85937-150-7	£14.99
Northumberland Tyne & Wear (pb)	1-85937-281-3	£9.99
Northumberland	1-85937-522-7	£14.99
Norwich (pb)	1-85937-194-9	£8.99
Nottingham (pb)	1-85937-324-0	£9.99
Nottinghamshire (pb)	1-85937-187-6	£9.99
Oxford (pb)	1-85937-411-5	£9.99
Oxfordshire (pb)	1-85937-430-1	£9.99
Oxfordshire Living Memories	1-85937-525-1	£14.99
Paignton (pb)	1-85937-374-7	£7.99
Peak District (pb)	1-85937-280-5	£9.99
Pembrokeshire	1-85937-262-7	£14.99
Penzance (pb)	1-85937-595-2	£9.99
Peterborough (pb)	1-85937-219-8	£9.99
Picturesque Harbours	1-85937-208-2	£14.99
Piers	1-85937-237-6	£17.99
Plymouth (pb)	1-85937-389-5	£9.99
Poole & Sandbanks (pb)	1-85937-251-1	£9.99
Preston (pb)	1-85937-212-0	£9.99
Reading (pb)	1-85937-238-4	£9.99
Redhill to Reigate (pb)	1-85937-596-0	£9.99
Ringwood (pb)	1-85937-384-4	£7.99
Romford (pb)	1-85937-319-4	£9.99
Royal Tunbridge Wells (pb)	1-85937-504-9	£9.99
Salisbury (pb)	1-85937-239-2	£9.99
Scarborough (pb)	1-85937-379-8	£9.99
Sevenoaks and Tonbridge (pb)	1-85937-392-5	£9.99
Sheffield & South Yorks (pb)	1-85937-267-8	£9.99
Sherborne (pb)	1-85937-301-1	£9.99
Shrewsbury (pb)	1-85937-325-9	£9.99
Shropshire (pb)	1-85937-326-7	£9.99
Shropshire Living Memories	1-85937-643-6	£14.99
Somerset	1-85937-153-1	£14.99
South Devon Coast	1-85937-107-8	£14.99
South Devon Living Memories (pb)	1-85937-609-6	£9.99
South East London (pb)	1-85937-263-5	£9.99
South Somerset	1-85937-318-6	£14.99
South Wales	1-85937-519-7	£14.99
Southampton (pb)	1-85937-427-1	£9.99
Southend (pb)	1-85937-313-5	£9.99
Southport (pb)	1-85937-425-5	£9.99
St Albans (pb)	1-85937-341-0	£9.99
St Ives (pb)	1-85937-415-8	£9.99
Stafford Living Memories (pb)	1-85937-503-0	£9.99
Staffordshire (pb)	1-85937-308-9	£9.99
Stourbridge (pb)	1-85937-530-8	£9.99
Stratford upon Avon (pb)	1-85937-388-7	£9.99
Suffolk (pb)	1-85937-221-x	£9.99
Suffolk Coast (pb)	1-85937-610-x	£9.99
Surrey (pb)	1-85937-240-6	£9.99
Surrey Living Memories	1-85937-328-3	£14.99
Sussex (pb)	1-85937-184-1	£9.99
Sutton (pb)	1-85937-337-2	£9.99
Swansea (pb)	1-85937-167-1	£9.99
Taunton (pb)	1-85937-314-3	£9.99
Tees Valley & Cleveland (pb)	1-85937-623-1	£9.99
Teignmouth (pb)	1-85937-370-4	£7.99
Thanet (pb)	1-85937-116-7	£9.99
Tiverton (pb)	1-85937-178-7	£9.99
Torbay (pb)	1-85937-597-9	£9.99
Truro (pb)	1-85937-598-7	£9.99
Victorian & Edwardian Dorset	1-85937-254-6	£14.99
Victorian & Edwardian Kent (pb)	1-85937-624-X	£9.99
Victorian & Edwardian Maritime Album (pb)	1-85937-622-3	£9.99
Victorian and Edwardian Sussex (pb)	1-85937-625-8	£9.99
Villages of Devon (pb)	1-85937-293-7	£9.99
Villages of Kent (pb)	1-85937-294-5	£9.99
Villages of Sussex (pb)	1-85937-295-3	£9.99
Warrington (pb)	1-85937-507-3	£9.99
Warwick (pb)	1-85937-518-9	£9.99
Warwickshire (pb)	1-85937-203-1	£9.99
Welsh Castles (pb)	1-85937-322-4	£9.99
West Midlands (pb)	1-85937-289-9	£9.99
West Sussex (pb)	1-85937-607-x	£9.99
West Yorkshire (pb)	1-85937-201-5	£9.99
Weston Super Mare (pb)	1-85937-306-2	£9.99
Weymouth (pb)	1-85937-209-0	£9.99
Wiltshire (pb)	1-85937-277-5	£9.99
Wiltshire Churches (pb)	1-85937-171-x	£9.99
Wiltshire Living Memories (pb)	1-85937-396-8	£9.99
Winchester (pb)	1-85937-428-x	£9.99
Windsor (pb)	1-85937-333-x	£9.99
Wokingham & Bracknell (pb)	1-85937-329-1	£9.99
Woodbridge (pb)	1-85937-498-0	£9.99
Worcester (pb)	1-85937-165-5	£9.99
Worcestershire Living Memories	1-85937-489-1	£14.99
Worcestershire	1-85937-152-3	£14.99
York (pb)	1-85937-199-x	£9.99
Yorkshire (pb)	1-85937-186-8	£9.99
Yorkshire Coastal Memories	1-85937-506-5	£14.99
Yorkshire Dales	1-85937-502-2	£14.99
Yorkshire Living Memories (pb)	1-85937-397-6	£9.99

FRITH PRODUCTS & SERVICES

Francis Frith would doubtless be pleased to know that the pioneering publishing venture he started in 1860 still continues today. Over a hundred and forty years later, The Francis Frith Collection continues in the same innovative tradition and is now one of the foremost publishers of vintage photographs in the world. Some of the current activities include:

Interior Decoration

Today Frith's photographs can be seen framed and as giant wall murals in thousands of pubs, restaurants, hotels, banks, retail stores and other public buildings throughout the country. In every case they enhance the unique local atmosphere of the places they depict and provide reminders of gentler days in an increasingly busy and frenetic world.

Product Promotions

Frith products are used by many major companies to promote the sales of their own products or to reinforce their own history and heritage. Frith promotions have been used by Hovis bread, Courage beers, Scots Porage Oats, Colman's mustard, Cadbury's foods, Mellow Birds coffee, Dunhill pipe tobacco, Guinness, and Bulmer's Cider.

Genealogy and Family History

As the interest in family history and roots grows world-wide, more and more people are turning to Frith's photographs of Great Britain for images of the towns, villages and streets where their ancestors lived; and, of course, photographs of the churches and chapels where their ancestors were christened, married and buried are an essential part of every genealogy tree and family album.

Frith Products

All Frith photographs are available Framed or just as Mounted Prints and Posters (size 23 x 16 inches). These may be ordered from the address below. From time to time other products - Address Books, Calendars, Table Mats, etc - are available.

The Internet

Already fifty thousand Frith photographs can be viewed and purchased on the internet through the Frith websites and a myriad of partner sites.

For more detailed information on Frith companies and products, look at these sites:

www.francisfrith.co.uk
www.francisfrith.com
(for North American visitors)

See the complete list of Frith Books at:

www.francisfrith.co.uk

This web site is regularly updated with the latest list of publications from the Frith Book Company. If you wish to buy books relating to another part of the country that your local bookshop does not stock, you may purchase on-line.

For further information, trade, or author enquiries please contact us at the address below:

The Francis Frith Collection, Frith's Barn, Teffont, Salisbury, Wiltshire, England SP3 5QP.
Tel: +44 (0)1722 716 376 Fax: +44 (0)1722 716 881 Email: sales@francisfrith.co.uk

See Frith books on the internet at www.francisfrith.co.uk

FREE PRINT OF YOUR CHOICE

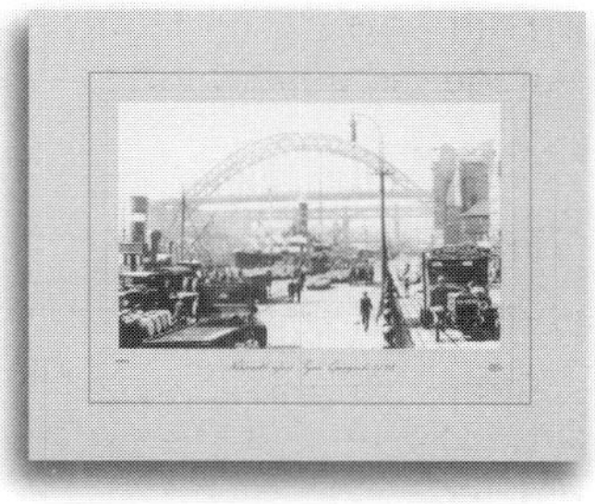

Mounted Print
Overall size 14 x 11 inches (355 x 280mm)

Choose any Frith photograph in this book. Simply complete the Voucher opposite and return it with your remittance for £2.25 (to cover postage and handling) and we will print the photograph of your choice in SEPIA (size 11 x 8 inches) and supply it in a cream mount with a burgundy rule line (overall size 14 x 11 inches). **Please note: photographs with a reference number starting with a "Z" are not Frith photographs and cannot be supplied under this offer.**
Offer valid for delivery to UK addresses only.

***PLUS:* Order additional Mounted Prints at HALF PRICE - £7.49 each** (normally £14.99)
If you would like to order more Frith prints from this book, possibly as gifts for friends and family, you can buy them at half price (with no additional postage and handling costs).

***PLUS:* Have your Mounted Prints framed**
For an extra £14.95 per print you can have your mounted print(s) framed in an elegant polished wood and gilt moulding, overall size 16 x 13 inches (no additional postage and handling required).

IMPORTANT!

These special prices are only available if you use this form to order. You must use the ORIGINAL VOUCHER on this page (no copies permitted). We can only despatch to one address. This offer cannot be combined with any other offer.

Send completed Voucher form to:
The Francis Frith Collection, Frith's Barn, Teffont, Salisbury, Wiltshire SP3 5QP

CHOOSE A PHOTOGRAPH FROM THIS BOOK

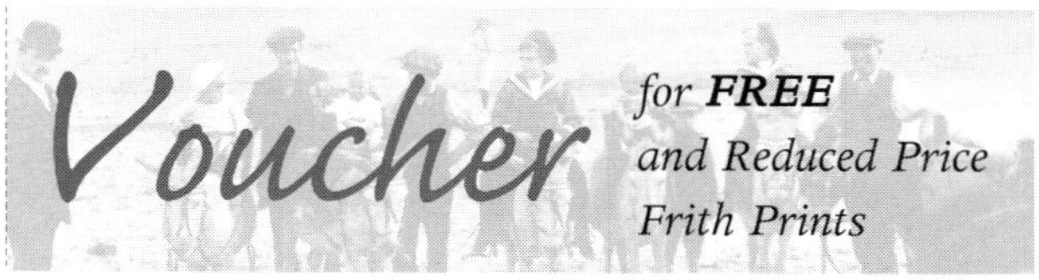

Please do not photocopy this voucher. Only the original is valid, so please fill it in, cut it out and return it to us with your order.

Picture ref no	Page no	Qty	Mounted @ £7.49	Framed + £14.95	Total Cost
		1	Free of charge*	£	£
			£7.49	£	£
			£7.49	£	£
			£7.49	£	£
			£7.49	£	£
			£7.49	£	£
Please allow 28 days for delivery			* Post & handling (UK)		£2.25
			Total Order Cost		£

Title of this book ....
I enclose a cheque/postal order for £ ....
made payable to 'The Francis Frith Collection'

OR please debit my Mastercard / Visa / Switch (Maestro) /Amex card
(credit cards please on all overseas orders), details below

Card Number

Issue No (Switch only) Valid from (Amex/Switch)

Expires Signature

Name Mr/Mrs/Ms ....
Address ....
....
....
.... Postcode ....
Daytime Tel No ....
Email ....

Valid to 31/12/07

Free Print - see overleaf

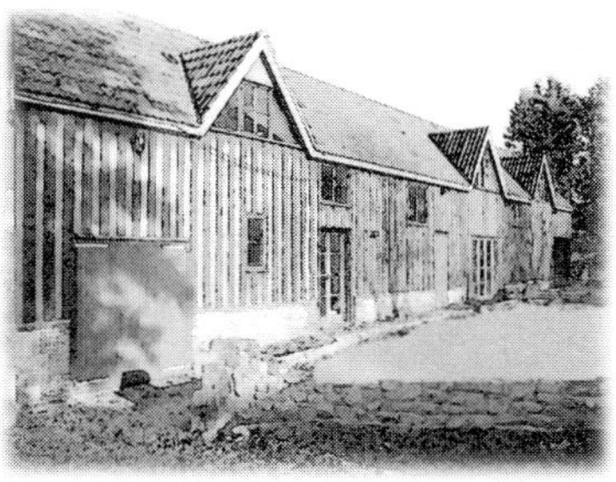

Would you like to find out more about Francis Frith?

We have recently recruited some entertaining speakers who are happy to visit local groups, clubs and societies to give an illustrated talk documenting Frith's travels and photographs. If you are a member of such a group and are interested in hosting a presentation, we would love to hear from you.

Our speakers bring with them a small selection of our local town and county books, together with sample prints. They are happy to take orders. A small proportion of the order value is donated to the group who have hosted the presentation. The talks are therefore an excellent way of fundraising for small groups and societies.

Can you help us with information about any of the Frith photographs in this book?

We are gradually compiling an historical record for each of the photographs in the Frith archive. It is always fascinating to find out the names of the people shown in the pictures, as well as insights into the shops, buildings and other features depicted.

If you recognize anyone in the photographs in this book, or if you have information not already included in the author's caption, do let us know. We would love to hear from you, and will try to publish it in future books or articles.

Our production team

Frith books are produced by a small dedicated team at offices in the converted Grade II listed 18th-century barn at Teffont near Salisbury, illustrated above. Most have worked with the Frith Collection for many years. All have in common one quality: they have a passion for the Frith Collection. The team is constantly expanding, but currently includes:

Paul Baron, Phillip Brennan, Jason Buck, John Buck, Ruth Butler, Heather Crisp, David Davies, Louis du Mont, Isobel Hall, Gareth Harris, Lucy Hart, Julian Hight, Peter Horne, James Kinnear, Karen Kinnear, Tina Leary, Stuart Login, David Marsh, Lesley-Ann Millard, Sue Molloy, Glenda Morgan, Wayne Morgan, Sarah Roberts, Kate Rotondetto, Dean Scource, Eliza Sackett, Terence Sackett, Sandra Sampson, Adrian Sanders, Sandra Sanger, Jan Scrivens, Julia Skinner, David Smith, Miles Smith, Lewis Taylor, Shelley Tolcher, Lorraine Tuck, Amanita Wainwright and Ricky Williams.